ADAM CLAYTON POWELL

About the Authors:

Neil Hickey graduated from Loyola College in 1953, and began his journalistic career as a reporter on Baltimore newspapers. He now lives and works in New York where he has been a contributor to and a staff member of various national magazines. His last book was a biography of Arthur Barry, "The Gentleman Was a Thief." Mr. Hickey, a former naval officer, is best known for his profiles of many leading figures in the political and entertainment fields.

Ed Edwin studied at Stanford University, the University of Maryland, and earned a master's degree from the School of International Affairs at Columbia University. A reporter for twenty years and a political analyst for nearly as long, he has developed election reporting systems for NBC News, written political guides for CBS News, and worked in government. It was during the abortive purge of Adam Clayton Powell, in 1958, that Mr. Edwin focussed on Harlem. In the years since he has interviewed nearly every major Negro American mass leader for television, and conducted a series of interviews for the Oral History Research Office of Columbia University.

ADAM CLAYTON POWELL

AND THE
POLITICS OF RACE

BY

Neil Hickey and Ed Edwin

FLEET PUBLISHING CORPORATION

NEW YORK

Library of Congress Catalog Card No.: 65-16313
PRINTED IN THE UNITED STATES OF AMERICA

The authors gratefully acknowledge permission to use the following quotations:

From *Marching Blacks* by Adam Clayton Powell, Jr. Copyright 1946 by Adam Clayton Powell, Jr. Reprinted by permission of the publishers, The Dial Press, Inc.

From "The Dangerous Road of Martin Luther King," by James Baldwin. © 1961, by Harper & Row, Publishers, Incorporated. Reprinted from *Harper's Magazine* by Special Permission.

From "Is the Race War Shaping Up?" by Arnold J. Toynbee. © 1963 by the New York Times Company. Reprinted by permission.

From *Montage of a Dream Deferred*, by Langston Hughes, the poem, "Harlem," published by Alfred A. Knopf. Copyright © 1951 by Langston Hughes. Reprinted by permission of Harold Ober Associates Incorporated.

Acknowledgment

The authors would like to thank the staff of the Schomburg Collection of the New York Public Library in Harlem for their generous assistance in making available their impressive archives. We thank also the superintendents, and their assistants, of the Periodical Galleries of the United States Senate and House of Representatives in Washington.

To the scores of persons important in political and interracial affairs in New York City, Washington, Puerto Rico, as well as in many other locations around the United States, whom we interviewed, we are most grateful; their impressions about the subject of this book, as well as about the life and progress of the American Negro over the last fifty years, have been invaluable.

NEIL HICKEY
ED EDWIN

New York, 1965

Contents

List of Illustrations

ADAM CLAYTON POWELL

1. The Symbol and the Struggle

Adam Clayton Powell must be counted among the most extraordinary public figures of our times. He has been praised as an agitator for Negro rights ever since the early 1930's. He was an abrasive force for the Negro masses before such names as Martin Luther King, James Farmer, or Malcolm X ever gained national currency. He has been denounced as a charlatan, demagogue, playboy, woman-chaser, opportunist, hypocrite, rabble-rouser, maverick, and master of the grandstand play; nonetheless, he has been elected every two years since 1944 to the United States Congress (often with hardly a campaign speech), and is chairman of the influential House Committee on Education and Labor. He is, in addition, pastor of a church having one of the largest Protestant congregations in the United States: Harlem's Abyssinian Baptist. In the words of one Harlemite, "How in hell you going to beat him? He has a parish with ten thousand people in it and every one is a potential campaign worker."

Many of Powell's detractors claim he is less a doer than an irritant—a symbol of the Negro struggle for equality in the United States. Joseph A. Bailey, one of his vanquished opponents for Congress, called him "the greatest Negro orator in the world today—a man who doesn't do anything practical about achieving civil rights, but he expresses our people's outcry against injustice—and they respond gratefully." Roy Wilkins, executive secretary of the National Association for the Advancement of Colored People, once wrote that "Powell is a master of all the tricks of rousing what he calls 'the masses.'"

Powell persistently defies the white man and for that he has the admiration, the gratitude—and even the adoration— of great numbers of Negroes. He enjoys "showing the flag" in such expensive New York restaurants as Sardi's and "21." His performance at such times is a study: word pervades the room that "Adam Powell is here" and at once heads turn and necks crane. He moves from table to table, appearing to know everyone, bestowing his luminous smile and warm hand-shake in several directions.

At home, Powell is a man of easygoing charm, a pipe-smoker who customarily indulges an unerring taste for lux-ury. "I go to the Salzburg Festival every year," he once told a New York Times interviewer, "and I never miss an opening night on Broadway if I can help it. All the producers save tickets for me."

His manner of living and his obvious pleasure in moving freely in the white man's world contrast sharply with the slum life of the average Negro, especially those in Harlem. He has plumbed deeper than any other Negro leader the vicarious sense of many lower-class Negroes. "When my peo-ple see a picture of me in '21,'" says Powell, "or some other downtown nightclub, they like it. They know I can pass for white, but that I'm as black in my thinking as the blackest of them."

This last remark suggests what is perhaps the greatest irony in the career of this most paradoxical of leaders: no one— not even Powell himself—is absolutely certain how much of his ancestry is Negro. In his book, Marching Blacks, published in 1945, Powell claimed that his earliest awareness of Negro-white differences occurred when, as a child, he stood on a chair and traced with his finger the letter "P" branded on his slave grandfather's back. Easier to establish is his Choctaw Indian, French, and German blood. It appears that, at least during one brief period of his life, he attempted to pass as white, but was found out. He told Ernest Dunbar, a senior editor of *Look* Magazine: "If I have all white blood and I'm doing what I am for the Negro, I deserve all the more credit."

Whether Negro or not, Powell is undeniably a product of the ghetto, with all that this implies—and it implies a great deal. Like the Reverend Dr. Martin Luther King, he is the son of a patriarchal and strong-minded Baptist minister father. Adam Clayton Powell, Sr. fought his way to Yale University and built Harlem's Abyssinian Baptist Church into the social and political fortress it has been for the last thirty years. Today, Powell and King speak to different regions of the Negro mind, a divergence which is historical, and which symbolizes some new directions in the yearnings of the great mass of Negroes in the United States. Powell is closer in his roots to Marcus Garvey—the "Black Moses" of the 1920's—who came to New York from Jamaica preaching a doctrine of black worthiness; whose explosive oratory made him the most sought-after Negro speaker of his day and whose Universal Negro Improvement Association labored to inflate the suspicion in the American Negro's mind that being black was not all bad; that it should, in fact, be a source of pride. Adam Clayton Powell is in that line of descent. Martin Luther King, on the other hand, is the archetype of the Negro leadership which was forged out of the events of the 1950's and early 1960's beginning with the Montgomery, Alabama, bus boycott of 1955. That eruption presaged a black revolution the dimensions of which were foreseen by only a perceptive few. There followed "freedom rides," sit-ins, enrollment assaults on all-white southern universities, and hundreds of street demonstrations.

For the first time in their 340-year tenure in the United States, large sections of the Negro masses were participating directly in efforts to improve their condition. The American Negro suddenly was an uncommon form on the world scene: one of the few groups still using non-violent methods to obtain social and political reforms from a hostile environment.

Remarkably, many Negroes discovered they were no longer afraid to stand up for their rights. Although few people recognized it at the time, a new Negro faith was being born. Louis Lomax, in his book *The Negro Revolt,* said, "This faith was the culmination of a hundred years of folk suffering . . . it was a hodgepodge, as every faith is, of every ethical principle absorbed by my people from other cultures. And so the best of Confucius, Moses, Jesus, Ghandi, and Thoreau was extracted, then mixed with the peculiar experience of the Negro in America."

At the forefront of these activities was a loosely connected cadre of Negroes who came to be called The Big Six. They were:

The Reverend Dr. Martin Luther King, president of the Southern Christian Leadership Conference (an organization that was born out of the Montgomery bus boycott).

A. Philip Randolph, international president of the Brotherhood of Sleeping Car Porters, the only Negro vice-president of the AFL-CIO, and founder of the Negro American Labor Council.

Roy Wilkins, executive secretary of the National Association for the Advancement of Colored People.

Whitney Young, executive director of the National Urban League.

James Farmer, national director of the Congress of Racial Equality.

John Lewis, the youthful chairman of the Student Non-Violent Coordinating Committee (SNICK).

These men were of differing temperaments, different generations and sometimes colliding ambitions; but together they succeeded to the task of laying down a strategy for the revolt, and of holding it on a properly militant and non-violent track.

Leadership of the black revolution devolved upon the Big Six rather than on the handful of Negro politicians around the country who held important elective office: Congressman William L. Dawson, for example, whose District on Chicago's tenemented South Side was 92 percent Negro; Congressman Robert N. C. Nix, of Pennsylvania; Congressman Charles C. Diggs, of Michigan; Hulan Jack, borough president of Manhattan; and Adam Clayton Powell, Congressman of Harlem. For patent reasons, those men appeared to have the most to lose by any concerted move toward full integration. They owed their existence to the ghetto system, or to the sufferance of white bosses of political organizations. Suddenly the Negro politician was projected as an ineffective instrument of the black revolution. He had never been a race leader anyway, but rather a special pleader for Negro betterment inside the ghetto "system," and an attentive ear for voters' grievances and supplications.

Adam Clayton Powell, for one, was quick to discern that, unless he were sure-footed, history would pass him by. But in implementing that realization—whether from perverseness or gross miscalculation—he was spectacularly unsuccessful. In the summer of 1962, he enraged his colleagues in Congress by junketing to Europe with two attractive female aides—ostensibly to study patterns of female employment abroad. Newspaper reports of his travels placed him consistently in the night-clubs, expensive restaurants, and boulevards of

Europe's grand tour cities, where he spent counterpart funds with the *élan* of a deposed Middle Eastern potentate. So savage was the outcry against his behavior that even Powell, accustomed to expressions of disapproval over his habits, was shocked. In an unusual action, Senator John J. Williams, Republican of Delaware, denounced Powell on the Senate floor as an "authority on adult delinquency" and the nation's editorialists took the occasion to pounce on Powell and criticize his whole life style. Powell's relations with his own party—which had not always been harmonious—deteriorated further when no voice was raised publicly in defense of his junket. This vacuum enraged him.

Then, on March 23, 1963, Powell shared a platform with Malcolm X, who was then chief strategist of the Black Muslims—before his estrangement from that sect, and his subsequent murder in Harlem on February 21, 1965—at a rally outside the Black Nationalist Bookstore on Harlem's Seventh Avenue. Powell savagely attacked the NAACP, CORE, SCLC, and the National Urban League for being white-dominated, and complained that the nominal Negro leadership of those groups was not the controlling leadership. This was not a new plaint with Powell, but the cyclorama against which he reasserted it gave it new weight and significance. He embraced Malcolm X as a "friend" and applauded the aims of the separatist Black Muslim movement. It was a shocking tactic and, whether motivated by petulance or revenge, it had the effect of announcing that the full force of Powell's impressive anger would be hurled at anyone who questioned his right to be a leader of the Negro people.

Six weeks after Powell's street corner performance with the Black Muslims, however, race violence broke out in Birmingham, Alabama. Newsphotos were broadcast to the world's press: police dogs lunging at fleeing Negroes; fire hoses blasting demonstrators and sending them sprawling; a

Negro woman pinned to the sidewalk, a policeman's knee at her throat. Finally, four Negro children were killed by a bomb hurled into the church where they were attending Sunday School. The hatred generated on Birmingham's streets moved one observer to remark that "the alternatives may not be those of the Civil War—indivisible union or irreparable separation—but they are no less stark and serious: total equality or total repression." Birmingham became the bench mark of the black revolution.

The violence had the effect of coalescing the major civil rights organizations and turning them toward the belief that only through their combined efforts could the goals of each be attained. Since the previous January, A. Philip Randolph had been urging that a massive demonstration be held in Washington to dramatize Negro demands. Few had taken him seriously. After Birmingham, everybody listened. On July 2, 1963, the Big Six—acting as a coalition for the first time—met in New York's Hotel Roosevelt and, after a two-hour conference, announced to the press that a mass civil rights march would be held in Washington on the following August 28th. Roy Wilkins said: "We have no intention of doing other than holding an orderly march in Washington. There is no projected plan for camping in the halls, for sit-ins in Senate offices or for lying down in the corridors." He declined to say how many persons might take part, but Martin Luther King predicted the number might be around 100,000.

Complex planning got underway. Some liberals were against the march, fearing that any eruptions of violence could only set back the cause of civil rights and give fuel to segregationists. But the Big Six, under the mediating guidance of Randolph, moved ahead cautiously, maintaining that the March for Freedom would be the most dramatic affirmation of the Negro's demands for equal opportunity since Emancipation.

Decisions about the conduct of events for the ceremony were not reached easily. What was to be the over-all tone of the March? Which aspects of the black revolution were to be accented, which underplayed? Toward the end of July, the headquarters of the March was swamped with requests from organizations and individuals who wanted to participate. The feeling was growing that the March would be memorable indeed, and that anybody who sought identification with Negro aims in the United States had better take part in it. It was apparent, however, that the formal part of the ceremony could not run on through the day. How many speakers could be accommodated in a three-hour program? Was it possible, for example, to exclude Adam Clayton Powell—the most powerful Negro politician in the country—a man who had, more conspicuously than any of them, been at the forefront of civil rights battles as far back as the early 1930's; a man who had propounded civil rights before John Lewis of SNICK, one of the March's organizers, had even been born? They decided it was not only possible, but desirable, since Powell had so recently flayed them publicly, pointedly lauded the separatist Malcolm X, and thus effectively alienated himself from the methods and aspirations of this new Negro leadership.

In their distrust of Powell, the Big Six were of a single mind. They knew from the past how a Powell oration could mesmerize a mass rally. Powell had displayed a sure talent— a compulsion, in fact—for upstaging any other leader he might join on a platform. This talent was incompatible with the concepts of the March. It was to be a demonstration of Negro dignity and self-discipline, as well as protest. The explosive potential of a hundred thousand Negro demonstraters was not lost upon the organizers.

"We can't trust him," one of the Big Six said. "He's dangerous. In fact we're not at all sure he won't walk right up to the microphone without an invitation." But such was not Powell's intention. In an exertion of that stunning unpredictability, which is the only predictable thing about Powell, he chose instead to reverse his field and, for one historical moment, to assume a posture that was at once humble and accommodating.

On Sunday, July 28, Powell was in Harlem conducting a forum, one of a series he was sponsoring at Abyssinian Baptist on the subject "The Black Revolution." (An earlier entry in the series had featured Malcolm X.) He was strangely good-willed toward the Big Six and, at length, announced dramatically that "On tomorrow, at 12:30, I will consult my leaders." (A. Philip Randolph, queried later as to whether he had ever heard Powell call anybody "my leaders," laughed, and said, "Not that I know of.")

Powell had arranged a conference telephone call with members of the Big Six, who were scattered at various points around the country. The purpose of the call, ostensibly, was to discuss ways and means of expediting civil rights legislation which was then before the House. It had the effect, at the same time, of reminding them of Powell's long-term association with the cause of civil rights, extending back to the 1930's, and announcing his willingness to lend his person to the historic demonstration. But the Big Six indicated no interest in having Powell share their day in the sun, a day for which all of them had such high expectations.

Powell made other efforts to align himself with this emerging Negro leadership. When Randolph addressed the National Press Club in Washington on the Monday before the March, Powell managed a guest invitation and contrived to sit near his "leader"—a display of the sort of accommodation, even sycophancy, which traditionally had been the attitude of the plantation "house Negro" in the United States; and a posture for which Powell himself had so often shown such terrible contempt.

But the organizers fortified their decision to deal Powell out by ruling that no politician, black or white, would be allowed to address the marchers. That solved the dilemma. Not even the Kennedy brothers, for whom an exception might reasonably have been made, were exempted from the ruling.

August 28, the day of the March, dawned clear and warm. In the early morning, the Capitol was still with anticipation. Government and private business, fearing traffic congestion, and even violence, had urged employees to take the day off. Bars and liquor stores were closed. Washington looked like an evacuated city, and many white families had, in fact, fled into temporary exile in Maryland and Virginia. Military police directed traffic while helmeted soldiers rumbled about in jeeps and command cars. Special trains and buses began rolling into the city from all parts of the United States.

It was apparent by 11:30 a.m., the scheduled time for the March to begin, that the demonstrators totalled over 200,000 —rather than the 100,000 that had been predicted. They began leaving the Washington Monument rallying point spontaneously by the tens of thousands to begin the trek down Constitution and Independence Avenues to the Lincoln Memorial. Many thousands waved placards that read: "We march for integrated schools *now*," "We demand voting rights *now*," "We demand decent housing *now*." Some marchers wept as they walked. There was little shouting or singing; only the muffled rumble of 200,000 marchers, about 15 percent of whom were white.

They reassembled under the brooding statue of Abraham Lincoln. (It was 100 years and 240 days since the signing of the Emancipation Proclamation.) Film stars and labor leaders milled about in the platform area waving and grinning for photographers. The gray-haired Randolph told the crowd: ". . . Jesus led the multitude into the streets of Judea. . . . Until *we* went into the streets, the Federal Government was indifferent to our demands. It wasn't until the streets and the jails were filled that Congress began to think about civil rights. . . . The March on Washington is not the climax of our struggle, but a new beginning."

James Farmer of CORE, languishing in a Louisiana jail, sent a message: "Two hundred and thirty-two freedom fighters jailed with me in Plaquemine, Louisiana . . . send greetings to you."

A small claque began to chant: "Let Adam speak! Let Adam speak!" But the chant was lost in applause for the organizers and their guests. Powell sat inconspicuously, a few dozen feet from the platform, in a section reserved for Congressmen. He smoked his pipe and, from time to time, joined in the applause. At a nearby hotel, Malcolm X was holding a press conference denouncing the Negro demonstrators for "seeking favors" from the "white man's Government."

Mahalia Jackson sang a gospel song called "I've Been 'Buked and I've Been Scorned":

> *I'm gonna tell my Lord*
> *When I get home,*
> *I'm gonna tell my Lord*
> *When I get home,*
> *Just how long you've*
> *Been treating me wrong.*

Then Martin Luther King—nicknamed "De Lawd" by some observers of the black revolution—was on the platform waving his arms for silence. It was on King that the crowd bestowed its most vocal and enthusiastic welcome. "The Negro," he told them, "lives on a lonely island of poverty in the midst of a vast ocean of material prosperity and finds himself an exile in his own land . ... This sweltering summer of the Negro's legitimate discontent will not pass until there is an invigorating autumn of freedom and equality." Great cheers and whistling arose from the crowd.

A few moments later the ceremonies were over and the marchers dropped their placards on the grass around the reflecting pond which stretches to the Washington Monument. Slowly they dispersed to the buses and trains that would take them back to their home towns.

In an avenging mood, Powell returned to Harlem a few days after the March. His role in the black revolution was now perilously ambiguous. His voice was being drowned out by the voices of these new leaders, and they appeared to have the ear of the masses. To attack the Big Six in their time of triumph would have been obvious folly. So Powell chose a target closer to home—J. Raymond Jones, the man who had been his campaign manager during an abortive purge of Powell by Tammany Hall in 1958; Jones was, in effect, the administrator of Powell's influence in the Harlem power base and an influential manipulator in his own right. (He is called "The Fox" by admirers of his expertise in organizational politics.)

Now Jones was running for a seat in the City Council. Harlem had become too small for both of them. In a breach occasioned as much by their squabbling over real estate deals as by politics, Powell called Jones "a traitor to the black revolution" and withdrew his support from Jones's candidacy. Jones was bent on "a personal grab for power," said Powell, and his campaign was supported by "a flood of white money."

Powell's remarks moved Jones to break a long and disciplined public silence. On Labor Day, 1963, the battle of the behemoths broke out in Harlem. "Powell is no longer considered a national leader of any importance in the civil rights movement," Jones said. "He can't even get into the conferences of the Negro leaders. Powell was no more important than any of the other two hundred thousand people at the March. I think he's through. He ought to be through."

Jones (who, a year later, was named leader of the New York County Democratic Executive Committee—the old Tammany Hall) and Powell were acting out a classic confrontation of the American experience: a pair of strong, willful men contending for supremacy in the same territory. Jones was unrelenting. "Powell can dish it out," he said. "Now we'll see if he can take it." He made public what had long been discussed privately among Negro leaders: Powell's disdain for the poverty-ridden masses that had thrust him to power.

"He has nothing but contempt for the Negro masses," Jones said. "In relaxed moments, Powell refers to Negroes as 'my slaves.' "

Jones hit everywhere. He talked of Powell and Puerto Rico, where the Congressman had maintained a residence for a half-dozen years. "Powell has had some difficulty deciding whether he is a Negro or a Puerto Rican," Jones said. "He wanted to take on Muñoz (Luis Muñoz Marín, Governor of Puerto Rico). Then the Puerto Ricans saw what he was up to and stoned his house, so he crawled back to Harlem."

Jones easily won the nomination over Powell's man and breezed to victory in the general election by a three-to-one margin. Powell's hegemony in Harlem had been seriously eroded.

Other influential Negroes protested Powell's apparent intention to "go it alone" at a time when the black revolution was gathering force in the land. Dr. Ralph Bunche, United Nations Undersecretary for Special Political Affairs, in a speech at Tougaloo Southern Christian College, attacked both Powell and the Black Muslims as carriers of a "black form of the racial virus." He regarded Powell's attacks on the NAACP as "revoltingly racist" and insisted that, for his own part, he refused to look to "some mythical, fanciful state of black men for my salvation."

The story of Adam Clayton Powell is one of the most rousing and, in some ways, one of the saddest stories in the American experience. It is possible to discover in it the elements of literary tragedy: the classic leader, the man of breadth and stature, whose ambitions take possession of him and whose fall is made inevitable by his own nature. But it is a fact that Powell still symbolizes the Negro protest for significant segments of black America.

The Negro literary renaissance and the Marcus Garvey militancy of the 1920's; the Harlem crusade for jobs in the 1930's; the ancient protests over housing, public accommodations, and schools: this is the arena in which Powell's character has been fashioned.

In the late 1950's, the nation suddenly became aware of King and Farmer and Randolph and Wilkins; but none of these men has been so thoroughly and so long identified in the public mind with the roots of Negro discontent in the United States. None of them has been more completely a denizen of that heart of darkness which we are now only beginning to understand.

2. North to Harlem

"Adam views himself as a joke on the whole white race," one of Powell's closest allies from the past has said. "They think he's a Negro. And he views himself as a joke on all Negroes. They think he's a Negro too." Powell has claimed that his maternal grandmother was an octoroon, the mistress of a white New York beer baron who lived for a time in Virginia. In *Marching Blacks* he wrote that his mother came from the Busters of West Virginia, "a fighting family of mountain people," and that his paternal grandmother was part Choctaw Indian. Yet he remembers his paternal grandfather as an ex-slave with a nine-inch high letter "P" branded into his back. He has described his paternal grandmother, Sally Powell, as a freed slave and a strong-willed woman; after being freed, she once was ordered off a path to a water-well by a white woman. Sally threw the woman to the ground, pulled her skirt over her head and doused her between the legs with a pail of cold water.

But like most Negro Americans—whose origins are be-clouded in a history of illegitimacy, arising chiefly out of the ancient claim of landmasters to the beds of their female slaves—Powell's ancestry is beyond reliable reconstruction. His father, the Reverend Adam Clayton Powell, Sr., wrote in his autobiography, *Against The Tide:* "On my paternal side, I know less than little about my ancestors. My maternal grandmother was dominated largely by Indian blood and traits. She was very fond of eating rats, and wanted to be going somewhere all the time. She was a great hunter of small game and taught me the art of hunting. My mother's father was German. I never saw him, but was told he was handsome and brilliant."

Powell senior was fair-skinned and patrician. Dr. Kenneth Clark, a Negro social psychologist, recalls: "When, as a child, I first saw him, I thought he was God." During the early 1940's, when a series of race riots had shocked the United States and race feeling was running high, Powell senior was in Detroit on a lecture tour. One day he wandered into a lunchroom in a Negro neighborhood. He sat down and ordered ice cream. The patrons nearby glared at him and moved away. The proprietor refused to serve him. He overheard vile comments about the white race, and suddenly realized that the Negroes in the lunchroom thought he was white. Nervously, he got up and backed toward the door. Running through his mind at that moment was the plight of a Chinese laundryman in Harlem during some particularly violent race riots in 1935. Marauding Negroes were smashing the display windows of the white shopkeepers in Harlem. The laundryman, observing an angry band approaching his store, hurried outside to defend his windows. He held up his arms and shouted: "Me colored too!" The Reverend Powell thought that had those Detroit Negroes started to accost him he would have emulated the Chinese shopkeeper and yelled: "Me colored too!"

Adam Powell, Sr. was born near Martin's Mill at the conflux of the Magotty and Soak Creeks in Franklin County, Virginia, in 1865, twenty-five days after Lee's surrender at Appomattox. His earliest recollections were of poverty: his mother, stepfather, and six other "inmates," as he called them, lived in a one-room log cabin on five acres of land. The rent was one dollar a month, and their toughest problem was to pay it, and to meet payments on a yoke of oxen they had bought on the installment plan. They all slept, ate, bathed, and entertained in the one room. At 6 a.m. each day, before going into the fields, they had a breakfast of fried pork and corn pone and coffee made of rye. One year the crops were so bad that the corn and wheat were used up by April, and they lived on dried apples and black-eyed peas for six weeks until the new crops matured.

In 1875, Powell's stepfather read in a Washington, D.C., newspaper that wages were higher in West Virginia—a Negro could make up to a dollar a day there. So the family sold its chickens, hogs, cows, and mules, and embarked on a two-day train ride to a tiny farm on the Kanawha River, opposite Colesburg, West Virginia. A year later, they moved on to a place called Paint Creek and Powell resumed his schooling.

On his way to the schoolhouse one winter morning, he overtook a six-year-old classmate named Mattie Fletcher Shaffer and assisted her over an open bridge covered with ice. They met at the bridge on many subsequent mornings, and Powell always helped her across with brotherly concern. Twelve years later, when he was a divinity student in Washington, they were married, and remained so until her death in 1945.

Aside from meeting Mattie, Powell's eight years in West Virginia were a "mental and moral disaster," he claimed. "If there were five men over 20 years of age living at the time in the Kanawha Valley between Malden and Hawksnest with high moral ideals or literary aspirations, I never met them," he wrote. "The chief aim of the average man was to possess a pistol, a pair of brass knuckles and a jug of hard liquor. Fights were numerous and life was cheap. . . . The itinerant preachers who stopped at our house exhorted me to seek the Lord, but I did not take them seriously because they could drink more liquor and eat more stolen chickens with less compunction of conscience than I." Work was scarce for young men, so he left home and went to nearby Rendville, Ohio, and took a job in a coal mine for $100 a month. According to Powell, he gambled it all away consistently and was among the leading "sinners" in Rendville. Then a week-long revival meeting came to the coal town and Powell, along with dozens of his fellow revellers, abruptly "got religion." He bought a new suit of clothes, stopped gambling, joined the local Sunday School, and eventually was appointed deputy marshall by the mayor. He had "made it to the harbor of Grace."

He determined on a career in the legislature, and applied for admission to Howard University Law School, in Washington, D.C., but was turned down for dearth of qualifications. He moved on to Washington anyway, and there, in the summer of 1888, was seized by a powerful desire to become a preacher. Wayland Seminary and College in the capital accepted him as a student. In order to finish in four years, he undertook nine hours of instruction on two days of the school week and seven on the other three. He paid his way by working summers and acting as headwaiter in the school dining room.

After graduation, he accepted an offer to be pastor of the tiny Ebenezer Baptist Church in Philadelphia, at a salary of $8 a week. He supplemented that income by working as a waiter during the summer in an Atlantic City Hotel. Within a year he was recommended for the pastorship of Immanuel Baptist Church in New Haven, Connecticut— an impoverished parish in the shadow of Yale University— which at the time had a congregation of 135.

Powell accepted the appointment, and for the next 15 years

he looked after the spiritual needs of the Immanuel Baptist congregation. He enrolled as a special student at the Yale Divinity school and continued the laborious process of self-education that had begun in the one-room log cabin in Franklin County, Virginia. He discovered in himself a pronounced oratorical talent and set about developing it. Soon he was in some small demand as a lecturer in and around New Haven, and was able to enhance his income by accepting speaking engagements. This increment was all the more welcome because his salary came from the collections taken up on the second and fourth Sundays of the month. If it rained on either or both of those days, nobody came to church and the pastor's income suffered accordingly. At such times, his wife Mattie summoned her ingenuity in providing food for the two of them.

Powell's first child—a daughter, Blanche Fletcher Powell—was born in New Haven on July 24, 1898. His second, Adam Clayton Powell, Jr., arrived on November 29, 1908, almost simultaneously with an invitation from New York's Abyssinian Baptist Church urging him to accept the pastorship of their congregation. He recalled, "I was too full of energy to remain long in New Haven. I needed a heavy load to steady me."

He was not prepared for the size of the load that was arranged about his shoulders in New York. Abyssinian Baptist had just celebrated its hundredth anniversary. It had started as a tiny parish on Worth Street in lower Manhattan in 1808, and then moved to Waverly Place in Greenwich Village. At the time Powell, Sr. arrived, it was located on 40th Street between 7th and 8th Avenues in one of the most rollicking red light districts in New York. Prostitutes prowled the streets at all hours; some were in the habit of standing on the sidewalk outside Abyssinian Baptist after services, their dresses half-unbuttoned, loudly soliciting. Others grabbed men's hats and ran into doorways in an attempt to get them to follow.

The pastor's apartment, it turned out, was a cold-water flat across the street from the church; the only other occupants of the building were streetwalkers. Powell made two major discoveries in his first days at Abyssinian Baptist: first, his appointment had not been the unanimous decision of the church's deacons—a vocal and militant minority was still trying to convince the previous pastor to change his mind and stay on; and secondly, the church was almost $150,000 in debt, its checking account was $300 overdrawn, and it had never had even the most elementary bookkeeping system.

Powell first tried to do something about the harlots: he complained to the mayor and wrote angry letters to the daily papers. As a result, anonymous threats were made on his life, and once, while he was walking on 40th Street with his young son Adam, an assailant hurled a paper bag full of human excrement from a nearby rooftop. It missed them, but the bag broke and splattered young Adam's clean white suit.

Eventually, Powell was able to rid the neighborhood of the more blatant prostitutes, and the congregation began to discern that their pastor was indeed an exceptional person. They moved him out of the dank cold-water flat into better quarters.

As early as 1911, it was apparent to Powell that Harlem, not Manhattan's West Side, was the destination of Abyssinian Baptist. "The great shoal of fish was four miles away [in Harlem]," he wrote, "and other schools by the thousands were swimming in that direction." Harlem was not then the Black Ghetto it became after World War I. It was instead an all-new community of well-constructed one-family houses north of Central Park, designed for the upper middle class New Yorker who wanted to escape the midtown marketplace at day's end. Two Negro families moved into 134th Street west

of Fifth Avenue in 1900 and from that seed grew the largest
Negro enclave in the world.

The elders of Abyssinian Baptist fought Reverend Powell's
effort to move the church to Harlem. They claimed that the
40th Street property could one day be sold for a million dollars. But World War I depressed property values on the West
Side and put an end to that argument.

At about the same time, the messianic figure of Marcus
Garvey arrived in Harlem from Jamaica and began preaching black nationalism with a fervor that left an indelible
mark on the Negro consciousness. "The coming to Harlem
of Garvey . . . was more significant to the Negro than the
World War, the Southern exodus and the fluctuation of property values," Reverend Powell wrote. "The cotton picker of
Alabama, bending over his basket, and the poor ignorant
Negro of the Mississippi Delta, crushed beneath a load of
prejudice, lifted their heads and said, 'Let's go to Harlem to
see this Black Moses.' "

In the spring of 1920, as a result of their pastor's strong
urging, the elders of Abyssinian Baptist bought six lots on
West 138th Street in Harlem. But the post-war price spiral
was so steep that $300,000 would be required to build the
kind of church which the pastor had in mind, and the deacons
were unwilling to undertake the debt. So the plan languished
for a year while Powell grew more impatient. Finally, in
December, 1921, he mounted his pulpit and blistered his
congregation for their penny-pinching and announced his
resignation "because you do not believe in progressive and
aggressive leadership."

They were shocked at the prospect of losing him. Fifteen
days later, the 40th Street property was sold for $190,000, and
building contracts were signed for a new, massive Abyssinian
Baptist Church, to be built in Harlem. In the astonishingly
short period of four years, the entire mortgage—a third of a

million dollars—was to be paid off, a testament to the energy and business astuteness of the senior Powell.

The Harlem of 1923 to which he brought his wife, Mattie, their 25-year-old daughter, Blanche, and their 15-year-old son, Adam, was not yet the Harlem of bleak tenements and pervasive poverty. The Depression was still six years away. A periodical called *The Harlem Monthly* had written in 1893: "It is evident to the most superficial observer that the centre of fashion, wealth, culture and intelligence must, in the near future, be found in the ancient and honorable village of Harlem. . . ." It was New York's first suburb. Working-class families, at the time, customarily paid ten to twenty dollars a month rent in other sections of New York; apartments in one row of Harlem brownstones in 1900 were renting for $100 a month, and were occupied by federal judges, prominent businessmen, and theatrical producers.

The major reason for Harlem's real estate boom was a proposed subway line that would link it with downtown Manhattan. It was taken as unassailable truth that property values would double and triple as soon as the subway was completed. William Waldorf Astor erected an apartment house on Seventh Avenue at a cost of half a million dollars; real estate sections of the Sunday newspapers were heavy with advertisements describing the gracious living available to New Yorkers having the means and the taste to take advantage of it. The speculation led to outlandish increases in the price of real estate; the get-rich-quick fever had hit the city. A piece of property bought for $10,000 one week was sold for $15,000 the next—and then re-sold for successively higher prices. And construction went on in spite of the uncertainty over how long it would take to complete the subway. Soon, well-built homes were standing vacant because there was no demand to match this new supply.

The bubble burst around 1905. Many real estate investors

were faced with financial ruin. Rather than suffer the losses, most of them were willing to rent their properties to Negroes, and collect the high rentals which Negroes customarily had to pay. Others simply threatened to rent to Negroes, and thus extorted the purchase price of homes from certain white residents of Harlem who were determined to keep their neighborhoods white. The first use of "blockbusting" occurred during this frantic period: shrewd operators "placed" Negro families in neighborhoods, then bought up adjacent homes at deflated prices when white residents fled.

When the Negroes of New York saw what was happening they hastened to Harlem where, for the first time in their lives, really fine housing was available to them. Many owners fought the "invasion" bitterly. They banded together in such groups as the Anglo-Saxon Realty Corporation, the Harlem Property Owners' Protective Association, the Committee of Thirty, and the Harlem Property Owners' Improvement Association. They signed covenants agreeing not to rent or sell to Negroes: "We herewith resolve that every colored real estate broker be notified as to the following: That the owners of this section have unanimously agreed not to rent their houses for colored occupancy. . . ." Negroes took special pride in "breaking" these Covenant Blocks and that manner of resistance soon proved ineffective.

There followed a period of panic selling. Between 1905 and 1915 there occurred a great erosion of resolve on the part of landowners as one block after another became totally inhabited by Negroes. The dilemma for the landlords was whether to take a hard line on the exclusion of Negroes and lose everything or rent to Negroes at higher prices and make a profit. Most of them chose the latter course.

Thus the Black Ghetto was born and grew. In 1915, 50,000 Negroes lived there in a 23-block area. It was a community, like many other Negro ghettos around the nation, which was "isolated from many of the impulses of the common life and little understood by the white world," as one writer put it. Still, Harlem was unique. For Negroes everywhere, it was a symbol of the good life: its avenues were broad and tree-lined, its homes capacious and well-made. A 1914 National Urban League report said: "Those of the race who desire to live in grand style . . . can now realize their cherished ambition."

The grand style was not destined to last. Between 1915 and 1925, millions of Negroes left the South to settle in northern cities; the largest bloc of them went to Harlem. Two main reasons accounted for the influx: World War I and Marcus Garvey.

For Black America, World War I was a dismal and disillusioning experience. The armed forces accepted 370,000 Negroes for service. The Marine Corps, however, would take none, and the Navy restricted black men to a few menial chores. The presence of Negroes in the Army created a whole new area for friction: Where would they be trained? Would they serve in the same units with whites, or be segregated in their own outfits? Would Negroes be allowed to become officers? At home, trade unions confined Negroes to unskilled jobs in war production factories.

Throughout the war, there were sordid conflicts between Negro and white soldiers (as well as between Negro and white factory workers in war plants). Brigadier General James B. Erwin forbade Negro soldiers of the 92nd division to speak to Frenchwomen, and American military police arrested Negroes caught breaking the order. General Pershing's headquarters issued a communique on August 7, 1918:

"To the French Military Mission Stationed with the American Army—Secret Information Concerning the Black American Troops.

"1. We must prevent the rise of any pronounced degree of intimacy between French officers and black officers. We may be courteous and amiable with the last, but we cannot deal with them on the same plane as with the white American officer without deeply wounding the latter. We must not eat with them, must not shake hands or seek to talk or meet with them outside the requirements of military service.

"2. We must not commend too highly the Negro American troops, particularly in the presence of [white] Americans.

"3. Make a point of keeping the native cantonment population from spoiling the Negroes. [White] Americans become greatly incensed at any public expression of intimacy between white women and black men."

In the United States, there were 54 lynchings in 1916, and 38 in 1917. The NAACP organized a silent parade down Fifth Avenue in New York in which 10,000 Negroes protested the killings. A. Philip Randolph was roaming the country making denunciatory speeches about the Negro's treatment in the war; the Justice Department had him jailed for a few days.

The Negro's post-war mood of cynicism and despair was the fertile ground in which Marcus Moziah Garvey flourished and built the first mass movement that American Negroes had known. Adam Powell, Sr. wrote of Garvey: "He is the only man that ever made Negroes who are not black ashamed of their color." Adam Powell, Jr. wrote in *Marching Blacks:* "Marcus Garvey was one of the greatest mass leaders of all time. He was misunderstood and maligned, but he brought to the Negro people for the first time a sense of pride in being black . . . backed by one million followers in splendid array he preached a program of Africa for the Africans. At the outset of his career he distrusted light Negroes and bitterly hated all whites. He combined all the Negro's former attitudes— escape from reality, religious fervor and sorrow songs—wove

them together in a dazzling pattern and cried out to the sub-
merged blacks, 'Any Negro is better than every white.' "

Powell was a young boy on Harlem's streets when Garvey
and his uniformed legions were holding their assemblages.
The pudgy Garvey arrived in the United States from Jamaica
in 1916, at the age of 28, and proceeded to build a mass following in an astonishingly short time. His remarkable oratorical powers, compounded of bombast and heroics, stoked
fires of Negro nationalism that persisted in such Harlem
groups as the African Nationalist Pioneer Movement, the
First Africa Corps, the Moorish Americans, the Garvey Club,
and the Nation of Islam, better known as the Black Muslims.
Garvey, who boasted he was a full-blooded black with no
"taint" of white blood in his veins, told Harlemites what they
most wanted to hear: that a black skin was a symbol of valued
heritage, not a badge of shame; that the Negro past was one
of triumphs and high accomplishments; that a new Negro
Israel would one day be established on the African continent
which would be a refuge for black men and a haven from
lynching and hatred. It was all heady stuff, fiercely chauvin-
istic; and Harlem bought it wholesale.

Garvey had read Booker T. Washington's autobiography,
Up From Slavery, and it had a profound effect on him.
". . . My doom—if I may so call it—dawned upon me . . . ,"
Garvey later wrote. "I asked: 'Where is the black man's Gov-
ernment? Where is his King and his Kingdom? Where is his
President, his country and his ambassador, his army, his navy,
his men of big affairs?' I could not find them, and then I de-
clared, 'I will help to make them.' " Garveyism had found its
origin, ironically, in the work of the American, Booker T.
Washington, a leader who was contemned by many American
Negro intellectuals as the worst of Uncle Toms.

Garvey had established his organization in 1914 in Jamaica
and hung on it a title worthy of an *Amos 'n Andy* radio

script: Universal Negro Improvement and Conservation Association and African Communities League. But it was not to be taken frivolously. Among its stated aims were:

"To establish a Universal Confraternity among the race; to promote the spirit of race pride and love; to reclaim the fallen of the race; to administer to and assist the needy; to assist in civilizing the backward tribes of Africa; to strengthen the imperialism of independent African States; to establish Commissionaries or Agencies in the principal countries of the world for the protection of all Negroes, irrespective of nationality; to promote a conscientious Christian worship among the native tribes of Africa; to establish Universities, Colleges and Secondary Schools for the further education and culture of the boys and girls of the race; to conduct a world-wide commercial and industrial intercourse."

Garvey's arrival in the United States barely preceded the industrial expansion of World War I and the concomitant arrival in Northern cities of Southern rural Negroes searching for jobs. Whole towns in the South were vacated as the migration gathered force. It was from those near-illiterate, disillusioned, and superstitious Negroes that Garvey derived his strongest support. They had come North in flight from feudal conditions and a downtrodden status, because they had heard rumors about the opportunities that awaited them. During the war, there were, in fact, jobs for many of them; but later, as the war boom waned, their high expectations gave way to discouragement when it became clear that even in the fabled North they were unwanted. They were unaccustomed to big-city living and soon were herded into black ghettos—the last to be hired and the first to be fired.

Riots occurred, even before the war was over, in New York, Chicago, Los Angeles, Detroit and other large cities. A few bloody months in 1919, during which there occurred 26 outbreaks in American cities, came to be called "The Red Summer." On July 27, 1919, a riot started in Chicago over the accidental drowning of a Negro boy in a white section of a Lake Michigan beach. Some Negroes insisted he had been murdered and the rumor was enough to set off violence that lasted thirteen days. At least 38 persons died in the fighting and hundreds more were injured. More than a thousand families, most of them Negroes, were homeless after the worst outbreak of racial strife in the nation's history.

One result of the episode was that this new breed of transplanted Negro was recognized as something different from the docile animal who had shuffled through Southern folklore for so many decades and who had inspired Mr. Dooley's remark that "th' black has manny fine qualities. He is joyous, lighthearted, an' aisily lynched."

Northern Negroes let it be known they were ready to defend themselves—with bullets if necessary. Harlem became the brain of Negro radicalism in the post-war years, home of such publications as the *Messenger,* the *Voice,* the *Crusader,* the *Challenge,* the *Emancipator* and *The Negro World,* all of which were thought sufficiently dangerous to be cited in a 1919 Department of Justice report on Negro radicalism and sedition. The *Challenge* published in every issue an oath swearing "never to love any flag simply for its color, nor any country for its name. . . . The flag of my affections must rest over me as a banner of protection, not as a sable shroud." The old Uncle Tom race leaders were being replaced by more militant spokesmen (Booker T. Washington had died in 1915). There were men such as A. Philip Randolph and Chandler Owen, in whose mouths the words "equality of the races" seemed to mean just that.

But, up to this time, no Negro organization had ever managed to fuse the Negro masses into any monolithic force for the betterment of Negro-white relations. The National Association for the Advancement of Colored People, which was 12 years old in 1920, and the National Urban League had done their best to help lower-class Negroes, but their principal support had come from upper-class whites—a chronic weakness which circumscribed their field of action. To whom was the more impatient Negro to turn for an articulation of his discouragement?

The time was right for a Marcus Garvey, and he was there. At first Harlemites were skeptical of his sidewalk harangues and dismissed him as another West Indian carpetbagger. But with the start of his newspaper, *The Negro World,* they began to take notice: its pages not only gave news of Negro affairs in the United States, but also described regal splendors in ancient Africa to which the American Negro could refer with pride. He wrote, sometimes in fanciful detail, of the heroism of such Negro slave dissidents as Nat Turner and Denmark Vesey, of the battles of Zulu and Hottentot warriors against their European rulers; he recounted the histories of Moorish and Ethiopian conquests, and the exploits of Toussaint L'Ouverture against the French in Haiti.

To this heady brew, Garvey added the spice of gaudy uniforms, parades down Harlem streets with banners and brass bands and a touch of the occult in the form of high-sounding titles. On ceremonial occasions, he appeared in a bright uniform with cocked hat and cockade, medals and ribbons on his chest, and was driven in humorless splendor through the streets in an open car.

Beginning in 1920, he held annual conventions of his Universal Negro Improvement Association in Harlem. The first of these was an extravaganza that brought delegates from 25 countries and filled Harlem's streets with marching bands and a uniformed "army," the African Legion, whose swords suggested that Negro deliverance might be achieved through force. It also brought the Black Cross Nurses, whose enthusiasm for Garvey's cause exceeded any medical training they might have. On the night of August 2, 1920, 25,000 Negroes met in Madison Square Garden and sang the new UNIA anthem, "Ethiopia, Thou Land of Our Fathers." Garvey mounted the platform and told them: "We are descendants of a suffering people. We are the descendants of a people determined to suffer no longer. . . . We shall now organize the 400,000,000 Negroes of the world into a vast organization to plant the banner of freedom on the great continent of Africa."

When the convention adjourned, Harlem was aware of a powerful new force. Not all Negroes, however, were enthusiastic about Garvey. A. Philip Randolph, who was already an important Negro leader in the early 1920's, said in a speech that "people are now fighting for the erection of democracies, not of empires," and that Negroes did not want "to be the victims of black despotism any more than white despotism." For his trouble, Randolph received in the mail a human hand and a note signed by the Ku Klux Klan telling him, "If you are not in favor with your own race movement, you can't be with ours. [The KKK] wants to see your name in your nigger improvement association as a member, paid up too, in about a week from now. Be careful . . . or we may have to send your hand to someone else." Randolph decided that the grisly package and its message had come from a Garveyite, not the KKK. He continued his criticism of the UNIA.

But the Garvey crusade was too emotional a venture to last. His downfall was occasioned by his plan to form an all-Negro steamship company—the Black Star Line—and involve American Negroes in commerce on a world-wide scale. It was a scheme that touched some primal ambition in American Negroes, and money for the purchase of ships poured in. Sale of Black Star stock was limited to Negroes and no individual could purchase more than two hundred shares. Garvey actually did buy three or four ships, and those rickety vessels

actually made a few voyages carrying cargo and passengers;
but the Black Star Line was at no time solvent and was, in
fact, the object of repeated warnings from the District Attorney that unless the company were organized properly as
a legitimate business venture, the sale of stock would be
halted. Garvey ignored the warnings, and was eventually
indicted for mail fraud—and convicted. While his request for
appeal was being considered, a second indictment, charging
perjury and income tax evasion, was returned. His request for
appeal in the mail fraud case was denied and Garvey was
spirited off to federal prison in Atlanta where he charged that
a conspiracy of the less militant Negro organizations, such as
the NAACP and the Urban League, was responsible for his
plight. President Coolidge commuted Garvey's sentence in
1927 and ordered his release. Since Garvey was not a United
States citizen, and had been convicted of a felony, immigration authorities demanded his deportation as an undesirable
alien. Thus, in December, 1927, the "Black Moses" of so
many exalted expectations, was put on a ship in New Orleans
and sent back to Jamaica where he continued his preaching
of black nationalism.

Retrospectively, the Negro press appraised Garvey's contribution to the Negro cause and found him something other
than a complete charlatan. "A movement that commands the
fanatical devotion of two million people—black or white, cul-
tured or crude—must have something in it more than red and
green uniforms," insisted the *Amsterdam News*. "It is because
Marcus Garvey made black people proud of their race. In a
world where black is despised, he taught them to admire and
praise black things and black people. . . . They rallied to him
because he heard and responded to the heart beat of his race."
Garvey himself said: "You will see from the start we tried to
dignify our race. If I am to be condemned for that, I am satisfied."

Adam Powell, Sr. and his family had arrived in Harlem at the height of Garvey's fame when the undercurrent of black nationalism was strong. In addition, the ghetto was entering its most lusty and carefree era, one which has come to be called the Negro Renaissance. It was a time of flowering for Negro artists, poets, and writers: Langston Hughes, Countee Cullen, Claude McKay, Jean Toomer, and James Weldon Johnson. Hughes wrote: "It was a period when local and visiting royalty were not at all uncommon in Harlem . . . it was a period when at least one charming colored chorus girl, amber enough to pass for a Latin American, was living in a penthouse, with all her bills paid by a gentleman whose name was banker's magic on Wall Street. It was a period when every season there was at least one hit play on Broadway acted by a Negro cast . . . it was the period when the Negro was in vogue."

Harlem in the giddy 1920's acquired a reputation for exoticism. Prohibition was a washout in the ghetto where speakeasies flourished by the scores: the Glory Hole, the Blue Room, Leroy's Basement, Brownie's Coal Bed, Small's, Happy Rhone's, and Lulu Belle's. Duke Ellington was at the Cotton Club and Louis Armstrong was at the Sunset. A Negro singer named Nora Holt sang "My Daddy Rocks Me With One Steady Roll" at a party for the Prince of Wales. A dowager rushed up to her afterwards exclaiming enthusiastically: "Oh, my dear! How beautifully you sing those Negro spirituals."

Every evening after dark, limousines emptied white patrons into Harlem's jazz joints. Paul Robeson starred in Eugene O'Neill's *All God's Chillun Got Wings* and rent parties offered more impromptu entertainment, along with chitterlings, pig snouts, black-eyed peas, and collard greens. Langston Hughes rhapsodized: "Harlem, like a Picasso painting in his cubistic period. . . . Melting pot Harlem—Harlem of honey and chocolate and caramel and rum and vinegar and lemon and lime and gall. Dusky dream Harlem rumbling into a nightmare tunnel where the subway from the Bronx keeps right on downtown, where the money from the night-clubs goes right back downtown, where the jazz is drained to Broadway, whence Josephine goes to Paris, Robeson to London . . . Garvey to the Atlanta Federal Penitentiary . . . but Duke Ellington to fame and fortune, Lena Horne to Broadway. . . ."

Adam Powell, Jr. was too young at the time to participate in the merriment. His childhood was a sheltered one and, by the standards of most Harlem children, more than comfortable. His father's dabbling in real estate added to the family's income. Adam attended Public School No. 5 and Townsend Harris High School—at that time a preferred school for gifted children. His grades were excellent. Abyssinian Baptist parishioners remember him as a "pretty" child and a handsome adolescent, who was pampered by the church members. The principal hazard of his young life was his fair skin, which made his situation in Harlem ambiguous. He told Dan Wakefield, a writer for *Esquire:* "When I was about twelve, we moved into 136th Street and we were one of the first Negro families there. Well, there were always fights between the Negroes and the Irish—we called 'em 'Micks.' I remember one night my mother sent me out to the bakery and I was stopped by a bunch of Negro kids and they beat me up because they thought I was white. The next night I went out and a gang of Irish kids beat me up because I was Negro. Later that week another group of Negroes stopped me and they said, 'What are you?' I said, 'Mixed.' Well, they thought I said 'Mick,' so they beat me up."

Three years after the move to Harlem, Powell's sister Blanche died at the age of 28. Recalling her death, Powell told acquaintances in 1963 that he was probably in love with her, psychologically speaking. Her death was, in any case, the first cloud of sorrow that entered his life. The next year, he graduated from Townsend Harris and enrolled in New York's City College. It was there, according to all accounts, that Powell discovered girls—an admitted preoccupation that has been near the center of his activities ever since. "Adam was a chaser even in his mid-teens," an acquaintance recalls, "but he didn't chase them any harder than they chased him. The girls just loved him, even then." Amid all the chasing, Adam promptly flunked out of City College in his second semester, in spite of his demonstrated high intelligence.

His father was bitterly disappointed. With the help of a family friend, Adam was enrolled in Colgate University in upstate New York. He decided on a pre-medical course of studies, with the intention of becoming a surgeon. One of his best college friends, star Negro athlete Ray Vaughn, was interviewed by the New York *World-Telegram* in April, 1963. He recalled how he and Powell bought a Model A Ford and used it for week-end junkets to New York. "I was often a guest at the Powells'," Vaughn said. "One night Adam's father called me into the living room. He told me he wanted Adam to follow him in the Church and take over some day, and asked me to try to persuade Adam to change from pre-med to a theology major. That night, as we drove back to school, I spoke to Adam about the advantages of going into the church—it was all set up for him, after all. He saw the point and, not long afterward, he dropped the pre-med and began to prepare for the ministry."

But the young man who one day would be a leader and articulator for the Negro people faced a crisis during his Colgate career which could have ruined him as a prospective Negro pastor, and certainly as an elected Negro official. Vaughn recalled: "When the fall term started, the track coach told me to hunt up a Negro boy named Powell who was supposed to be a good 440-yard-dash prospect." Vaughn was unable to find him. Then, a few weeks later, Vaughn's German professor was reseating his students in alphabetical order, and in so doing, called out the name "Powell." Vaughn looked at the freshman student, and thought "That can't be my 440 man. He's white." But then he looked harder and decided that Powell was, in fact, a Negro.

"He was passing as white," Vaughn said. School authorities had put Powell in a room with white students; ordinarily, Negro students roomed together. Also, he had been pledged by a white fraternity. According to Vaughn, it was the fraternity pledge which ended Powell's brief term as a "white" man. A routine check of his background by his fraternity turned up the information that Powell's home was in Harlem and that his father was pastor of a Negro congregation. The student board of governors voted to send him to coventry, according to Vaughn, and nobody on the campus, white or Negro, would speak to him. A few days later, Vaughn said, Powell came to his room and announced: "I think I've made a mistake."

"Boy, you sure did," Vaughn answered. Powell enlisted Vaughn's aid in salvaging the situation and switching to a Negro fraternity, thereby putting an end to the episode. Still, Vaughn's recollection of Powell in those days remains friendly. "Adam was a likable guy," he said, "and a great one with the girls."

Powell graduated from Colgate with a respectable record. So great was the relief and satisfaction of Adam senior that he sent the new graduate on a three-month, 16,000-mile tour to the Holy Land, Europe, and Egypt.

By then the honeymoon of the bumptious 1920's was over; the Depression was settling over Harlem like a cold embrace, and Adam Powell was on the brink of his public career.

3. Depression and Protest in the Ghetto

Negroes were, as the 1920's ended, beginning to believe that the Northern ghetto system, while not the Utopia it had seemed from the South, was at least bearable and, with agitation, might improve. But as the Depression hardened, it became apparent that Negroes would be the ones to suffer most. Almost half of the relatively skilled Negro males in the nation lost their jobs during the years 1930-1936. Negro men sat on curbstones in Harlem and dumbly read their dismissal slips. Day by day, the streets filled up with the idle. What was to be the outcome? Starvation? Death by exposure? New York had no Department of Public Welfare to prevent such disasters. It was a time of "appalling suffering and privation, of grown men crying, and women wringing their hands in empty kitchens." As *Ebony* magazine described it, a time ". . . of battered furniture standing on concrete curbs, of crowds protesting and Communists organizing the discontent, of big government trucks cruising through Negro neighborhoods and dropping off Navy beans and powdered milk, a time of locusts and a mood of despair."

In the spring of 1931, the firing of five Negro doctors from the Harlem Hospital supplied the impetus for Adam Clayton Powell, Jr.'s first public performance as a Harlem leader. His entry into the ministry, on April 24 of that year, had been an event in Harlem, filling Abyssinian Baptist with well-wishers. No fewer than 200 ministers attended the reception to meet the promising son of their old friend. Adam, at the time, was acting as business manager of Abyssinian Baptist Church, and director of its social and educational program. Simultaneously, he was taking courses at nearby Columbia University toward a Master of Arts degree. Harlem Hospital was a poorly-staffed and under-equipped institution called "the butcher shop" by Harlemites. It was, in addition, riven with caste feeling. Graduates of Negro universities and medical schools were deemed less qualified than those from white schools. The discharged doctors, from Howard and Meharry Universities, claimed they were treated as second-class practitioners.

Powell was acquainted with the doctors and advised them to fight the decision. They picketed, protested, formed committees, and sent angry delegations to the hospital superintendent's office. Nothing worked. They wrote to the Board of Aldermen for an appointment, but were refused. Finally, a large group of protesters, Powell among them, descended on City Hall by car, bus, and subway train. The Board of Estimate was in session. Leaving the marchers at the steps of City Hall, Powell and a committee made their way to the board room, were halted briefly by the acting Mayor, and finally invited in by the President of the Board of Aldermen. They stated their case, went away peacefully, and the five doctors subsequently were reinstated. Powell claimed that the demonstration at City Hall resulted in a general clean-up of the hospital, investigation of the nurses' training school, and construction of a women's pavilion. But, in fact, conditions at the hospital remained so bad that a full scale scandal erupted over them a few years later during the LaGuardia administration. The hospital's rate of infant mortality continued to be the highest in the city: 120 per 1000 births.

Adam Powell, Sr. was deeply involved with relief work during those years. He set up a free soup kitchen in the basement of Abyssinian Baptist, contributed a thousand dollars to get it started, and put his son in charge. Adam junior, with the help of college friends and church volunteers, handed out thousands of pieces of clothing and shoes and often fed a thousand people a day. Married men applying at the church were given three days work a week at $3 a day and the community house was opened as sleeping quarters for the homeless. It was, according to Powell senior, "the largest relief bureau ever set up by colored people." The pastor asked his church employees to contribute one-fifth of their salaries to the relief work. At the same time, he chided ministers all around the country for not throwing their whole-hearted efforts into the desperately-needed welfare work. A *New York Age* article reported his declaring "that preachers have robbed people under the guise of religion and should return the loot." He quoted from an Urban League survey showing that "about one-fourth of the colored people in the twenty-five large cities are out of work and hungry. This is not only a most pathetic challenge to every race leader and race organization, but to every Negro individual who has a job and is living comfortably. If the churches do not answer their challenge, they ought to shut up and close up."

His remarks caused a national dispute in religious circles. One minister said Powell was "fortunate in being pastor of one of the richest congregations in this country," and regretted that he had sullied the good reputations of Negro ministers everywhere. "If Reverend Powell's assertions are true," the man said, "then 30,000 Negro preachers should be in jail." Powell claimed at that point that he was too busy feeding and clothing the poor to get any further embroiled in the discussion.

It was during Easter Week of 1932 when the Depression was in full flower, that Adam junior met a pretty Savannah girl named Isabel Washington. She had been a Cotton Club chorine and later a dancer on Broadway. The young minister promptly fell in love and began an elaborate campaign to make Miss Washington his wife. The elder Powell met this exercise in young love with high disapproval, as did the deacons of Abyssinian Baptist Church. Not only was Miss Washington an actress but also a divorcee with a young son. Powell senior saw all his hopes and high expectations for Adam junior going awry and fought the romance. Adam would not be turned. He was in love with Isabel Washington, he said, and that was all—even if it meant giving up his right to the prestigious and lucrative pastorship of Abyssinian Baptist.

Adam Powell, Sr. relented finally when he recognized that his son was determined to marry. He performed the ceremony himself on March 8, 1933. Thousands of church members stood outside Abyssinian Baptist in the rain for a glimpse of the glamorous couple; thousands more queued up at the reception to congratulate them. Adam Powell had performed his first conspicuous act of independence and prevailed so satisfyingly that the lesson would remain with him all his life.

Isabel Washington, as it happened, confounded the church deacons' notions about showgirls by immersing herself in the affairs of Abyssinian Baptist. She abandoned the stage and set about organizing choirs and committees to abet the work of her husband and her father-in-law. Powell adopted the child of her former marriage and settled into the life of a big-city preacher.

The Harlem in which he moved was a mean and deflated community. In the middle 1930's, Harlem newspaper readers were fed a diet of five major ingredients: the Scottsboro boys, Ethiopia, Father Divine, Joe Louis, and mayhem. Headlines in the ghetto press featured kidnappings, murder, banditry and knifings. The ghetto at that time ran from 110th to 155th Street, and from the Harlem River to Amsterdam Avenue, an area of almost one thousand acres. Besides native-born Negroes, it was home to Ethiopians, West Indians, Spaniards, and Puerto Ricans, almost all of whom earned their living outside Harlem as waiters, cooks, porters, doormen, handymen, longshoremen, and house servants. Before the Depression, Harlem had been an active community and, to a superficial eye, a happy one. It had, in addition, been a Republican stronghold (Adam Powell, Sr. for example, was an active Republican until the middle 1930's). In the state elections of 1930, Harlem went Democratic, re-electing Franklin D. Roosevelt governor and Herbert H. Lehman lieutenant governor.

The stranglehold of landlords gave rise to the "rent party." Tenants invited in neighbors and passers-by. They sold whiskey, played the numbers game, and danced. In the thirties the scores of rent parties in Harlem on any evening were often the scene of dope pushing and impromptu prostitution.

Prices for food stayed high in Harlem in spite of the surrounding economic collapse. "Whale stations" began to appear on 7th and 8th Avenues where six pieces of fried fish and some french fried potatoes could be bought for fifteen cents. Restaurants were closing down, but basement-front lunchrooms—where a meal could be had for twenty-five cents —proliferated.

The downtown press was not kind to Harlem in those days, reflecting a general disillusionment with the ghetto as an exotic midway of "high yaller" women, jazz music, and frenetic dancing. Harlem was unmasked, and shown for what it had been all along. The tens of thousands of black South-

erners who had come to Harlem fifteen years earlier to hear
the sweet encouragement of Marcus Garvey and who stayed
to see their dream take tentative root in the promised prosperity of World War I, stood on Harlem's streetcorners now
and peered out from her grimy vestibules, watching their
hopes being sullied over and finally lost in the refuse heaps
of a city that never wanted them. Langston Hughes wondered:

> *What happens to a dream deferred?*
> *Does it dry up*
> *Like a raisin in the sun?*
> *Or fester like a sore—*
> *And then run?*
> *Does it stink like rotten meat?*
> *Or crust and sugar over—*
> *Like a syrupy sweet?*
> *Maybe it just sags*
> *Like a heavy load*
> *Or does it explode?*

Harlem exploded. On March 19, 1935, the ghetto erupted
in a race riot in which four were killed, scores injured, display windows smashed, and damage suffered to the extent of
a quarter of a million dollars. It was the bitterest night of
Harlem's experience. Recalling it, Adam Powell wrote that
". . . Harlem burst into flames. The fuel had long been ready.
It had dried with the wind of the ghetto as the years went by.
The depression, the bitter memories of the South and the
constant reminders by the press of the misdeeds of Mason-
Dixon fascists made it possible for an insignificant spark to
ignite the center of Negro America."

At 4 p.m. on the day of the riot, a 16-year-old boy was
caught stealing a ten-cent penknife in Kress's dime store on
125th Street. A store detective hustled the boy into a back

room and, in so doing, threatened him loudly with a beating. A Negro woman observed the scene and hurried outside to spread word that the store's white owners were about to man-handle the youth. Soon, a group of picketers from the left-wing Young Liberators League appeared with hastily-printed signs reading "Kress Brutality Beats Negro Child" and "Kress Brutality Seriously Injured Negro Child." A Negro man erected a platform outside the store and began haranguing passers-by, not only about the supposed brutality, but about the intransigence of white store owners all along 125th Street in giving jobs to Negroes.

Then someone in the crowd threw bottles through two large plate glass windows. The mob enlarged to more than three thousand persons. The police emergency squad, an advance guard of the more than 500 policemen who eventu-ally entered the fray, deployed in the shopping district, combed rooftops and fired shots in the air in efforts to restore order. But the mob would not be headed.

A woman shouted: "There's a hearse! It's come to take the boy's body out the back door!" A hearse indeed passed nearby, but on a mission unrelated to Kress's capture of the petty thief. That, however, was all the crowd needed. Their fury intensified, and they surged forward to smash hundreds of windows and loot stores.

Spontaneously, the mob atomized into marauding bands. They assaulted white pedestrians and raged over a one square mile area looking for property and persons on whom to exor-cise their wrath. Hundreds, black and white, were injured in knifings and fist fights. At 1:00 a.m., a Negro man was shot fatally in the stomach at 121st Street and Seventh Avenue. A New York *Daily News* photographer was beaten by Negroes outside the Hotel Theresa. Another man was shot in the chest while attempting to loot an A&P store. Jails were filling up as police arrested looters. The Harlem Merchants' Association hurriedly wired Governor Herbert Lehman advising him that the city police were unable to quell the violence and asking for "military assistance." Lehman refused.

Reports of other fatalities filtered in as the terrible night wore on. Mayor Fiorello LaGuardia kept a vigil at his home, issuing intermittent orders to the battle zone. Meanwhile, the apprehended youth at Kress's five-and-dime store had been ushered out the back door after a stern warning. Nonetheless, rumors of his murder outran attempts to gainsay it, and the great pent-up fury of Harlem continued to spend itself into the morning hours.

At dawn, the spectacle of 125th Street was sickening, with great shards of glass covering the sidewalks for blocks, and dazed men stumbling home as though numbed from orgiastic pleasures.

The District Attorney, William Copeland Dodge, told reporters he saw a Red plot. "My purpose is to let the Communists know they cannot come into this country and upset our laws," he said. The *Daily Worker* did, in fact, make capital of the catastrophe with a six-column headline, "NEGRO HARLEM TERRORIZED." But Roy Wilkins, then editor of the NAACP organ, *Crisis*, insisted that authorities would make "a great mistake to dismiss the riot as a demonstration of a few communists and agitators." The violence, he argued, was induced by discrimination against Negroes in employment and housing.

Reporters sought out the young assistant pastor at Abyssinian Baptist and queried him for an interpretation of the violence. Job discrimination and economic maladjustment were the main causes, he told them. He also pointed to the Scottsboro case (in which nine young Alabama Negroes were accused of raping two white women) and to the invasion of Ethiopia by Mussolini—a power play condemned by Negro intellectuals as racist, and which had caused minor but bitter skirmishes between Harlem Negroes and local Italians. "The trouble seems to be over for the time being," Powell said during a meeting at his home at 666 St. Nicholas Avenue, "but it may break out in a month or even in a week unless our people get some assurance of economic adjustment to end the discrimination against them." He recalled that two years earlier, Negro churchmen had warned Harlem shopkeepers that they must employ Negro help since they were making their livelihoods from Negroes in a Negro community. "They think of all the milk used in Harlem," he said, "yet not one bottle of it is delivered by Negroes. We see our boys and girls come out of college, well-trained, compelled to go on relief or work as redcaps." He also seized the opportunity to complain that rents in Harlem were 25% higher than anywhere else in the city.

Mayor LaGuardia's report on the riot was perceptive: "This sudden breach in the public order was the result of a highly emotional situation among the colored people of Harlem due in large part to the nervous strain of years of unemployment and insecurity," it insisted.

Harlem quieted to a tentative peace after the Black Ides of March. Describing the incident in *Marching Blacks*, Powell exclaimed: "The Harlem riot was a revolt of the common man against the tyranny of a bastard democracy. It focused worldwide attention on New York's black ghetto. Out of it came new schools, new hospitals, an investigation and inquiry by the Governor, but more than that—out of it came a new Negro."

Powell was emerging as an articulate and energetic spokesman for the underdog black. He was about to embark on a phase of conspicuous social action in Harlem's streets and political clubhouses. This phase would put him in picket lines and protest meetings with Communists and rightists—visionaries of every political coloration—and would thrust him into the center of an extended civil rights campaign that would persist until the opening of World War II.

Eleven months after the Harlem riot, on February 15, 1936, Powell began writing a newspaper column for the weekly *Amsterdam News*. As a title, he chose the traditional symbol of political exhortation—"The Soap Box." The column appeared prominently on the *Amsterdam News* editorial page accompanied by an inset picture of its 28-year-old author. The paper introduced Powell's first journalistic effort with the heading: "Our newest columnist is a graduate of Colgate University and is junior minister of historic Abyssinian Baptist Church. His liberal column will cover a wide range of social and economic subjects." Powell announced straightaway: "What Harlem needs is a year-round, air-conditioned soap box. It is my intention to try to supply this need. I hereby set up my soap box in this corner."

In subsequent weeks, he got down to the business of establishing his own political posture, and it was markedly leftist. "Boys and girls, political party days are over. All groups are rapidly concentrating at the two opposite poles—laborers and leisurers. As a race 98% working class—God knows what the other 2% are—we must go left with the laborers. We must cast our voting powers to those who offer the laboring class most. . . . Negroes, we are at the crossroads. Left or right? Freedom or oppression? Quo vadis?"

"The Soap Box" treated every subject that might interest Harlemites, from the quality of the shows at the Apollo Theater to the rise of Nazism in Germany to the Negro church, which he insisted "has the potentiality of being the greatest force in our race. . . . Let us stop commercializing the church and make the church an instrument, keen and rugged, fighting exploitation and raising the standards of our race along the entire battlefront of human liberties. Upon this basis only does the church deserve to survive."

He scolded Negroes for upsetting the fruit stands of Italian merchants and breaking the windows of Italian tailors in reprisals for Mussolini's surprise assault on Ethiopia. "When fascism is defeated—and it will be in my lifetime—it is going to be defeated by the masses of the liberty loving who refuse to be puppets of capitalism. Fascism is capitalism making its last stand. . . . It works upon man's oldest prejudices—race and religion—and plays the masses against each other. Fascism is Death and Hunger riding at night into the home of every soul that sits quiescently by. . . . Only world brotherhood of working peoples united, despite color and creed, will stop fascism."

Among Powell's other principal targets were William Randolph Hearst (he suggested Negroes boycott all Hearst newspapers, magazines, and the movie theaters that showed Hearst's *Metrotone News*), Mayor LaGuardia (often called "the Little Flower") and Father Divine, the sensationalist preacher who frequently called himself "God." "LaGuardia and Father Divine are linking up for the fall political fight," Powell wrote. ". . . 'God' and Mammon together at last. That's an unbeatable combination—the Little Flower for Mayor and 'God' for President of the Board of Aldermen. . . . Put this in your scrapbook: beware of Greeks bearing gifts, colored men looking for loans, and whites who understand the Negro."

Powell's column was a goad to the Harlem conscience. He instructed his readers dutifully, like a New England schoolmaster, in spite of his youth and inexperience. His precocity was apparent in every column: the well-developed historical sense, the cosmic concerns that extended far beyond the bounds of parochial Harlem politics, the recurring light touch and easy communicativeness. "I pity Broun and Pegler, not to mention Mrs. Roosevelt," he wrote. "It must be an awful grind turning out a column each and every day. These few words of mine once a week frequently call for mental acrobatics. To have to turn out the same amount day in and day out would wear me down to a mere shadow. I guess that's why Broun is so emaciated looking. Some day you will meet on the Avenue a thin little runt and say 'There goes Ad Powell. He writes for a daily now.' My 206 pounds will have been dropped by the wayside."

Even when he and Isabel fled Harlem in the summertime for a retreat on Martha's Vineyard, Powell mailed his weekly column back to the ghetto. He advised sweltering Harlemites about books they should read (*I Write As I Please,* by Walter Duranty, and *It Can't Happen Here,* by Sinclair Lewis), and complained that his own summer reading inevitably fell off from its midwinter pace of two books and 17 periodicals a week. "I have a wife who follows the Izaak Walton trail avidly," he wrote. "She also manages to outfish me by the simple process of refusing to bait her hook and refusing to take her fish off when caught." He and Isabel shared happy days on Martha's Vineyard in those summers—swimming, boating, and wandering the island. Still, politics had a way of cropping up, even then. "For seven weeks I let my beard grow until I looked like Balboa. It finally reached such terrifying proportions that I took it to a barber to get it cut. While reclining in the chair I learned the barber was Italian. When he started to shave my neck, he began to talk about Mussolini. Just about the time his razor was sliding back and forth over my Adam's apple, he asked, 'Don't you think Mussolini is the greatest man in the world?' I answered quickly with an eye on the razor. 'Yes, Sir.' "

The most insistent note in Powell's journalism was the exhortation to Harlem Negroes that they meld with the worldwide drift to the political left and unite with workers everywhere, black and white, to assure themselves first-class citizenship. His admiration for the Russian experiment was pronounced and he hammered at the notion that Negroes—more than any other segment of the working classes—were in need of the guidance and inspiration the Soviets could proffer. He flayed Negroes who clung to their middle-class, white-inspired aspirations; who failed to swim out boldly into the main currents of a historical stream he was certain would hasten the Negro to a better life. "The hour has struck for a purge within our race," he insisted. "A purging of so-called Negro society. Away with a caste system within this race of ours. Away with those who feel they are better. Away with our Sugar Hill and Strivers Row complexes. The Negro in the valley is hungry and despised, humiliated, oppressed and he's ready to march."

A purge of quite a different sort was in progress in the Soviet Union, and it caused the first public expression of disappointment over Soviet policies to creep into Powell's writing. Stalin's wholesale obliteration of political enemies came as a shock to many fellow travelers, and Powell too was affected by it. In July, 1937, he wrote: "You know I lean left when it comes to the Soviet. It can sin far greater than any other nation and yet there's always an understanding. But the recent bloody purges have been unable to gain a hearing for even my calmer moments. The cry of 'Trotskyites, Trotskyites!' doesn't strike the same chord it used to. I don't know what it is, but Soviet Russia has seemingly gone berserk." Nonetheless, Powell continued to press upon his readers the doctrine that the sharply leftward path was still the Negro's best hope.

During this period, Powell's aging father was avidly trying to resign the pastorship of Abyssinian Baptist. Two months after the 1935 riot, at the age of 70, he wrote his resignation and sent it to the church deacons. They refused to accept it. Instead, they sent him and his wife on a six-month cruise to Cuba and Panama. After he had rested, they hoped, he would be willing to carry on with his duties. But the following year, the pastor was back with another resignation. It too was refused. Finally, in September, 1937, he declared he would retire in two months whether his resignation was accepted or not and suggested the elders start thinking about holding an election to replace him.

The announcement cast Abyssinian's church members into turmoil. Years earlier it had been assumed that Adam junior would one day succeed his father as a matter of course. But now that he had grown into an ardent leftist, if not a radical, that assumption was weakened. Abyssinian Baptist, placed as it was on West 138th Street, was dependent for its support on many of the Sugar Hill and Strivers Row residents—Harlem's more affluent citizens—whom Powell had been pummelling so remorselessly in his column. Abyssinian's membership divided neatly between the younger liberals and the older conservatives. The *Amsterdam News* took notice of the crisis: "The elders . . . are even more determined that the young Mr. Powell will never become their pastor."

But Adam Powell, Sr. with his consummate powers of conciliation managed to keep the rift from widening in public view. He met with the elders privately and argued that his son's clamorous liberalism was little more than youthful high spirits and would in no way impinge upon his administration of the church's affairs. Gradually, the rumors of dissension in Harlem's most populous and wealthy congregation faded.

At a nominating session in Abyssinian's meeting hall, one of the deacons offered young Adam's name, extolling his contributions and those of his wife to the church's growth: "He organized and directed relief for all Harlem during the years 1930, 1931, and 1932. . . . It has been generally conceded by both officers and members that no individual member in the past five years has made a larger contribution to the program of this institution than has been made by the wife of our junior pastor. . . . We, your Pulpit Committee . . . feel that no one in training or experience can qualify like the Reverend Adam Clayton Powell, Jr. to become the successor of his father. . . ." When the moderator asked for other nominations, a ripple of laughter ran through the audience.

Adam junior made his acceptance speech at a testimonial dinner for his father, attended by Mayor LaGuardia and a number of high city dignitaries. "This is a victory not for me but for the forces of liberalism within the church," he said. "I have never played politics with any so-called controlling group in the church. For the future, I promise to preserve at all cost my individual integrity and to champion liberation in the church."

The *Amsterdam News* editorialized: "Well done . . . ," to the retiring pastor and added, hopefully, "We also pray that his successor will prove to be as worthy of his trust. . . ." An editorial on the same page looked forward longingly to the day when Negroes would unite sufficiently to send a Negro to the City Council of New York, which only recently had supplanted the Board of Aldermen as New York's legislative body.

Thus Adam junior became the 18th pastor of Abyssinian, to the conspicuous approval of his father. In a closing sermon, the elder Powell declared, "Tomorrow the mantle falls upon Adam Clayton Powell, Jr. . . . God is my witness that I did not ask anybody to vote for him or work for his election. I gave him an opportunity seven years ago and he has made good. Since he is elected, I can say now without fear of being misunderstood that there is no other preacher in the world so well qualified to continue the great work at Abyssinian Baptist as Adam Clayton Powell, Jr." The old pastor grew nostalgic. "It is a long way from a one-room log cabin and a brush arbor church in Franklin County, Virginia," he said, "to . . . the most beautiful marble pulpit in America and the largest Protestant church in the world."

Such was his legacy to Adam junior. But the young man already was casting his eye beyond the boundaries of the Abyssinian Church. "The time was ripe for someone, a new and dyamic leader," he recalled in *Marching Blacks,* written eight years later. "The masses were distrustful but hungry for leadership." He now had a power base in his own right, one which projected him as a bright candidate to assume that leadership himself—and be thrust to unexampled power at the head of his army of marching blacks.

4. "On My Journey Now"

One word fairly describes Negro civil rights aspirations in the years just preceding World War II—jobs. Full integration was still too sophisticated a notion to command any real devotion from the Negro masses.

In Harlem, the job crisis found its focus on 125th Street, the ghetto's commercial main drag—a half-dozen blocks of broad thoroughfare, lined with 250 stores: jewelers, furriers, five and dime stores, restaurants, haberdashers, shoe stores, and saloons. Almost all of these were owned and operated by whites. Their patronage, however, was 90% Negro. Into this breach flew a covey of protest groups: the Citizen's Committee, the Harlem Labor Union, the Harlem Job Committee and the band of rabid protesters led by the rightist Sufi—called "Black Hitler." Each was avid for the biggest share of glory, the right to claim they had "broken the back" of 125th Street.

Late in 1937, Powell became embroiled in a controversy with the Negro poet-novelist Claude McKay over the conduct of the 125th Street campaign. Powell had claimed for the Citizen's Committee, headed by one Ira Kemp, certain gains against 125th Street merchants. McKay insisted that Sufi ought to get the credit, and denounced the "exuberant young minister" for inconsistency and opportunism in the 125th Street picketing. "I know all about the Citizen's Committee," wrote McKay in the *Amsterdam News,* "and the dubious role of Adam Powell, Jr. who marched in Sufi's picket line after Sufi had denounced him from a stepladder on Seventh Avenue." McKay recalled that Powell had supported Kemp—a rabid anti-communist—for Assemblyman and, not long after, given permission to the Communist Party to hold a rally in Abyssinian Baptist Church. When the church elders heard about the proposed rally, they angrily withdrew the permission and the Communists picketed Abyssinian Baptist. "This incident illuminates the opportunistic, careeristic character of the preacher-columnist—a man who flirts with reds on one hand and on the other supports red-baiters such as Ira Kemp," wrote McKay. He called Powell a "political acrobatic," and insisted that "it would be expecting the impossible of the young student of theology, who caters to the most fundamental form of Negro religion on Sunday, that he should understand my type of mind."

A few months later, on Lincoln's Birthday, 1938, Powell and a mixed bag of Harlem intellectuals announced the formation of the Greater New York Coordinating Committee for Unemployment, a corps which was destined to enjoy the most spectacular successes of any of the Harlem protest groups active at the time. Co-chairman with Powell was The Reverend William Lloyd Imes, minister of St. James Presbyterian Church. Other members were James W. Ford, perennial vice-presidential candidate of the Communist Party; Arnold Johnson, a suave, handsome black Cuban; Captain A. L. King, head of Marcus Garvey's old UNIA; Ira Kemp; Arthur Reid; a number of Negro socialites from Sugar Hill and a few sympathetic white Wall Street brokers. The Committee claimed to represent 206 organizations with a total membership of 155,000, and declared its intention of breaking down discrimination against Negroes in public utilities and other industrial fields, as well as in the 125th Street sector.

Recalling that first flush of militancy and high expectation, Powell wrote later: "There was no difficulty in selling the Coordinating Committee to the masses. Poor, hungry, evicted and dispossessed blacks had been marching with me for seven years. Radical organizations were ready because I had co-operated with them, especially in the great fight for the freedom of the Scottsboro boys. Black nationalists joined because I always stood four square on the proposition that Negroes must come together before they can be integrated into American life. West Indians cooperated because we saw no difference in each other. Mulattoes regarded me as one of them. Even Striver's Row was willing because the depression had begun to pinch the pocket of even the most economically secure. It was the marching blacks' hour, time and place."

They set out to blitzkrieg 125th Street. They browbeat Harlemites into the belief that it was a disgrace to cross a picket line. They chanted, "Don't buy where you can't work," in front of dozens of stores simultaneously. Gradually the ghetto dwellers began to honor the picket lines until the Committee could be sure of starving out almost any store they chose to boycott. Some merchants approached Committee leaders secretly and tried to buy them off. But it was too late for that. Uncle Tom was dead, the leaders declared. Their price was jobs and plenty of them.

While the 125th Street siege was in progress, the Committee also was badgering the Consolidated Edison (gas and electric) Company, the New York Telephone Company, the beverage industry, bread companies, and pharmaceutical houses. Consolidated Edison, under the threat of picketing and the more direct threat of a lightless day a week imposed by Negroes, signed an agreement to the effect that, in the future, "an appreciable percentage of all new Con Ed employees will be Negroes." Powell called it "the first victory in our campaign for white collar jobs for Negroes in industry." In exerting pressure on the Telephone Company, the Coordinating Committee threatened to have thousands of Harlemites abjure the dialling of telephone numbers when making a call and, instead, to ask the operator to put the call through for them. It was a ploy designed to necessitate the hiring of many more operators. The Telephone Company, like Con Edison, gave its assurance that more Negroes would be hired in the future. Both companies, however, kept their word only to the extent of a few token hirings.

In the middle of the campaign, Powell departed the field momentarily to travel to Shaw University in Raleigh, North Carolina, where he delivered the commencement address and was awarded an honorary Doctor of Divinity degree. He returned to Harlem just before the Coördinating Committee's most spectacular breakthrough came to light. After four months of negotiations with the Uptown Chamber of Commerce—a trade organization representing most of the 125th Street merchants—the Committee announced on August 7, that a pact had been signed guaranteeing one-third of all white-collar jobs in Harlem stores to Negroes. The Committee suspended picketing and boycotts until unresolved charges of discrimination were referred to a joint committee. Mayor LaGuardia hastily termed the pact "a tribute to common sense and justice." Both sides called it a "historic step" and "the first agreement of its kind ever negotiated." The Uptown Chamber of Commerce predicted the agreement would abolish prejudice among Negro workers and bring a more peaceful era to Harlem: "As more and more colored workers are transferred from relief rolls to the security of decent paying jobs in private industry, we shall see a vast improvement in the social, living and economic conditions of Harlem."

Suddenly, Powell, as chairman of the Coördinating Committee, was the object of widespread approval and acclaim in Harlem. He came to the attention, as a force that needed to be reckoned with, of the Borough President, the City Council, and the National Labor Relations Board.

Shortly afterwards, President Franklin D. Roosevelt unwittingly handed Powell the opportunity for his most conspicuous act of protest up to that time. Roosevelt's birthday was about to be celebrated—a benefit party for children afflicted with infantile paralysis. The organizers asked Powell to lend his name and newfound prestige to the occasion. Powell wrote the committee and hotly refused. "Many thanks for your kind invitation to become a member of the distinguished group to be known as the Church Council," he told them. "I would gladly pledge full cooperation of not only myself but all the members of this, the largest Protestant Church in America, if it were not for the rigid practice of discrimination against crippled Negro children and youth now being practiced at Warm Springs, Georgia. If your organization has arrived at any practical plan to include the Negro victims of infantile paralysis, I shall be only too glad to serve."

Neither Roosevelt nor his committee replied, but the tactic delighted Harlem and made front page headlines in the ghetto newspapers. "ADAM POWELL SNUBS ROOSEVELT," shouted the eight-column streamers. Powell quickly followed up his advantage with a demand that Roosevelt make some statement about the lynching in Mississippi of a 24-year-old Negro —the eighth such murder in 1938. "What if a Jew is lynched in Germany, the Chinese slaughtered in Nanking, Ethiopia pillaged in Africa, 13 million of Loyalist Spain dying from pellagra or a black boy hanging from a tree in Mississippi. It is all the same. Suffering is suffering; persecution is persecution."

Powell's radical leftist tendencies were well established in the Harlem public mind by this time. He used "The Soap

Box" column to spray over Harlem the grapeshot of his wrath at rightist derelictions at home and in Europe. "Fascism draws closer," he proclaimed. "Throughout the world it is rearing its ugly head of oppression, militarism and cruelty. The anti-Fascist forces of the world have their last chance now. . . . Today, Fascism is on the march. . . . Loins must be girded. Minds must be purged of divisive prejudice. . . . Alert we must be to strike at every evidence of things fascist. With a solidarity of race and with a unity of workers of all colors, pray God Fascism shall not come."

Powell stopped short of being a Communist, of making a total commitment to the Marxist dogma. He announced himself a member of the American Labor Party and declared that ". . . the political hope of the Negro and the masses is bound up in a working class movement. . . . I do not feel there is any future for the Negro in either of the old line major parties."

But the great awakening came to Powell in September, 1939, as it did to thousands of liberals all over the world who had cherished dreams of a socialist Utopia for more than 20 years. It was the Hitler-Stalin non-aggression pact which united the proletarian godhead with the racist dictator. Powell's own denunciation found it "the most classic double-cross in history. Karl Marx now becomes the world's greatest international refugee. The united front, the popular front, the league for this, the association for that; all have been given a swift kick in the pants by the grandpappy of it—Stalin himself. The only thing left in the world for the masses to depend on is what we started out with—democracy. Weak, inadequate, imperfect, unjust—yes, but still the cream of the crop."

The lament ran on in "The Soap Box" until late in 1939: "Frankly, to an impartial observer of the scene, American communism is just about finished."

And again: "As we say goodbye to the barricades, boys, it cannot be without a tinge of regret. . . . It was a swell time while it lasted. . . . We can hear the death cry of the Loyalist cause in Spain, of the Ethiopian cause in Africa." The dirge, Powell suggested, was supplied by the cries of the Abraham Lincoln Brigade—Americans fighting for Spanish Republicanism—who were shot down by German planes.

Thereafter, "The Soap Box" lost its fervor. The Hitler-Stalin pact had deflated Powell's militancy in behalf of the Soviets, and he was suddenly a singer without a song. He stopped writing the column in the middle of 1940—at about the same time Marcus Garvey died in London. In one of his last columns, Powell declared: "I am not a politician, nor am I interested in politics any more than as a decent citizen. . . . It is high time that we demanded and obtained a Negro Congressman. . . . Not only do we need Negroes in Congress, but the white race needs them as well."

A Congressman from Harlem was not possible at that time. Reapportionment was a dream of Harlem from the time it first became apparent that the New York enclave was becoming the world's largest ghetto. But Harlem could not elect its own representatives under the patchwork districting that prevailed in the 1930's. Harlem's press, clergy, and professional men were eager for the carving out of a new district that would run through the heart of Harlem and comprise 170,000 voters, 85 percent of them Negro. A reapportionment amendment to the state constitution was on the ballot in the 1938 elections, but was defeated. Harlem remained optimistic. Reapportionment, they were certain, would come naturally in its own time.

Powell's father published his autobiography, *Against the Tide,* that same year. It was a cry for justice for Negroes, as well as a sketchy dramatization of his life in the ministry. He urged Negroes to help themselves, to become more economically respectable in the eyes of whites, to stop throwing refuse into Harlem's streets. He regretted that only two colleges in the United States were supported by Negro money; the others, such as Tuskegee, Hampton, Spellman, Morehouse, Fish, and Virginia Union, existed through the generosity of whites.

In spite of his insistence that ". . . there is not a man living who knows the desires, ambitions and aspirations of the Negro better than I," he misread the Negro temper. "Other things being equal," wrote the elder Powell, "they [Negroes] would rather live in communities by themselves than to be scattered over wide areas." He thereby sanctioned the perpetuation of ghettos in the United States. Similarly, he was prepared to accept the separate-but-equal doctrine for schools—a notion repulsive to the civil rights fighters of a few decades later. ". . . These segregated schools must have equally prepared instructors, the same curriculum and appropriations for their maintenance. It is not the separate school that the Negro objects to, but the separate *inferior school.*"

The senior Powell who was even more physically imposing than his son had a pride to equal his size. *Against the Tide* was a self-serving book, compounded of reminiscence, exhortation and an extended catalogue of tributes to himself. The old pastor had carefully clipped all newspaper reports of his lectures and sermons, all editorials lauding him for public service, the complete texts of testimonials tendered him at dinners in his honor. These he scrupulously included in *Against the Tide* in page after page of verbatim transcription. Yet it was precisely this prideful thrust that made him so tireless a worker for Negro betterment. He could say, with considerable truth, "I am . . . speaking with authority which comes from long years of the most intimate contact, south and north, when I say that Negroes want equality; nothing else will satisfy them and nothing else will help them to help themselves out of their present low estate."

In Manhattan, the Negroes' low estate consisted of their living in less than one sixteenth of the borough's area although they comprised more than one tenth of its population. In one section of Harlem, a single block had 3,871 residents—the equivalent of many small American towns.

Adam Powell, Jr.'s Coördinating Committee moved on to another battlefield: the New York World's Fair Corporation. Grover Whalen and the World's Fair organizers were busy popularizing a slogan, "Building the World of Tomorrow." Powell and the Coördinating Committee insisted that the kind of world which Whalen and his confederates were limning would hasten World War II—a world of race hostility. The Fair Corporation had been conspicuously reluctant to hire Negroes except as menials.

For the first time, the Committee moved its picket lines downtown. Under placards that read "No discrimination in the World of Tomorrow," they marched in front of the Empire State Building, which housed the World's Fair headquarters. Each Thursday, a "death watch" marched through the night, swelled by Negro performers coming from their theaters in Harlem or on Broadway. Chorus girls, judges, and shoe shine boys marched side by side. Finally, the World's Fair organizers relented and hired a few score Negroes in positions other than as porters and maids. It was another token victory—but it was a victory, and New York's Negroes were beginning to impress their need for jobs on the minds of "downtowners."

The battle surged on. The Coördinating Committee's cold gaze next fell on the New York City Omnibus Company, which included nearly all the north-south bus lines servicing

Harlem's broad thoroughfares. No Negro had ever worked as a bus driver and only a handful had jobs as cleaners in the garages. This discrimination was perpetuated by an unwritten agreement between the Omnibus Company and the Transport Workers Union, headed by the fiery and voluble Irishman, Mike Quill, one of New York's most successful labor leaders. Practically all of the bus company drivers and mechanics were Irish. Powell and the Coördinating Committee decided to break this stranglehold. They were joined by both the Harlem Labor Union and the National Negro Congress. The display of solidarity resulted in formation of the United Negro Bus Committee, with headquarters at Abyssinian Baptist. Harlemites went there to register for picket duty. The theatrical division of the committee included Duke Ellington, Jimmie Lunceford, Canada Lee, Jimmy Mordecai, and a talented young pianist named Hazel Scott.

In March of 1940, Quill was involved in a dispute with the Omnibus Company over wages. After an eleven day strike, he secured an improved contract for his workers. Five hours after the strike was over, the Negroes struck the strikers. At a mass rally in Abyssinian Baptist, Powell reminded an audience of several thousand that they had been deprived of bus service during Quill's strike and, as a result, the white drivers and mechanics had achieved a better standard of living. "Now we are asking that you stay off the buses so that the black man may have a decent standard of living also," he told them. "It may be longer than eleven days. It may be eleven years, but by the Grace of God and the power of the mass, one day a black man is going to roll a bus up Seventh Avenue."

He demanded that the bus company hire at least 200 Negro chauffeurs and mechanics. The Committee forbade Negroes to ride the buses until this goal was achieved. "Beginning tomorrow," shouted Powell, "every Negro that rides on a bus is lynching the Negro race." He added, "But don't be hard on any Negroes you see on the buses this week. By next Monday if there are still people who have not seen the light yet, then convert them—one way or another." The veiled suggestion of sanctioned violence was not lost on the Negro community. The buses traveling through Harlem emptied.

The bus committee requested a meeting with the Omnibus Company and was refused. They sent thousands of pickets into the streets and threatened to march on the bus company's downtown offices. When the bad publicity and loss of revenue began to hurt, the bus company sent for representatives of the Committee. This time it was total victory. Powell, acting for the Committee, signed a tri-party agreement with the bus company and the union guaranteeing the hiring of 210 Negroes as drivers and high-grade mechanics. Powell, at the center of the bus fight, had won his biggest victory so far.

By now, Powell was a real force in the life of Harlem. The 1930's had been a time of genuine achievement and growth for the young pastor. He was energetic, articulate, and was discovering in himself impressive leadership qualities. With Abyssinian Baptist as a base, he had a voice and a platform inside the ghetto. Some Negro leaders, especially clergymen, were finding him uncongenial and too ambitious (the charge sometimes was made that he appeared on picket lines only long enough to have his picture taken); but his achievements were palpable and his potential as a political leader were apparent even to his detractors. It was obvious, even then, that politics, not religion, would claim his best efforts; that social action, not theology, was his element. There would be no office worth running for, however, until the City Council elections of the following year.

It fell to another leader, meanwhile, to make the sort of grand gesture of protest which would have crowned Powell's young career and brought him to national attention for the first time. America was not yet in the war, but its defense establishment was already expanding. Important Negro labor leaders—among them A. Philip Randolph, head of the Brotherhood of Sleeping Car Porters—had few illusions about white largesse in the employment boom that was growing more imminent every day. Randolph decided to dramatize Negro demands for a proportionate share of war production jobs. He called for a march on Washington.

Randolph first set about mustering the support of Negro labor unions, fraternal and church organizations, and the disparate strength of Negro political clubs. He concluded, at length, that he could produce 100,000 marchers and convene them in Washington in what would be the most dramatic protest demonstration the nation had ever seen. He set the date for July 1, 1941, then requested a meeting with President Roosevelt.

Roosevelt received Randolph on June 21. The labor leader demanded that Roosevelt issue an executive order establishing a fair employment practices commission with the power to impose penalties against defense contractors who were discriminatory in their hiring. Roosevelt bridled. He pointed out to Randolph that he had already issued a strong statement condemning jim crowism in defense hiring. It wasn't enough, said Randolph. Nothing short of an executive order, with teeth in it, was acceptable. Roosevelt asked Randolph to put himself in the President's shoes and imagine the hostility such an order would excite among defense contractors both in the North and South. Randolph was unmoved. Roosevelt stood his ground.

After the meeting, Randolph told reporters grimly: "The March will go on." He wrote a letter to Roosevelt subsequently confirming his determination.

Roosevelt was discomfited by the threat to his good reputation among Negroes. He resolved to use every means to convince Randolph that the proposed March was a mistake. A few days later, Randolph received the following letter from Eleanor Roosevelt:

My dear Mr. Randolph:

I have talked over your letter with the President and I feel very strongly that your group is making a very grave mistake at the present time to allow this march to take place. I am afraid it will set back the progress which is being made, in the Army, at least, toward better opportunities and less segregation.

I feel that if an incident occurs as a result of this, it may engender so much bitterness that it will create in Congress even more solid opposition from certain groups than we have had in the past.

I know that crusades are valuable and necessary sometimes, but undertaken when the temper is as tense as it is at present, it seems to me unfortunate. To run the risk which a meeting such as this carries with it is unwise. You know that I am deeply concerned about the rights of Negro people but I think one must face situations as they are and not as one wishes them to be. I think this is a very serious decision for you to take.

Randolph was undeterred. He renewed his demand for an executive order banning discrimination in war production. Mrs. Roosevelt hastened to New York for a meeting with Randolph and Mayor LaGuardia, who also opposed the march. Randolph not only stood firm, but told LaGuardia during the meeting that he had decided to march on New York's City Hall on June 27, three days prior to the scheduled Washington demonstration.

LaGuardia was startled. "What for?" he cried. "What have I done?"

"Nothing," Randolph said. "But I'd like you to petition the President to issue the executive order."

Roosevelt sent Secretary of War Stimson and Secretary of

the Navy Knox to reason with Randolph, but they enjoyed no greater success than had Mrs. Roosevelt. At length with the threat of an angry demonstration hanging over him, the President relented; he admitted that Randolph's power play was more formidable than the defenses the administration could muster. On June 25, 1941, he issued Executive Order Number 8802 establishing a fair employment practices commission with authority to exact penalties against defense contractors guilty of discriminatory hiring practices.

It was the first time since the Emancipation Proclamation that a President had issued an order affecting the status of Negroes.

The Negro community was jubilant. Randolph suddenly was the most popular Negro in the nation. He had learned an important lesson about the uses of power, a lesson that would serve him well in similar circumstances 22 years later. The Harlem press celebrated his steadfastness and dignity. The *Amsterdam News* editorialized:

"The rise of A. Philip Randolph to a new and loftier position in the affairs of the race appears to presage the passage of the leadership that has controlled the Negro's destiny for 25 years. Other organizations and other leaders have done some good work, but because their support has not come from the masses . . . this leadership has been weak and ineffectual. For many years, the Negro has been groping for leadership that could be trusted. It seems now that leadership is being ushered in. We regard A. Philip Randolph as the man of the hour."

Harlem—the font and wellspring of civil protest for all Black America—was in painful transition between the Depression and a war economy. The ghetto's worst crime wave was in progress. "A murder a day" was the plaint of Harlem's police, many of whom, it was revealed, were in the ghetto as punishment for drunkenness or laziness. The New York Urban League described the position of Negroes in New York as "tragic." At the end of 1940, 40 percent of New York's Negro population was getting direct relief or was dependent on temporary jobs supplied out of Federal subsidies. Freewheeling prostitution was the norm along 125th Street and Harlem's other main arteries. Arrests were rare because the white "johns" customarily refused to make complaints. White teachers requested police protection to get them safely out of their school buildings at the end of the day. Insurance companies curtailed service because their collectors were robbed so frequently. White storekeepers allowed Negro children to get away with petty pilfering, fearing another riot such as had erupted in 1935. District Attorney Thomas E. Dewey said that most of Harlem's crimes were being committed by children between 8 and 16. Murders were almost always committed by knifing and were rarely premeditated. The crime wave got city-wide attention after a Negro man succeeded in burglarizing an apartment directly across the hall from Mayor LaGuardia's, who was living at 1274 Fifth Avenue, at 109th Street, on the southern edge of Harlem.

Reporters from downtown papers sought out Powell for an explanation of the mayhem that was in progress. "The so-called crime wave will not be stopped by the police," he told them, "but by calls for the united efforts of all the people of the city to improve the miserable living conditions in Harlem.

"The so-called recent crime wave is neither a crime wave nor is it recent. It is not a crime wave in the accepted sense because it is not being conducted by criminals. It is not recent because it dates to the beginning of the Depression. In the past 25 years, the population of Harlem has increased fivefold, yet facilities for recreation, education and health haven't even been doubled. Into this ghetto have been crowded people living in century-old tenements, making less money, but paying higher rents and higher prices for foodstuffs than any other group in the city."

Rent parties still flourished with their concomitant evils. Rich whites from midtown Manhattan were once again flocking to the ghetto after dark in search of thrills. They were fed a diet of staged theatrics, lewd dances, and hired blacks who filled every empty table as stage dressing and behaved in buffoonish fashion, as was expected of them. Slumming parties were a big business in Harlem and the Negroes were careful to give them what they came to see.

In broad daylight, when the slummers had returned to their eyries beyond Central Park, Harlem got on with its real business. It could boast one Negro police lieutenant, scores of Negro policemen and firemen and a few hundred colored city nurses. There were 1100 amusement places charging admission, 6000 beauty parlors, 5 newspapers, a Young Poets' Club, 100 lodges of 20 secret organizations, various social and political clubs and 1300 churches, from Abyssinian Baptist— the largest and richest—to the tiny pentecostal storefront churches that flourished on almost every block.

In this arena and at this historical instant, Adam Powell decided to enter the political sector and run for the New York City Council. During the summer of 1941, petitions bearing his name began to appear on Harlem's streets.

New York City had abandoned its Board of Aldermen, who had been elected from apportioned districts. It had been extremely difficult under this apportionment for a Negro to be elected. A new City Charter provided for the election of any candidate who polled 75,000 votes. Powell estimated that he could win that many votes from Negroes, and be assured victory.

Under the aegis of a new protest group, The People's Committee (an outgrowth of the Coördinating Committee, which became moribund as street demonstrations lessened with the onset of World War II), and a new slogan, "One People! One Fight! One Victory!", Powell began fashioning his campaign machinery. He described it as being composed of "about the finest bunch of honest thieves and corrupt Christians in captivity."

He eschewed affiliation with any one of the three major parties, but set about convincing each of them that they must withdraw their own Negro candidates and solidify Negro voting strength behind him; that only in this way could Manhattan's Negroes be assured representation on the Council. His powers of persuasiveness were with him. All three recognized that he would be a formidable candidate, drawing strength from his home base at Abyssinian Baptist, and able to capitalize on the years of protest in the streets with which he had become identified.

As autumn wore round to the November elections, Powell garnered impressive added support: the CIO Trade Union Council, the League of Women Voters, the Trade Union Committee to Elect Labor's Candidates, the United City Party, and the Transport Workers Union.

Powell was tireless in wooing these groups and assuring them that a Harlem with a voice of its own in the city administration was to everybody's advantage. Repeatedly, he told streetcorner audiences and civic groups: "I am not seeking a political job. I am fighting for the chance to give my people the best representation in the affairs of their city, to help make Harlem the number one community of New York." It was his baptism as a campaigner and a moment of discovery for both himself and the Harlem voters. The latter were struck by his energy, his apparent sophistication, and his determination to beard the white man in his own arena—in this case, the City Council chamber.

Powell's organization distributed 200,000 sample ballots to assure that Harlem's voters were properly instructed in the manner of recording their votes. (It paid off. In Harlem, only 12% of the proportional representation ballots were thrown out, while in the rest of the city the ratio was 19%.)

So well-oiled was Powell's campaign machinery that opposition to him largely dissolved. On election day, he coasted into office with 64,043 votes, third highest among six successful candidates from Manhattan. He was the first Negro ever elected to that body.

Powell's victory statement applauded the united front Negroes had fashioned to elect him: "This is the greatest power we possess, unity of the masses. With it we can do all things."

Harlem, generally, was jubilant at this new boon to its aspirations. Certain intellectual elements in the ghetto, however, were more reserved and watchful; they were uncertain about the true nature of Powell's ambitions, and not yet convinced that he owned the selflessness and utter dedication which the times called for. The *Amsterdam News* editorialized: "With an earnest, kindly word of caution, we congratulate New York's first colored Councilman . . . as he begins his two year term in office. It is a grand opportunity for service to his people, city, and country that confronts him. He has the ability, courage, and popular support to render that service. . . . How effective his tenure in office will be depends entirely on how effectively, in and out of the Council chamber, he uses these natural advantages."

The nation was at war now, and Negroes everywhere were in need of spokesmen in high place to articulate their demands for a full share of the war's burdens as well as of the jobs it created. Powell, as he later related, thought of his victory in terms of an old Negro spiritual:

> On my journey now, Mount Zion
> On my journey now, Mount Zion
> And I won't take nothing, Mount Zion
> On my journey now!

5. Wars, Riots, and Ruins

To most Americans, World War II was an elementary exercise in right and wrong; to America's Negroes, it was a vast ambiguity. One Negro said, "Just carve on my tombstone, 'Here lies a black man killed fighting a yellow man for the protection of a white man.'" In a letter to the editor of a Raleigh, North Carolina, newspaper, another Negro wrote, "The Negro races on earth are very suspicious of the white man's good intentions. This is very likely to be the last war that the white man will be able to lead humanity to wage for plausible platitudes."

Many Americans found their real or imagined interests threatened by the change in the Negro's status which the war inevitably brought—as it became apparent the country would need all its available manpower. This realization thrust into the foreground all the basic unresolved issues surrounding the American Negro, as well as the animosity and indifference which characterized most Americans' dealings with the black community in their midst.

World War II was advertised to Americans as a war of ideologies; a crusade to achieve the Four Freedoms for people everywhere; a struggle of democracies against fascist states and an indictment of Germanic theories of racism. Negroes, especially, were eager to refute the notion that a dictator could, with impunity, destroy an "undesirable" race—genocide by executive order. At the same time, they had to puzzle out the meaning of a number of disparate facts at home. The Red Cross was segregating Negro blood donations from white, to assure that no wounded or dying white soldier would be infused with "black" blood. Japanese-Americans were rounded up and placed in internment camps on the West Coast, while German and Italian immigrants—who were white men—remained free. Negroes were not admitted into the Marines nor the Air Force, and in the Navy they were given duties as stewards and mess boys. In the Army, they served in segregated engineer and construction battalions; they were not allowed to fight. At home, many defense plants refused to hire Negroes even though some of their machinery was idle and unproductive. The chairman of the New York State War Council made a survey which indicated that 90 percent of plants engaged in war production in New York were reluctant to hire Negroes.

While the fighting was in progress in Europe and the Pacific, in the United States there was the Silent War, the Secret War, or as Adam Powell called it—Civil War II. Soldiers and sailors who had come from remote areas of the South and had never experienced the cruder forms of bigotry, were facing it for the first time and were bewildered by it.

At Army camps in the United States, Negro soldiers were having pitched battles with white soldiers and civilians determined to keep the black men "in their place." Violence broke out at Fort Bragg, Fort Benning, Camp Stewart, Camp Gibbon, Camp Davis, and Jackson Barracks, as well as in many towns near military installations both in the United States and overseas where soldiers went to relax. One newsman estimated that 50 Negro soldiers were killed in the United States during the war as result of the bitterness of recalcitrant whites. Judge William Hastie, Negro Assistant to the Secretary of War, resigned in protest against the Army's soft-line policy against such crimes. Other Negroes complained that wounded white service men were recuperating at such resorts as Palm Beach, Miami Beach, Lake Placid, and Hot Springs, while Negro wounded were sent to the Hotel Theresa in Harlem.

Meanwhile, the FEPC was proving inadequate to the task of insuring the Negro's full share of war production employment. "The President will move only when Negroes make him move," A. Philip Randolph declared angrily on April 4, 1942. "He is not going to take action on the Negro's problem unless he is compelled to."

When the defense program got underway, the Negro was a bystander in American industrial life and he appeared to be losing ground daily. His prospects were dim. He was discouraged. The forces of racial reaction felt their position to be secure. Robert C. Weaver, in his definitive study of Negro wartime employment patterns, *Negro Labor,* said: "That a nation at war would delay the use of its total manpower resources for three years is the most striking instance of the tenacity with which America had clung to its established color-caste system." But that is what happened. In April, 1940, there were close to six million non-whites (95 percent of them Negro) in the labor market. One million, three hundred thousand of those, or 22 percent of the total, were unemployed. At the same time, 17 percent of the total whites were unemployed. In the succeeding six months, the figure for whites declined to 13 percent, while the proportion of non-whites fell only one-tenth of one percent. Negroes were turned away at the gates of defense plants while employers bemoaned the acute shortage of skilled workers. In June 1942, the situation was so bad that Secretary Knox of the Navy Department sent a telegram to several New York ordnance plants condemning the refusal of whites to work side by side with Negroes. He called it disloyalty to the government and said those involved "are not only subject to immediate dismissal but may be prevented from obtaining employment in other establishments engaged in war production."

In this atmosphere of national bitterness over the Negro's forced emergence into the social consciousness of white America, Adam Clayton Powell, Jr. assumed his first public office, as an independent in New York's City Council. He commenced agitation immediately on a broad front, demanding resolutions condemning alleged discrimination in a dozen areas. He attacked the federal government for its internment of Japanese-Americans. He declaimed against the treatment of Negroes in the armed forces and in war production. When the city of New York agreed to turn over to the Navy the campus of Hunter College as a training center for WAVES and SPARS—outfits which refused to accept Negro women—Powell introduced a resolution, which was passed, condemning the pact. He demanded impeachment of Mayor LaGuardia for approving construction of the Stuyvesant Town housing development after it became apparent that the project's managers intended to enforce a jim crow policy. He announced that not a single Negro was among the 2,232 faculty members of New York's city-supported colleges—Brooklyn College, Queens College, City College, and Hunter College—and managed to have the presidents of those institutions interrogated before a committee of the Council. He introduced a resolution to forbid newspapers from using words to identify the race of criminals.

The energy of Powell's denunciations left an impression of high activity and accomplishment on his Harlem constituents. The Harlem press, however, frequently accused him of failing to follow up on his attacks, of losing interest in a cause once the speeches had been made and the news coverage exhausted. He was not, in fact, well-liked by many of his fellow councilmen, but the reasons were less racial than parliamentary: he was voluble from the outset instead of maintaining the customary freshman's reticence. He later explained his record this way: "As an independent in the City Council I did not get the coöperation that I would have received if I had been elected through the regular channels of the major party in control. What was more important than coöperation, however, was the fact that I could speak fearlessly on any subject and so focus attention on wrongs that would have to be righted. In the early months of my term whatever legislation I proposed was either defeated, tabled or emasculated. Regardless, however, of the immediate outcome, every legislative objective I set up eventually came through victoriously in one way or another."

Part of the Council's hesitancy to take Powell to their bosom was founded in their uncertainty over the young pastor's political ambition. Barely 18 months after entering the Council, he announced at a mass meeting in Madison Square Garden that he intended to run for Congress as soon as the state legislature in Albany redrew district lines to make of Harlem a near-homogeneous Congressional entity. In the last days of the legislature under Governor Herbert Lehman, the reapportionment bill came up. In spite of dire predictions in the white press that the bill was doomed, the Negro community and its allies exerted sufficient pressure to get the bill out of committee and before the legislature, where it was passed. It was a momentous occasion for New York's Negroes. The bill established the 22nd Congressional District in the heart of Harlem, consisting of 300,000 people, 90 percent of them Negro. (In 1952, this district was reapportioned, and designated the 16th; then, in 1962, it was changed to the 18th.) For the first time, it was possible that a Negro from the eastern seaboard would represent his people in Washington.

In order to press his campaign for that honor, Powell
needed a medium through which to address an even broader
audience than he commanded at Abyssinian Baptist and in
the New York City Council. He found it in a new newspaper
called *The People's Voice,* a smaller-than-tabloid sized weekly
which appeared suddenly on February 14, 1942, bearing
Powell's name as editor-in-chief and that of one Charles
Buchanan as publisher. Other Negro newspapers in and out
of Harlem had heralded the new journal with cryptic suggestions of "white intrusion" and "sell-out" to forces inimical to
genuine Negro betterment. The *Amsterdam News,* for example, told its readers in a front page editorial that the new
journal would be "edited and managed in front by certain
ambitious, mercenary colored political newcomers—that it is
to be backed from behind by certain designing white capital."
The *Amsterdam News,* an essentially conservative newspaper,
was not eager for the competition of a liberal organ in the
ghetto, and certainly not one fronted by its former columnist,
Adam Clayton Powell, Jr. who now appeared bent on an
even larger career of energetic, liberal political action.

Most knowledgeable Harlemites were convinced that *The
People's Voice* was supported in its early stages by money
from Marshall Field, the Chicago philanthropist-publisher,
who was then backing the ultra-liberal newspaper *PM*. Powell
was quoted by *Time* magazine, in 1942, as disclosing at a
Negro publishers' conference that Field had granted him "another $25,000 of credit." Field wrote to *Time* denying that
he had extended credit to *The People's Voice,* while admit-
ting that the paper was printed on *PM*'s presses under an
undefined contractual arrangement.

The People's Voice appeared a harmless enough journal.
In spite of its splashy front page dominated by twin V's (one
for victory over the Axis powers, the other for victory
over totalitarian-minded forces at home), the paper carried

sports, theater and society news, a column by Mary McLeod
Bethune, women's feature pages and a lot of local news.
Powell resurrected "The Soap Box," spreading it over five
columns on an early page, and also contributed a signed editorial to each issue. But most of the radicalism was gone. His
plaints were high-sounding abstractions about Negro betterment and goals in the post-war world. The Powell energy and
vigor were still there, but his targets were easier ones—fascism
at home and abroad, the litany of inequities against Negroes
which finally was beginning to reach the consciousness of
white America. A few scant months after its birth, *The People's Voice* was claiming a circulation of more than 50,000.

Perhaps the most remarkable aspect of Powell's career in
those years was that he was functioning in at least four jobs,
any one of which would have been a full-time preoccupation
for a lesser man: City Councilman, Baptist pastor, newspaper
editor, and leader of the People's Committee, one of Harlem's
most militant protest groups. He was making scores of
speeches, both in Harlem and in the City Council attacking
wartime treatment of Negroes.

His wife, Isabel, devoted herself to the affairs of Abyssinian
Baptist. But as Powell waded further into the political mainstream, the first tiny discords in his domestic life began to be
apparent. He was seen at times with Hazel Scott, the jazz
pianist who had contributed her time to several of Powell's
protest committees.

There was much in public life to engage Powell's vigor and
distract him from home life, as well as from the pastoral routine of a Harlem minister.

All over America, hostility to the emerging Negro was heading toward some finale. It came in the summer of 1943, when
four major race riots erupted in 26 days.

On June 6, the "zoot suit" riot broke out in Los Angeles

between sailors and Mexican teen-agers and raged over parts of the city for almost a week. In Mobile, Alabama, a dozen Negroes were upgraded to welders in the yards of the Alabama Dry Dock and Shipbuilding Company, causing 20,000 workers, both white and Negro, to leave their jobs for four days and indulge in an orgy of violence that ended only after troops were called in. In Beaumont, Texas, a Negro neighborhood was razed and several men were killed after a false rumor circulated that a Negro had raped a white woman. But the worst of them, and perhaps the worst race riot in United States history, came in Detroit on June 16. Race relations were already exacerbated in that city by the influx of Negroes looking for war production jobs. Once again, a false rumor triggered the violence: a Negro woman had been drowned by a white man, came the report, and her baby slain. The story enlarged as it spread to Paradise Valley, Detroit's Negro ghetto. Black men marched out and were met by whites carrying sticks and pistols. Fights broke out wherever the races came together and soon whole sections of the city were engulfed in rioting. Negroes pillaged pawn shops for guns and knives. Bricks flew and automobiles were overturned. Trolley cars were halted and boarded and Negro passengers hauled into the street and beaten. A band of armed Negro men—one of them with a submachine gun—barricaded themselves in the Vernor Hotel in Paradise Valley and shot it out with policemen. Tear gas bombs dislodged them and they raced into the streets, still firing.

President Roosevelt ordered Federal troops from nearby Fort Custer to hasten to Detroit and quell the riot. Negro troops at the Fort already were trying to commandeer trucks and arms to go to the aid of their friends in the city. With machine guns and bayonets, the soldiers enforced order in Detroit after a day and a night of violence. But 34 were dead—25 Negroes and nine whites—700 were injured and wounded, and 1,300 arrested.

It was apparent that the nation was not done with violence, that new pitched battles were bound to break out in this atmosphere of high resentment. In New York, Adam Powell accused Mayor LaGuardia and Police Commissioner Lewis J. Valentine of refusing to discuss with him plans to prevent similar misfortunes from befalling the city. In a speech to the City Council, he said, "I now say, fellow Councilmen, that the riots of Detroit can be easily duplicated here in New York City. If any riot breaks out here, the blood of innocent people, white and Negro, will rest upon the heads of Mayor LaGuardia and Police Commissioner Valentine, who have refused to see representative citizens to discuss means of combatting outbreaks in New York. The Mayor says that he is ready. Ready for what? Ready after it is too late? We want to be ready now, beforehand."

His remarks were prophetic. Six weeks after the Detroit riot, violence came to Harlem—the worst it had ever known. At 7:00 p.m. on Sunday, August 1, a white policeman was called to the Hotel Braddock on West 126th Street to arrest a colored woman on a charge of disorderly conduct. A Negro soldier observed the arrest and objected to it. He twisted the night stick from the patrolman's hand and beat him over the head with it, then raced for the door. The patrolman rose, drew his revolver, and shot the soldier in the shoulder. He then took the wounded man to Sydenham Hospital for treatment and later to Bellevue Hospital for confinement. Word spread in Harlem like a firestorm that a white cop had shot a Negro soldier. Crowds gathered in front of the 123rd Street precinct station, and at Sydenham. The inevitable pattern of rumor and elaboration recurred. Some said the soldier was dying, though his wound was, in fact, a slight one. Others claimed that a vengeful band of whites was marching on

Harlem. Disputes broke out among Negroes themselves over what was the truth of the matter. Some wanted to rush Sydenham and free the soldier. In the supercharged atmosphere, a few fights broke out with passing whites, and Negroes began heaving stones through the display windows of stores assumed to be owned by white men. On that sweltering August evening, other Negroes hurried from their tenements to discover the nature of the disturbance, thus swelling the mobs which then surged along 125th Street and up Lenox and Seventh Avenues in search of whites and white-owned businesses. Many of the rioters were armed with knives, a few with pistols. They set upon slumming parties, white bill collectors, truck drivers, and policemen. Some of the marchers pulled the levers in all fire alarm boxes they passed. The confusion heightened as fire engines raced crazily through the streets on false alarms. One Negro ran at a policeman and shouted, "Shoot me! I would rather die here for my people than in Germany!"

When the rioters reached 138th Street on their march, it was apparent suddenly that the violence had been transmuted from racial protest into an orgy of criminality, looting, and pillaging. Harlem was being raped by her own citizens. Looters now were crashing through storefronts indiscriminately in a contagion of greed and hatred. Some merchants had hurriedly pasted signs on their windows, "Colored Ownership Only," but these were ignored. Hardly a storefront was spared on Harlem's main streets. Whole supermarkets were picked clean and their shelvings and cash registers stolen as well. Liquor stores were a prime target. Negroes paraded Seventh Avenue drunkenly in stolen opera hats, tails, and gaudy jewelry. The naked torsos of mannequins and dismembered arms lay in the broken glass outside furrier shops on 125th Street. One woman passed a store where Negroes were handing groceries through a smashed window.

"Help yourself," one of the men shouted. "It's all free!"

"I can't," said the woman. "I've got religion."

"I'm religious myself," the man said. "This has nothing to do with religion!"

"Well, praise the Lord and pass me a can of peas," she answered.

It was the biggest and most destructive revel in Harlem's history. Mayor LaGuardia hurried from his home to tour Harlem in a sound truck, shouting: "Go back to your homes! This is not a race riot. All looters will be prosecuted!" Harlemites booed him, and hastened their pillaging, each avid for his share of the booty. LaGuardia then made a series of radio broadcasts, speaking soothingly, insisting that the violence in progress was not a race riot, nor part of one, but the work of vandals, scavengers and opportunists. "I am very sorry if I am interrupting any program, but I am sure you will bear with me, because if I did not deem this of the utmost importance, I would not importune you at this time," said the Little Flower in his most reassuring manner. He closed Harlem's main streets to traffic. The wartime dim-out, enforced throughout New York City, was lifted for Harlem, and suddenly the ghetto was a brilliantly-lighted enclave shining in the heart of a somber metropolis. Five thousand policemen and squads of soldiers moved through Harlem arresting looters and dispersing crowds. LaGuardia opened the National Guard Armory at Park Avenue and 94th Street to contain the prisoners who were overflowing Harlem's jails.

At dawn, the ghetto's streetcorners were crowded with Negroes bartering their loot, selling bottles of whiskey for a dollar, wine for fifteen cents; hams, jewelry, musical instruments, furs, canned goods, typewriters, hardware, shoes, sporting equipment, firearms, furniture, and cameras—all were fodder for this floating, surreptitious marketplace.

Also at dawn, the score was tallied: five dead, 500 injured,

600 arrested. No accurate count could be made of the businesses that were ruined. Eight thousand members of the National Guard were mobilized to stand by in state armories against a resurgence of the violence. Also standing by were 1,500 civilian volunteers, 6000 police, MP's, and air raid wardens. National Guardsmen patrolled Harlem's streets in two's, crunching over the broken glass, their rifles held ahead of them. Police searched rooftops for stolen goods, sometimes marching the occupants of whole buildings into the street when a large cache was found. A sleepless LaGuardia continued to broadcast at intervals. He ordered Harlem's taverns closed for an indefinite period and imposed a 10:30 p.m. curfew on the ghetto.

Food was unobtainable, and commercial distributors were reluctant to send in their trucks. City-owned vehicles brought milk to the children and distributed a few essentials to the aged. One local preacher said that Harlem had brought "the greatest disgrace on the honest, hard-working members of their own race since the Negro landed at Jamestown, Virginia."

Explanations for the outburst covered a wide range of speculation. Adam Powell blamed it on "blind, smoldering and unorganized resentment against jim crow treatment of Negro men in the Armed Forces and the unusual high rents and cost of living forced upon Negroes in Harlem."

His father, Adam Powell, Sr., called it "the most puzzling . . . of all the riots in the United States since the Civil War. . . . These window-smashers were not looters, they were race rioters expressing their pent-up hatred of the white man's pagan civilization, called Christian. If those rioters smashed a window of a colored man's place of business, it was done ignorantly. If they touched a colored policeman it was because he was meddling in their business."

The New York Times editorialized: "No friend of the

Negro will defend the Harlem rioters. The overwhelming majority of Harlem's law-abiding people, who are as good and useful citizens as can be found anywhere, do not defend them. . . . Immediate causes for [the riot] can be found in a sense of grievance fanned into flame by sinister agitators, lies deliberately spread; in an ignorance that might be diminished if white people in this city took a more friendly interest in the welfare of the new additions to our Negro population."

The newspaper *PM* drew these conclusions: "The city and the nation would make a grave mistake if they tried to shake off this incident as just another riot. . . . It stems from essentially the same sources as created the bloody outbreaks in Mobile, Beaumont and Detroit. In part, it climaxes the mounting tensions within the Harlem community itself, the piled-up resentments against the segregation and discrimination, against the pushing around the Negro has been getting in civil and military life."

Roy Wilkins wrote in *The Crisis,* the NAACP organ: "A soldier in uniform was shot by a policeman in Harlem. The question of who was right and who wrong at the moment did not interest the mob. Mobs, white or black, don't reason. . . . Negro soldiers have been shot down by civilian policemen in Alexandria, Louisiana; in Little Rock, Arkansas; in Baltimore, Maryland; in Beaumont, Texas and beaten in countless instances. The Harlem mob knew all this. It hated all this. It could not reach the Arkansas cop who fired a full magazine of his revolver into the prone body of a Negro sergeant, or any of the others, so it tore up Harlem."

After the riot, a foundation announced it was going to spend $285,000 studying every angle of the Negro problem in New York. Sociologists, psychiatrists, and psychologists would pool their expertise, said the foundation, and come up with the best answer yet on just what needed to be done. Adam Powell, Sr. in his book published in 1945, *Riots and Ruins,* scoffed at such measures. "How wonderful," he exclaimed. "Every Negro has known this since General Lee surrendered. Some of these expert sociologists will be college Negroes. These Negroes knew the problem before they wrote a thesis. If the white men who are spending this huge sum . . . don't know what the Negro problem is, any ten-year-old black boy in the South or in Harlem will tell them without even expecting a ten-cent tip. . . . All the Negro wants or deserves is the same chance the white man has. . . . Until this is done, there are going to be riots, ruin and hell. Since the white man knows the solution, why doesn't he stop beating the devil around the bush and apply the remedy? Because it is much easier to spend money on surveys looking for solutions that they know are not in heaven or on earth than it is to do the things they know will settle the problem until doomsday. Investigation is an excuse for delaying action. 'We know this is right and we want to do it, but we can't do it until we find out the best way to do it.' This is an abominable American trait."

So the Violent Summer of 1943 passed.

In the November elections, Powell declined to run for re-election to the City Council, naming the Communist, Benjamin Davis, as "my logical successor." Davis campaigned and won. Powell's eye was firmly fixed on Washington; Congress was the highest political office to which he might reasonably aspire at that time. Privately, he had said that "The man who gets into Congress from this District can stay in there for the rest of his life." The one man who might have blocked Powell's single-minded assault on Congress, A. Philip Randolph, had a demonstrated aversion to involvement in partisan politics, and refused to compete for the seat. (Powell's own father had said of Randolph: "There is not a more heroic spirit in America than the one which dwells in A.

Philip Randolph's body. He is our nearest approach to John Brown because he has always sacrificed any selfish ambition for the good of his race.") A number of aspirants emerged, none of them distinguished, all of them ambitious. Each claimed a broad base of support, and each made Powell the prime target of his salvos.

Powell tuned his campaign to the ear of the masses. His platform planks included the demanding of an end to segregation in the armed forces, a permanent FEPC, a federal law prohibiting discrimination in interstate travel, the end of the poll tax and the white primary. In the spring and early summer of 1944, he campaigned vigorously on street corners and before civic clubs. Although his record of public service was impressive enough on its own merits, Powell regularly succumbed to hyperbole, indulging extravagant claims about his public accomplishments which succeeded only in enraging his opponents, especially one Mrs. Sara P. Speaks, who was the favorite aspirant of the *Amsterdam News*. Mrs. Speaks accused Powell of "talking through his hat" and of taking credit for civil rights victories gained by others while he "was still a playboy in college." "Some of us have good memories," she said, "and can't allow the work of others to be passed over lightly by the over-ambitious political preacher and editor. . . . It ill becomes a minister to deliberately distort the truth, even though he might have ambitions to become the political czar of Harlem."

The several hopefuls paced their campaigns to peak shortly before the August 1 primary, which, in effect, would decide the whole contest. Powell's organization ran smoothly and effectively. He persuaded Tammany Hall and the American Labor Party to support him, as well as the CIO and its Political Action Committee, the Transport Workers Union, large groups of Negro theatrical workers, and the Communist Party. In late July, Mrs. Speaks said she was confident "that the rank and file voters will not be fooled by Reverend Powell's oratory. His record is replete with irresponsible, ill-considered, and inflammatory actions and utterances. . . . His term on the City Council was strangely unproductive of legislation for the good of the community. . . . My opponent's technique for solving all problems is protest, protest, protest. . . . He is essentially a dreamer, a visionary, a prophet of a 'New World A'coming.' . . ."

Mrs. Speaks—the only candidate who mounted any real opposition to Powell—intensified her attacks as primary day approached: "Powell believes in the theory that one gets what one can take and keeps what he can hold. . . . Gradually, truth is beginning to pierce the fog of bombast which Adam Powell has fed the people of Harlem. It is regrettable that a young man with so much promise has failed so completely and has chosen to pursue a policy of fooling the people rather than providing them with forthright leadership. But, as he himself has preached, with dire warning to the ungodly, 'Beware, your sins will find you out.' "

Mrs. Speaks had righteous anger on her side, but Powell had style on his. A few days before the primary, he left Harlem for his annual vacation on Martha's Vineyard, leaving behind the impression that his election was a *fait accompli*. He was correct. On August 1, with his name on Democratic, Republican, and ALP ballots, he swept to victory in all three primaries, polling a meager 11,000 votes. Harlem's lack of interest in primary elections—even those in which Powell ran —was impressive, but the vote was sufficient to launch Powell into the national arena for the first time. (Since 1901, only three Negroes had sat in Congress: Oscar de Priest, Arthur W. Mitchell, and William L. Dawson. All three were from the Illinois First District in Chicago; Dawson was still serving.) In the November general election, Powell ran unopposed and took office along with Franklin D. Roosevelt and Harry S. Truman.

As Powell's political career prospered, his domestic life foundered. A few days after the election, Isabel Washington filed suit for separation charging that Powell had lost interest in her because of "his infatuation with a woman nightclub entertainer. . . . He has visited her at the nightclub at which she performs. He has met her at the Roxy Theater where she had an engagement. He has visited her at her home in White Plains and his association with this woman is a matter of common knowledge." The suit claimed abandonment, cruel and inhuman conduct, and failure to support her. Powell had indeed been seen frequently with the beautiful 23-year-old pianist Hazel Scott, but his countercharges took a different tack. He requested a divorce charging that Isabel was opposed to his political career, that she nagged him, and was responsible for his not having children. "I fear I just outgrew her," said the new Congressman. She wanted him "to live the cloistered life of a monk" so he had left their home at 732 St. Nicholas Avenue. His pastoral duties, Powell explained, often necessitated his visiting females in their homes, and that sometimes they became "demonstrative," but it was all in the line of duty. Isabel told reporters she was "flabbergasted" when Powell told her that "my actions toward him had driven him to the arms of another woman and that he could no longer live with me. I pleaded with him to make good our marriage in view of the fact he was sure to be elected to Congress. He seized me solemnly by the shoulders and said it was too late."

Isabel had, in fact, fought her husband's growing involvement with politics. She was convinced he could be a far greater force for good as pastor of Abyssinian Baptist than as a political leader, and had greeted his election to the City Council and his campaign for Congress with restrained enthusiasm.

She grew even more fearful when Powell mused to her one day that he saw no reason why he should not sometime be mayor of New York City and thereafter governor of the state.

Isabel, by her devotion to church work, had long ago made the deacons of Abyssinian forget she was a showgirl; by the same efforts she was losing her husband. "Ministers' wives frequently plunge into church work up to their eyes," said Powell, "invariably to the annoyance and discomfort of their husbands."

Powell's manly appeal received some of its most glowing endorsements during this period. Isabel claimed that right up to the moment he left their home she "never doubted Adam loved me as completely as I loved him." Later, in spite of all the bitterness, she was able to say that Powell had been "an ideal husband, affectionate and generous and capable of giving more happiness in five years than other men could in fifty." Hazel Scott, meanwhile, confronted with the reports of her "other woman" role in the tableau, said, "If and when he's free someday, I'd think myself an extremely lucky young lady to be his wife. He is one of the great men of our time. Really, he is the finest man I know." She said she had never met Isabel, but that Powell and she had been good friends for several years. "We are active together in many organizations in which our mutual fight is against jim crow. He has advised me on many details and, together with Barney Josephson, my manager, we've held many conferences on what would and wouldn't be good for me insofar as my future on the stage and screen is concerned."

Powell told friends he was willing to give up his church if necessary to marry Hazel. She was, indeed, a great prize for a number of reasons: a celebrity, a concert and jazz pianist, star of the show at the 58th Street nightclub, Cafe Society Uptown. Her earnings were $75,000 a year. She owned an elaborate home in Westchester County and was in demand for movie roles. In a short time, Powell was calling her "curlytop" and she was calling him "bunny."

Powell left Harlem in December to take up his duties with the 79th Congress. Hazel was present in the capital at his swearing in, although Powell's divorce proceedings were still in an early stage.

Adam Powell, Sr. continued to be a strong influence on his son. The retired pastor had been a delegate to the Republican state convention in the 1920's, but had become a Democrat in the early days of the New Deal. Now, in his 70's, he was more liberal than ever, and wrote in *Riots and Ruins:* "The Negro's only political hope is to register with the American Labor Party that is nearest to communism in its liberal attitude toward colored people." He warned that Negroes were ganging up at the left of the political spectrum and would soon be a concerted political force. He claimed that—after Franklin D. Roosevelt—Joseph Stalin was the most popular world figure with Negroes. He urged his race to stop being a political football for both of the old-line parties, and to understand that "Eighty percent of the members of Congress are incurably dishonest in their dealings with the Negro. . . ."

The words were not lost on Adam Powell, Jr. as he began his career in Washington.

6. A Black Voice in Congress

In 1945, there was no single, charismatic leader in whom Negroes could invest their aspirations, who would be their spokesman, dramatist, confessor, benefactor and defender: no Garvey, DuBois, Washington, or Douglass. The leadership was atomized and the charge continually made that Negroes couldn't even agree among themselves about what they wanted, much less about how to get it. The NAACP and its Legal Defense and Educational Fund was winning some important decisions with regard to restrictive covenants, Negro schoolteachers' salaries, public school facilities. It was preparing the now-celebrated public school segregation case which broke over the nation with the Supreme Court decision of May 17, 1954. With the passing of Nazism there was released in the United States a great urge toward the guaranteeing of civil liberties and civil rights. Social change was as imminent as sunrise.

Adam Powell arrived in the national capital at this moment. Knowledge of his personal magnetism, his oratory and his brilliance had preceded him. Many of his new colleagues in Congress wondered if he was not to be the Negro leader for which the times seemed ready and around whom would muster all the disparate forces of Negro dissatisfaction.

Powell's emergence as a national figure was celebrated with publication of his book *Marching Blacks,* a shrill polemic *cum* autobiography which sketched in the American Negro's history and attempted, by the energy of its exhortation, to get America's black men "on their feet and marching up Freedom Road." Neo-Marxist in coloration, the book tied the Negro's destiny to that of the working class. "I distrust people in high places, but have implicit faith in the masses of folk both black and white," wrote Powell.

His solution for the Negro's dilemma in the South was simply that they "pack up and move" to the North in "the greatest migration that America has ever witnessed within its shores." A million had already left during the war, said Powell, and ten million more should follow. That recommendation, he claimed, represented the considered conclusion that most parts of the South were hopeless and Negroes living there should "turn their backs on Egyptland!" The North is not quite the Promised Land, he said, but there is no lynching and no poll tax; there are schools and hospitals and even Northern slums are better than sharecroppers' huts. "It does not matter how you come, brother, but come. Come flying, riding or walking. The great Hegira has begun. The American Exodus is on its way—GLORY HALLELUJAH!" He even had a master plan to accomplish the evacuation. He divided the South into three sections: seaboard, inland-delta, and Southwest. The seaboard Negroes of Florida, Georgia, South Carolina, North Carolina, and Virginia would trek to Philadelphia and New York, with Boston absorbing the overflow; inland-delta Negroes of Alabama, Arkansas, Louisiana, Mississippi, Kentucky, and Tennessee would aim for Detroit and Chicago, with Ohio and Indiana receiving some immigrants; Southwest Negroes, concentrated mostly in Texas, would move to Los Angeles and San Diego, with others pushing on to San Francisco, Seattle and Spokane. The great migration actually would aid the South in the long run, Powell claimed, since the land barons would then have to turn their attention to building an economy more in tune with the modern world. They would probably fail, said Powell, but the breath of change would be good for both North and South.

He made bitter thrusts at the Southland: "If Bilbo doesn't want us in Mississippi and [Senator] 'Cotton Ed' [Smith] doesn't want us in South Carolina, then let them keep their illegitimate economy whelped by the great whore lynchoc-racy. . . . The South will soon learn that some of the men that they have sent to the nation's capital have been a dis-grace not only to the nation, but to their section as well. . . . Rankin . . . comes from a country of three hundred thousand people where not even a score of thousands vote." He allowed that a growing group of white Southern congressmen were beginning to be disgusted with the status quo. "Already this new South is beginning to caucus against the old. . . . Their revolt may break into the open any day. When it does, a people's democracy will have arrived."

If *Marching Blacks* was a romantic statement of the "New World A'coming" mystique, it served, at the same time, to define Powell for his new colleagues in the Congress and to prepare them for this burr that would rest under the saddles of many of them—this irritant that would reside in their midst for many sessions to come.

No new Congressman could have begun his tenure in more commanding style than did Adam Clayton Powell, Jr. Elected on tickets of three parties, his mandate was unencumbered. He acted immediately with all the authority implicit in such a mandate and behaved as the overwhelming majority of Harlemites would have him behave. White leaders would soon be criticizing him hotly, as the force of his dissent gath-ered momentum. Their criticisms, however, would be final proof to black America that Adam Powell truly represented it, and it alone. He was the black man's only black man in Congress. As such, he was determined to emblazon a record during his first term.

Customarily, in the House of Representatives, a freshman member is seen but not heard. Powell was both, and quickly. He introduced measures supporting a permanent FEPC, legislation abolishing segregation on railways, and the giving to Virgin Islanders the right to vote. He bombarded military service heads with demands that Negro nurses be accepted, that Negro journalists be allowed to sit in Congressional press galleries. (Washington at the time was a fervently jim crow city; no downtown hotel or movie theater would receive a Negro. Hazel Scott was turned away from a theater where *Rhapsody in Blue* was playing, a film in which she had an important role.) The only other Negro in Congress at the time was William L. Dawson of Chicago's South Side. Dawson had docilely accepted the unwritten discriminatory practice which excluded him from practically all Congressional facilities such as the steam room, gymnasium, and barber shop. From the first, Powell used all these facilities and even directed his staff to go to the House cafeteria and eat whether they were hungry or not.

Only days after his swearing-in, Powell delivered his maiden speech. It concerned labor legislation. Under consideration was the permanent FEPC bill, but Powell felt conservatives had so diluted the draft legislation that it would be meaningless. "[Senator Robert A.] Taft's milk and water bill would set up a voluntary FEPC which would provide for some more studies on discrimination," Powell said. "Have not Taft and his GOP colleagues realized yet that minority groups are sick and tired of being studied and now demand action?" He voted against the measure and, ironically, found himself in the same voting column with white supremacist John E. Rankin of Mississippi. Powell had voted against the

FEPC bill because it was too weak; Rankin because he was unwilling to accept any FEPC at all.

The Harlem press proudly reported that their representative was being accepted in high Washington circles, a judgement based on his being among the "select group of notables" invited to a White House luncheon following Roosevelt's inauguration. As a Congressman, of course, his name was automatically on such invitation lists and his presence at the affair implied no special distinction. But the day was not far off when even this minimal protocol would be violated by the striking of his name from standard invitation lists.

White supremacists did not have long to wait before the new Congressman assaulted them. If he needed living symbols against which he could rally the black masses in Harlem —and, indeed, throughout the country—he found the ideal "political beast" in John Rankin of Mississippi. Rankin conveniently embodied the key issues: white supremacy and ultra-conservatism. The latter was no less grist for Powell's mill, for he had chosen the path of high liberalism and was as likely to thrust against "American fascists" and foreign "imperialists" (in which he included Winston Churchill) as he was against Negro-haters. When Congress convened in January, 1945, Rankin declared: "I won't sit by Powell." Powell said, "That makes it mutual," and called Rankin a "Fascist."

"As far as democracy is concerned," Powell said, "Rankin is a degenerate. He is the leader of American fascism. His presence in the House of Representatives is the most serious obstacle to America's part in winning a People's War or a people's peace. I am happy that Rankin will not sit by me because that makes it mutual. The only people with whom he is qualified to sit are Hitler and Mussolini." Powell took a swipe at the opposition party, while attacking Rankin, a Democrat. "It's too bad that the Republicans have deserted

their party and produced followers of a Southern fascism. . . .
The recent committee on un-American activities should investigate Rankin first, for he and his majority lead America
in illiteracy and mass-murder lynching." In March, 1945,
Powell even went so far as to call for Rankin's impeachment
after the Mississippian had engaged in a brief fistfight with a
Michigan Congressman. Powell's running battle with Rankin
often included Senator Theodore G. (The Man) Bilbo, also
of Mississippi.

His "Soap Box" column in *The People's Voice* was another
battlefront of his war: "American fighting men are coming
back from the foxholes of the earth to meet American fascists
emerging from ratholes," he wrote. "[Bilbo and Rankin] are
two political degenerates and rat-hole Americans. . . . The
time has arrived, however, for an active campaign to be put
on by the national leadership of the Democratic party to
purge rats from public office." He demanded that New York's
United States Senators Robert F. Wagner, Sr. and James M.
Mead act against Bilbo, since a member of the lower chamber
was obliged not to attack a member of the upper chamber.
Powell made an early re-election pledge: "I am going back to
Congress for the next two years if for no other reason than
the fact that Bilbo once called me a 'bad Negro' and Rankin
would rather have anyone else in Harlem than me."

In Washington, Powell was becoming the subject of heated
conversation for still another reason: he made frontal attacks
on the jim crow practices of the District of Columbia. As
early as January 20, 1945, he advised Harlemites: "In Washington, D.C., the capital of the world, segregation is no less
pronounced than in the Deep South, and not much more
subtle. The Negro rates close to 30 percent of the population
and he is rigidly jimcrowed on every side. The time-worn
excuses cannot hold water . . . for here the Negro has probably the highest per capita educational status in the country

and his education ranks with that of whites, if not superior. ... Except for the transportation system, the pattern is identical with that of the Deepest South. ... Negroes and whites are rigidly separated in school systems. ... The theaters and restaurants in Washington rigidly exclude all members of the Negro group. Medical and health facilities are on a separate basis. ... In some [federal] departments, Negro and white workers still cannot use Government facilities together. In the Capitol itself, Negro congressional and senatorial employees are barred from the cafeterias."

He proposed a four-point program, including equal and unsegregated schools, desegregated federal buildings, a civil rights bill for the District of Columbia and the enfranchisement of Washingtonians (who finally voted for President for the first time in 1964).

That he intended to speak for Negroes everywhere—not only those in Harlem—became increasingly apparent. In June, 1945, he commented on a report of the Atlanta Urban League: "Read a few of these terrible discrepancies. There is one school for every 855 white children in Atlanta, but one for every 2,040 Negroes. Two thousand one hundred and fifty-six dollars is spent in buildings and land for each white school, but only $887 for each Negro. The white child goes to school six and one-half hours each day, but the Negro child spends three and one-half hours a day in school, due to the overcrowded conditions and the need for double sessions." Powell had put his finger on a fact which informed Negroes knew well, but which would not come home to most Americans for another decade: the separate-but-equal doctrine, which was the law of the land, was hypocritical. Negro schools were separate but far from equal.

Foreign affairs were not outside the new Congressman's purview. He complained again about the treatment given Japanese as compared with captured Germans, discerning in it the familiar dynamic of white supremacy. "When the war began," he said, "we locked up all Japanese-Americans even though they were born here in America and were of unquestioned loyalty and herded them together with Jap fascists in concentration camps. This we did not do with the Germans, or with the Italians for that matter. We front-paged every horror story; we headlined every atrocity committed by the yellow men. We prided ourselves that in combat, very few were taken prisoner. On the other hand, we have pampered Germans every step of the way. . . . We brought to America German prisoners and allowed them to ride on trains in better accommodations than Negro people, who were forced to ride in jim crow cars and eat in jim crow corners of diners. We let them fraternize with American girls and even allowed that fraternizing to go further than just a mere smile. If a Negro had done the same thing he would immediately be strung by a mob to the limb of a tree for 'rape.' " He warned that "there were people in America who tried to make this a white man's war from the beginning and if we don't watch out they are going to make it a white man's peace. . . ."

An early trademark of the new Congressman was the thoroughly-publicized telegram—a ploy he would use to needle several Presidents. On March 6, 1945, he sent one to President Roosevelt, asking him to commission Joe Louis, who was then an army sergeant. Powell observed that white boxing champions, notably Gene Tunney, Jack Dempsey, and James Braddock, had served as officers. Secretary of War Henry Stimson responded that no more direct commissions were being granted. But Powell had scored his point.

Powell's first return to Harlem after going to Washington was an opportunity for the sort of theatricality cherished by the Congressman. He held public court in the offices of *The People's Voice* surrounded by a battery of lawyers, ministers, social workers, secretaries, and newsmen. He entertained constituents' problems and made on-the-spot contact with the necessary city agencies by telephone, telegram, and messenger. Problems of old-age pensions, jobs, rents, and contracts were handled with a flair, even if results were not always forthcoming. His homecoming was celebrated with a party at the Golden Gate Ballroom attended by district leaders, theatrical figures, and consular functionaries.

In spite of Powell's ultra-liberalism, his relations with liberals were not without complication. He was always quick to spot liberal dualism. In a "Soap Box" column during his first term, he wrote: "True, there is no overt jim crow of Negro people in liberal movements, but I charge tonight that there is an intellectual jim crow. I am consistently at work telephoning, writing various great American liberals, demanding that they keep the Negro in the forefront where he once was, demanding that they stop using Negro Uncle Toms as stooges."

Powell's detractors often criticized him for not showing tangible results such as enacted legislation. He responded this way: "The way of the legislator is hard and especially so if he is black. If he happens to be a Negro he must virtually build a way out of no way. For one thing, however, there can never be an excuse—and that is silence. In these days of challenge, silence is no longer golden."

Thus, Powell began in Washington as the very model of the angry young man. He spoke in the same terms as the early Rooseveltian ultra-liberals who were angered by the Depression and outraged by the excesses of fascism and nazism in Europe. He vocalized his indignation no more vehemently than the Americans for Democratic Action, or labor union political actionists. Nor were his habits—abrasive though they were—any more abrasive than those of some liberals who emerged as spokesmen for organized labor. These latter enjoyed places of stature within the established power structure, even though they too were often controversial. But they were white. Powell was of an out-group, the non-accommodating blacks who would never consent to being "house Negroes." He aimed for a share of their power; they declined to cut him in.

Powell's mother died in her sleep on April 22, 1945, at the age of 73. She had been a preacher's wife all her adult life and had followed her husband from threadbare poverty to the affluence and position of Abyssinian Baptist. Her influence on her son is an ambiguous one, since he rarely mentioned her in public or in his writings. She was always something of a shadowy presence. Her husband, Adam senior, was destined to be a widower for only a year before his remarriage.

Late in July, Adam Powell, Jr. announced he would marry Hazel Scott on August 1. He had asked permission of his congregation, he said, and they had approved enthusiastically. He was 36, she 25.

The wedding day went less than smoothly. Powell had a flat tire driving to the church in Stamford, Connecticut, and had to be rescued by a Merritt Parkway tollhouse attendant, who rushed him to the ceremony 28 minutes late. Afterwards, he and Hazel sped back to New York to a crowded reception at Cafe Society Uptown, where thousands waited to meet the famous couple. News photographers clamored for pictures. Powell, however, had contracted for an exclusive sitting with a national picture magazine. The discrimination enraged the other news photographers and shouted complaints preceded the throwing of a few ineffectual blows. Powell angrily ordered one of the newsmen out of the club. Hazel fainted. The festivities got national press attention.

Two months to the day after the wedding, Hazel was in the

headlines again, this time with a *cause célèbre,* the repercussions from which were felt all the way to the White House. The Daughters of the American Revolution refused her the use of Constitution Hall because she was a Negro. The action called down upon the heads of the DAR the wrath of liberals everywhere. Powell shot off a telegram to President Truman asking him to intervene. Truman deplored the DAR's action, comparing their policy to that of the Nazis, who had banned the public appearance of artists and musicians whose religion or origin was "repugnant" to the Master Race. At the same time, he said that he could not interfere in the affairs of a private institution. Powell retorted that Constitution Hall was a public institution insofar as it was tax-exempt. *The New York Times* agreed in an editorial: "The DAR exists under a Congressional act of incorporation for the purpose, among others cited, of 'securing for all mankind the blessings of liberty.' "

The American Labor Party asked Senator Bilbo, chairman of the Senate Committee for the District of Columbia, to investigate. The controversy broke onto the House floor in bitter debate. Representative Rankin shouted that the attacks on the DAR were of Communist origin and that "we have come to a hell of a pass" if a group of ladies can't say who will or who won't appear in their hall. Representative Helen Gahagan Douglas of California introduced a bill to withdraw tax exemption from the DAR, and Representative Emanuel Celler of New York offered a measure to repeal the act of Congress of 1896 incorporating the group. Representative Clare Boothe Luce wired her DAR local chapter in Greenwich, Connecticut, for a draft resolution opposing the action and threatened that she would resign from the organization if no such resolution were forthcoming. Her chapter voted 48 to 2 to sustain the action banning Hazel Scott from Constitution Hall. Mrs. Luce did not resign, but suggested she would transfer her membership to some chapter that *had* opposed the discrimination, if one could be found.

Powell sent a letter to Mrs. Truman asking her to cancel a scheduled tea she planned to attend with leaders of the DAR. (Mrs. Roosevelt had resigned from the DAR in 1939 after it had refused Negro singer Marian Anderson permission to perform in Constitution Hall.) Mrs. Truman declined to boycott the tea, insisting in her reply to Powell that "my acceptance of the hospitality is not related to the merits of the issue which has since arisen." Powell countered: "From now on, Mrs. Truman is the Last Lady. . . . The excuse given by Mrs. Truman doesn't bear up when compared with Mrs. Eleanor Roosevelt's withdrawal from the DAR." Powell thus earned the undying enmity of President Truman.

The Trumans continued to attend concerts at Constitution Hall and Hazel never appeared there. But Powell had the last word. "I don't see how anyone can compare the action of the DAR with Nazism and then let his wife sit down and have tea with the Hitlers." Hazel, later that year, refused to perform at the National Press Club because Negro newspapermen were at that time barred from the club as well as from the press galleries of the Senate and House.

The marriage of Powell and Hazel appeared to be an ideal one. She described it as "Utopia" and he once told an audience that "We live together like we're company every day. She dresses for dinner and expects me to shave. Unfailingly, she has tall candles, flowers, sterling, and the rest every day. She knows I like them." On another occasion, he said: "My life with Hazel has been chockful of the kind of experiences that would excite the average American husband—warm, golden brown hot cakes on a winter morning; lazy summer afternoons on our Long Island beach; beer and crackers and cheese on our terrace; relaxing evenings at the neighborhood movie house and in the living room before the fire, with

Rachmaninoff's Second Piano Concerto coming out of the phonograph. I cite these things not because they are the typical pleasures of people everywhere in our country, but because they represent to me the little things of which my marriage to Hazel is made." They were, at the same time, precisely the "little things" to which many post-war Negroes aspired—the symbols of middle class respectability—and, if they couldn't have them in fact, they could have them vicariously in Powell.

Hazel introduced Powell to an inner circle of theatrical sophisticates. She abandoned her lucrative nightclub career to become a concert soloist and appeared with the New York Philharmonic, the Philadelphia, Los Angeles, and Milwaukee symphonies, among others. She was soon earning more from this activity than she had in night clubs—$100,000 a year, Powell claimed. Their real estate holdings began to be impressive: the house at 25 Monroe Place in White Plains, New York; apartments in Manhattan and Washington; a house on the south shore of Long Island at Westhampton; and several apartment buildings in Harlem. Their life was as different from that of Powell's constituency in Harlem as could be imagined: fine clothes and cars, luxury cruises to Europe and the Caribbean, Broadway openings, expensive presents. As a couple, they were idolized and celebrated by Harlem's tenemented blacks. Their arrivals and departures were unfailingly covered in pictures by the Harlem press.

When it was announced early in 1946 that Hazel was pregnant, Harlem was jubilant. As the day approached, hundreds of Harlemites telephoned the local papers daily to get news of Hazel's condition. "Lawd, Lawd," one old Negro woman sighed to an editor, "That Adam Powell is certainly a mess. He's got me putting a nickel in this phone box every day. At night I can't sleep for thinking. But watch out for a girl if it doesn't rain before Friday." The baby was born by Caesarian section and for a brief time Hazel's condition was reported critical. Powell told reporters: "I can't smile until I see Hazel smile. She was asleep when I left upstairs, but I intend to remain here until she smiles again." Hazel recovered, and the baby, which weighed eight pounds, was promptly named Adam Clayton Powell III. Asked by a reporter if the baby had any comment on the forthcoming election campaign, Powell said his first words had been "Vote for Daddy." Flowers and telegrams flooded the hospital; a Washington man sent a gold spoon, saying he had always wanted to see a Negro baby born with a gold spoon in his mouth. Powell told reporters the baby "has big feet, a big head and a big mouth like his daddy."

The birth of Adam III—nicknamed Skipper—wasn't the only event of domestic importance in the Powell family that year. Adam senior, at the age of 80, married a retired trained nurse named Inez Cottrell, who was many years younger than he. Adam junior said: "I am very happy that my father has someone like her to make easy these years."

All was not felicity in Powell's professional life. Other Negro leaders in the national sector already were beginning to believe that the new Congressman was determined on a career of lone wolf agitation over civil rights causes, and would never meld gracefully with their own efforts. A. Philip Randolph, at the head of a group called the National Council for a Permanent FEPC (which habitually excluded whites from its membership), was once again planning a march on Washington. Powell was not invited either to the march or to a giant preparatory rally in Madison Square Garden. His anger at the slight was quick and unambiguous: "It cannot be said that I was uninvited for the reason that strong speakers are feared," he claimed, "because what we need nowadays is, above all, a crying aloud and sparing none." Powell also doubted that his exclusion was based on criticism in *March-*

ing Blacks of earlier march-on-Washington attempts and his condemnation of the barring of whites from the ranks of the FEPC agitators. Time had proved him correct, said Powell, "because the only thing that is going to pass the FEPC in Congress is the white vote. . . . Undoubtedly Mr. Randolph does not know that his organization is playing politics with the bread and butter of the Negro people." Powell recounted his credits as a voice for civil rights in the Congress and complained that "despite all this" he had not been asked to be a part of the 1946 march-on-Washington movement. That particular march never materialized, but 18 years later, Randolph kept Powell at a distance from a march that did.

As the elections of 1946 approached, Powell was eager to keep his mandate intact by once again garnering the nominations of all three parties; however, there were persistent rumors of challenge. A Harvard-educated journalist, Earl Brown—the man who twelve years later would be impressed into running against Powell in the abortive Tammany purge —caught the political flavor of that election year: "The Democrats would dearly love to ditch Powell—from President Truman to Eddie Laughlin, the Tammany Hall leader—but they can't because Congressman Powell would win, even if neither party backed him. The Communists thought seriously of putting Councilman Ben Davis, their darling, against the pulpiteer, but they wisely thought better of the idea and so they are going with him again. He is one of the few politicians extant who is not wanted by any party, but is sought by practically all of them. If he were only sound, serious, and responsible, he would indeed be a whale of a guy. Unfortunately, these qualities don't mix with demagoguery." Brown also called Powell "the champ soapbox demagogue. . . . He can even make a preacher part with a dollar bill."

Only the Republicans mounted a campaign; they proposed Grant Reynolds, a minister, former army captain and commissioner of the New York Department of Correction. Many Harlem GOP leaders admitted privately that they preferred not to come to grips with Powell, but that "downtown" bosses had forced a candidate upon them. Powell did, in fact, lose the Republican primary to Reynolds by 500 votes—the only election the Harlem Congressman ever lost—but easily captured the Democratic and ALP nominations: his grand total of primary votes stood in a four to one ratio to Reynolds: 9,811 to 2,858.

Many ghetto dwellers saw Reynolds giving Powell his first real test in the general election; the campaign was advertised as "giant versus giant" and "the battle of the preachers." Political reporter Julius J. Adams called them "men who are alike in that both are aggressive, gregarious, and cosmopolitan; yet decidedly unalike, in that Reynolds is logical, studious, and gives close attention to form and strategy, while Powell is rash, blustering, strong-willed, and is constantly off on a tangent and half-cocked. . . . Reynolds works methodically for permanent and lasting gains; Powell is more opportunistic and will capitalize on a situation for temporary advantage." That the campaign would be colorful and theatrical also was obvious. "Both," Adams continued, "are strapping fellows, of the Clark Gable type of glamor boy. Both are excellent speakers, though Reynolds is probably the better in straight forensics, while Powell is the better 'shouter.' . . . Both have a flair for the dramatic and might have gone far on the stage or screen. . . . In the past, the dynamics of Powell's personality have been enough to drive all opposition to cover. . . . Nobody, it seems, has been willing to move in and trade punches with the champion phrasemaker—apparently afraid of his acid tongue and blistering attacks."

Earl Brown also described the contest in its glamorous, apolitical dimension: "Adam and 'Pretty Boy' Grant have practically unlimited appeal to the females. Some overstater has said, in fact, that the Reverend Powell slithered into the House on the kisses he has implanted on Abyssinian's glassy-eyed sisters every Sunday morning. The Reverend Grant, always superbly bedecked, is famous for his rather hard-to-get air. The lady voters fall for this and it is predicted that he will cut deeply into Adam's distaff preserves on election day." But Brown supposed it was "doubtful that [Grant] can out-bellow Adam either about God or mere man and his mundane matters. For Adam is in a class by himself when it comes to generating sheer noise."

Powell's announcement came early in June. The Abyssinian Church became his election organization and Joseph E. Ford his campaign manager. He announced endorsements from both Henry Wallace and Father Divine. He listed Joe Louis as one of his honorary chairmen. The ex-champion counter-punched: "If Powell used my name in any way it was without consulting me and without my consent." Reynolds was his candidate, said Louis. A similiar confusion occurred with the Reverend George H. Sims, Jr., pastor of the Union Baptist Church and President of the Empire State Baptist Convention. Powell claimed the clergyman was in his corner, but Sims said Powell's use of his name was an "unmitigated falsehood. My candidate is Reynolds."

Powell's campaign pitch was "I stand on my record." Prominently listed among his achievements was the fact that he had called Senator Bilbo "a rat"; his fight for FEPC, his arranging "hundreds of jobs" for Negroes in government and private industry, his intercession in "over eight hundred" armed forces courts-martial cases with every sentence said to have been reduced or the serviceman released.

Powell also laid heavy emphasis on passage of an early version of the "Powell Amendment" which he had attached to the Flanagan School Lunch Bill, providing $100,000,000 in

free lunches for school children. Powell's rider barred allocation of funds to any state refusing free lunches to Negro children—although it was not known that any state intended to
try excluding Negro children. As a result of the passage of the
amendment, Powell portrayed himself as "the first Negro
since Reconstruction to have any legislation made into law."
He also called attention to the bills he had introduced: several measures for naturalization of Virgin Islanders, Filipinos,
Koreans, and American Indians; measures abolishing lynching and poll taxes, providing for a permanent FEPC, elim-
inating armed forces segregation and providing sick and
annual leave for postal employees. According to Powell's
account, he had been an energetic sleuth in learning about
injustices in the courts-martial of Negroes, including WACS.
In what was described as a "partial report on justice won for
Negro GIs in over 800 courts-martial cases," he detailed instances of commuted or reduced sentences. Two GIs sentenced to death for rape in Germany were listed as freed.
One captain sentenced to 50 years had been and returned to
active duty. Negro rights in prisons had also been of concern
to him, he said, and reported that his complaint had brought
an end to segregation in a Danbury, Connecticut, prison.

Not all the issues he pressed were racial; some were purely
economic. The price control question attracted his frequent
attention. He was "furious," he claimed, at the failure of the
House "to stand by the people when it was slashing the OPA
[Office of Price Administration] to shreds." He said the
House had "betrayed the little people because of the pressures of big people—big industry and the big money boys." It
was big business that was out to defeat him in the 1946 election, said Powell. "Big business is giving the Republican
Party millions of dollars to defeat our candidates for re-election. But we can beat them because the people are on our
side."

He called Grant Reynolds "[Governor Thomas E.] Dewey's Uncle Tom," "a handkerchief head," and "the darling of the big Negroes who hate the little Negroes." In a radio broadcast, he claimed it was a contest of "an Uncle Tom against the New Negro." *The People's Voice* quoted Reynolds as saying "Forget Bilbo and work" and Powell as countering, "Remember Bilbo and fight." Powell heaped scorn on his opponent, charging that he had failed to end discrimination in Sing Sing prison while Commissioner of Correction, on grounds that he was only one man and thus could not force reforms through. Powell wondered then how Reynolds expected to accomplish anything as only one man among 432 Representatives in the Congress.

Reynolds, in his turn, slapped Powell on his absenteeism, claiming he had "abandoned the people" by being away at important moments. Personal gain, he charged, had led Powell to the lecture circuit at $500 an appearance, when he should have been on The Hill. Powell refused Reynolds' challenge to a debate on grounds that it would "give Reynolds more publicity than he deserves." Reynolds's own campaign was based on appeals for low-rent housing, slum clearance, a 75-cent minimum wage, and protection for veterans and their widows.

On election day, Powell polled 32,573 votes (22,641 Democratic and 9,932 American Labor Party) to 19,514 for Reynolds. Compared with later campaigns, it was a strong showing for the Republicans, but not good enough to keep Powell from crowing. "My easy victory," he said, "indicates the solid support of the people in Harlem. . . . The thousands of dollars poured into Harlem could not buy the Negro vote. We have served notice on cheap politicians to stay out of Harlem." Reynolds reported campaign expenditures of over $6000. Powell admitted receiving only one campaign contribution—for $50.

Overwork was the reason Powell gave, early in 1946, for retiring from participation in the affairs of *The People's Voice*. In a prepared statement, he said: "I have tried during the first year of my service in Congress to maintain as far as possible my duties as Editor-in-Chief. . . . I find, however, that this is impossible. . . . I begin a leave of absence from *The People's Voice* for the rest of my term in Congress." Powell said he would continue to be a contributor, but would not take any responsibility for the paper's editorial policy and news presentation. (He wrote "Soap Box" columns almost until the paper's demise in 1948.) At first he said his decision followed a conference with Negro leaders who advised him to end his ties with left-wing groups so as not to compromise his position in the Republican-controlled 80th Congress. Later, however, he branded "absolutely a lie" a report that he had resigned from the paper because it was "loaded with pro-Moscow party members." He called the report "one more attempt to disrupt the growing unity of the Negro people and of Negroes with their progressive white allies."

But it was a fact that, by the spring of 1947, the Communist line was becoming more and more apparent in the paper's pages. Phrases such as "American imperialism" and "fascist terror" and bitter condemnations of anyone favoring outlawing the Communist Party were appearing regularly. The paper began showing signs of moribundity early in 1948. Powell's "Soap Box" column disappeared. The last issue of *The People's Voice* was not labeled as such, but an editorial revealed the infighting. Titled, "Deceit, Betrayal, Trickery," it began: "Because of these ugly words and the more ugly strength they carry, *The People's Voice* recently failed to come out on time. . . . Here we are back again, effective on all fronts." But it was verbal rigor mortis. No further edition appeared. *The People's Voice* simply had not achieved financial success nor acceptance on Harlem's newstands. In addition, internal bickering between communists and non-communist elements of the staff—and finally among the communists themselves—contributed to the paper's collapse.

7. "New World A'Coming"

A recession in 1947—coming on the heels of the lifting of price controls and the concomitant inflation—hit Harlem hard. Relief rolls fattened and food prices went higher. The Abyssinian church opened a non-profit store to sell food at prices Harlemites could afford to pay. Mrs. Hattie Dodson, Powell's secretary, ran the store.

Inflation was not the only problem facing the 80th Congress as it convened. Until 1947, Powell had always worked in legislative bodies controlled by Democrats. But the general elections of 1946 produced Republican majorities in both chambers of Congress. Powell wasted no time in addressing himself to the new power structure: "I have come back to Washington to insist that the Republicans keep their campaign promises to the Negro people," he declared in "The Soap Box." "For the past years we have been repeatedly told that worthwhile legislation advancing the case of a people could not be passed because Congress was controlled by Southerners! Now this is no longer true. The Republicans are the bosses of both the House and the Senate. The Northerners are in power."

Almost immediately, however, the traditional coalition of Republicans and Southern Democrats hardened. Republican parliamentarians, including House Speaker Joseph Martin of Massachusetts, were not inclined to alienate their southern allies in racial tilting. Powell tested the coalition early in the session through an exchange with his favorite symbol of white supremacy, John Rankin. Rankin customarily used the word "nigger" on the floor of the House. Powell rose one day and objected:

Powell: Mr. Speaker, a parliamentary inquiry.
Speaker: Will the gentleman yield for a parliamentary inquiry?
Rankin: No.
Powell: Mr. Speaker, a point of order.
Speaker: The gentleman will state his point of order.
Powell: Is it within the rules of this Congress to refer to any group of our nation in disparaging terms?
Rankin: It is not disparaging to call Negroes niggers as all respectable Negroes know.
Powell: I am addressing the speaker.
Speaker: The chair is not aware of the disparaging term used.
Powell: He used the term "nigger" in referring to a group.
Speaker: The chair understood the gentleman to say "Negro."
Rankin: Mr. Speaker, I said what I always say and what I am always going to say when referring to these people.

Powell had made his point. In the past, the House stenographer had always written "Negro" when Rankin actually had said "nigger." Now Powell—by forcing the exchange with Rankin and, subsequently, by editing the stenographer's transcript before its inclusion in the *Congressional Record*—was able to set the *Record* straight. Powell claimed later that Speaker Martin was "the first speaker in Congress to legalize the use of the word 'nigger' by a Congressman. I would especially like to know if the Republican leaders in Harlem are going to let this go unprotested." He added, in a lighter vein, "I never consider Congress really open until I have an opening skirmish with Rankin."

His bouts with the coalition continued as the session progressed. He fought the Taft-Hartley Bill and accused the Republicans of being a rubber stamp for the National Association of Manufacturers, desirous of returning "American workers to chattel slavery."

Early in 1947, Powell was felled by a heart attack while travelling by car with Hazel between Manhattan and their Westchester home. His physician called the attack "severe." In July, Powell had a second attack and retreated for recuperation to his house at Westhampton, Long Island. A rumor of his death swept Harlem briefly, causing hundreds to telephone newspaper offices for corroboration. Adam Powell, Sr. amused his son with a story that fifteen New York morticians had volunteered to bury him free of charge, which suggested the number of people who would have been glad to see the Congressman gone from the scene.

Powell's abrasiveness was indeed making him personally repugnant to many whites, a considerable number of blacks, and the President of the United States. Powell's contempt for Truman was evident from the start and the relationship was aggravated by the DAR incident. As early as 1945, Powell was suggesting Henry Wallace as an acceptable 1948 nominee and predicting a Republican victory "unless the administration gets back in step with the Roosevelt way of a people's democracy." He called Truman the "Little Man in the White House."

It was not surprising, then, that presidential reception lists began omitting Powell's name. He resorted to a favorite cry: he was being snubbed because of racial bias in the White House. A reporter asked Assistant Press Secretary Eben Ayers, "It's rather odd, isn't it, to exclude a congressman from the list because he is a Negro?" Ayers would say only, "There were other Negro congressmen invited."

Powell's attitude toward Truman mirrored, at least to some degree, the sentiments of his constituents. Truman was not popular in Harlem; but a mellowing of that attitude began after the President's appointment of Judge William H. Hastie, dean of Howard University School of Law, as Governor of the Virgin Islands. Powell said: "Mr. Hastie's nomination . . . proves that a Negro need not be a 'handkerchief head' to get ahead in this country, even in government circles."

The nomination by the Republicans of Governor Thomas E. Dewey for President left Powell without a candidate to whom he could lend unqualified support. He finally announced himself in favor of "the Democratic ticket" on October 30. Although he declined to mention Truman by name, he did condemn Dewey, attacking him for an alleged indifference to police brutality. As for Powell's own re-election, it was typical of many to come. He made only one major speech and predicted a three-to-one victory for himself. Running as the candidate of both the Democrats and the American Labor Party, he polled four-to-one over his opponent, long-time Republican stalwart, Harold C. Burton.

From an examination of Powell's power base in Harlem, and the ease with which he won elections there, it began to be apparent to many whites that the Negro Congressman shared with his black constituents some secret which white men could only guess at. His victory margins mounted, in spite of a growing reputation for absenteeism, and charges against him that there was often more sound than substance in his cries of anger over racial injustice. The more expensive clothing, cars, and houses he bought, the more time he spent travelling first-class on junkets to Europe, the more frequently he appeared at Broadway opening nights and plushy night clubs

—the greater his popularity became with lower caste Negroes. Similarly, the more he was criticized by whites, the more certain were these tenemented blacks that he was indeed their best friend and spokesman. To whites, it was an egregious dilemma. Sensitive ears—as the decade of the 1950's began—were already discerning the first, subterranean rumblings of the black revolution. It was going to be important that Americans understand this implacable ten percent in their midst.

Social scientists were applying new tools to that task. A study titled *Mark of Oppression,* for example, attempted no less a task than psychoanalyzing black America and inquiring if there was indeed a basic personality for the Negro, a common and discoverable habit of mind among black men. The authors, Abram Kardiner and Lionel Ovesey, of Columbia University, concluded that there was, and close to the heart of this basic personality was the chronic low self-esteem in which Negroes customarily held themselves as the result of the ordinary hostile behavior of whites toward them. So omnipresent and unrelieved a condition is this low self-esteem, they said, that it lies well below the level of the Negro's consciousness, and, in order to retain the capacity to function at all, the Negro constructs about himself a facade of attitude and behavior, the maintenance of which makes him chronically mistrustful, lacking in confidence, and ill-at-ease.

Schematically, the Negro's internal state was described thus:

Low self-esteem = self-contempt ⟶ idealization of
the white ⟶ frantic efforts to be white = unattainable

hostility to whites
introjected white ideal ⟶
(⟶) self hatred ⟶ projected on to other Negroes =
hatred of Negroes.

His low self-esteem also produces apathy, hedonism, and criminality, the study insisted. His rage, in turn, gives birth to a fear of its consequences. Kardiner and Ovesey claimed that "Fear and rage become almost interchangeable. When the manifestations of rage are continually suppressed, ultimately the individual may cease to be aware of the emotion. In some subjects, the only manifestation of rage may be fear." Many Negroes work off their rage by replacing it with submissiveness, compliancy, and bowing and scraping. But the two most common products of a Negro's lifelong attempts to control aggression are low self-esteem and depression.

A Negro lives with the intuition that the world is hostile, said the study; that he is not essentially a creature who can command love. Many lower class Negroes thus become addictive "joiners" of clubs, lodges, and secret fraternities having exotic names and gaudy uniforms. A related dilemma for the Negro is represented by the question: "Whom do I want to be like?" His parents are members of a despised minority and thus are flawed as possible ideals. Inevitably, his ideal becomes the white ideal and he thus ties himself to goals that are unattainable—with the concomitant frustration which that predicament implies. He can *never* become white, but in trying, he frequently becomes a caricature of white and loses what pride he might have had in his own value as a human being.

Negroes discover varying ways for bolstering their self-esteem: flashy dressing, the use of skin bleaches, and treatments to straighten kinky hair. Many others, the study pointed out, simply insulate themselves against their hostile surroundings by the use of alcohol and drugs. (Alcoholic psychoses are twice as common among Negroes as among whites.) Gambling is another form of narcotic for many Negroes, especially numbers-playing, where even the most downtrodden can live daily with the tantalizing prospect of winning a pot of gold.

Similarly, most lower class Negroes are inclined to indulge in spending sprees when a few extra dollars are available, and to trap themselves in credit buying to the limits, and beyond, of their ability to pay—thus creating the illusion, if not the substance, of affluent living.

This death of self-esteem in America's Negroes was something Adam Powell knew intuitively and something which has been known to every important black nationalist from Marcus Garvey to Elijah Muhammad and Malcolm X. When Garvey was on trial for fraud after the failure of his Black Star shipping line, his defense attorney said: "If every Negro could have put every dime, every penny, into the sea, and if he might get in exchange the knowledge that he was somebody, that he meant something in the world, he would gladly do it. . . . The Black Star Line was a loss in money but it was a gain in soul." When Adam Powell defied the white man, challenged his ancient prejudices, shouted him down in the halls of Congress, surmounted attempts by white men to purge him from political life, and lived with greater style and enjoyment than most white men—then did the poor black "gain in soul" and capture a glimmering of his own importance as a human thing.

Powell's legislative activity gathered momentum in the Truman years. In 1948, he was adamant in his refusal to support appropriations for the House Un-American Activities Committee on grounds that it failed to investigate un-American pursuits across the board. "I said last year and I say again today," Powell declaimed on the House floor, "that when this committee really investigates un-American activities on all fronts, then I will vote for an appropriation." He complained that the committee had ignored Ku Klux Klan terrorism in Johnston County, Georgia, only one week previously when

the Klan had interfered with the attempts of 400 duly registered Negroes to vote.

When Powell, in the same speech, accused Mississippi police of lynch murders, Representative Rankin of that state
rose and angrily demanded that "those words be taken down."
There was not "a word of truth in that statement," said
Rankin, "and everybody familiar with the situation knows
that there is no truth in it." But Powell persisted, and exclaimed that he was against "red baiting, Negro hating, and
anti-Semitism." He would support the House Un-American
Activities Committee, he said, when they had ferreted out the
Klan, as well as "the Gerald Smiths, the police lynchers, the
Jew haters, and all the rats of our land. . . ."

In 1949, he continued to hammer away at these issues, and
such others as housing discrimination. On June 29, he casti-
gated the Federal Housing Administration, calling it a disgrace, and pointing to such housing developments as Levittown, New York. Although Levittown was the beneficiary of
federal monies, Powell said, it was for "Caucasians only." The
FHA had told members of the Banking and Currency Committee that such practices had stopped, but that was "a lie,"
Powell said. "The FHA . . . is supporting jim crow in New
York."

Also in 1949, Powell spoke against job discrimination, the
privation of citizens' rights in the District of Columbia and
the Virgin Islands, segregation in the armed forces, discrimination in immigration laws, mob violence and lynching, and
the poll tax. In 1950, he persisted in his efforts to get anti-
discrimination bills and resolutions before the Congress, and
took an important role in the consideration of fair employment practices legislation. One of his causes in 1951, was a bill
stipulating more stringent regulation of narcotic sales.

Powell's first serious brush with the law—the first of many—
came in 1952 when the Internal Revenue Service charged he

had underestimated his 1945 tax obligation by $2,749. The government finally accepted $1,193 in settlement, but that did not end the matter. In fact it started an incredibly complex investigation into his finances that was to last for many years to come. He and Hazel had been filing joint returns since their marriage, and claiming heavy professional expenses. But the opulent manner of their existence was calculated to arouse the curiosity of even the most complaisant tax collector.

In 1954, Powell was involved publicly in a mysterious exchange with a non-profit organization called the Tenants Protective Association, of which he momentarily found himself the president. In that year, a Senate Committee was investigating the Federal Housing Authority and, in so doing, learned that a contractor named David Kent had, in 1952, asked Powell to help in selling some coöperative apartments in an inter-racial housing project. Powell sent two of his congressional secretaries, Acy Lennon and William Hampton, to lend Kent a hand.

Later that year, Powell borrowed $3000 from Kent at one percent interest and gave Kent a note, payable on demand at any time after six months had elapsed. Then in 1954—just before the FHA investigation was announced—Powell gave Kent a check for $30, one year's interest on the loan. The Senate committee was eager to discover why Kent had allowed two years to go by without asking Powell to pay back the $3000. Kent said: "I am not in the business of making loans to friends. In fact, when Congressman Powell comes to me and pays me this $3000 I intend to return this check [for $30] to him."

Such magnanimity once again attracted the attention of the Justice Department to Powell's statement of earnings and, in a preliminary thrust, his two aides, Lennon and Hampton, along with a third congressional secretary, Mrs. Hattie Freeman Dodson, were indicted for tax evasion. Testimony revealed that in 1952 Kent had given Lennon a check for $3000 (not the same $3000 loaned to Powell), made out to the Tenants Protective Association and intended to cover commissions to Lennon and Hampton for their selling chores. Three days after the check was deposited to the account of TPA, a check was drawn in the same sum to the order of a man named Paul Klein, reportedly a friend of Powell's. TPA's treasurer swore he hadn't known of the existence of the money (in spite of the fact that TPA's bank account usually averaged around $25). In addition, all of TPA's checks had to carry the signatures of two of its three officers—the president, who was Powell, the treasurer, and co-treasurer. Both the treasurer and co-treasurer swore they had never signed such a check—forcing the conclusion that either forgery or perjury was being committed. Nobody—neither Powell, the TPA, Lennon, Hampton nor Klein—had reported the money as income. The Justice Department was interested to know who owed a tax on the disappearing $3000.

Klein said he had "no personal recollection" of having received the money, but, upon the urging of Lennon and Hampton, admitted he might have received it. "I thought I certainly would remember a loan of that sum," he said, "especially when I was broke." Powell came forward to testify that the money had not been *lent* to Klein, but was a payment for many old services. The court asked Powell to produce the cancelled check, along with his other records: Powell demurred. The Treasury Department had some of his records, he said. They did not, said the Treasury. Others, Powell said, had been stolen, and the rest burnt in a fire at Abyssinian Baptist. Alas, he had nothing to show them.

In the trial of Mrs. Hattie Freeman Dodson, another Powell aide and an official of the Abyssinian Baptist Church, the government charged that she had evaded $5000 in taxes and received $2000 in illegal refunds from 1948 to 1952; that she went to Washington with Powell in 1945 and was placed on the payroll, but returned to Harlem at the end of the year and continued to draw her salary. Joseph E. Ford, had appeared as a prosecution witness and testified that Mrs. Dodson kicked back her salary to Powell from 1948 to 1952, and that Powell had told her she could keep any refunds from her withholding tax. Ford, formerly a Democratic leader of the 12th Assembly District who had managed Powell's 1946 campaign, was operating a tax-consulting service out of the Abyssinian Baptist Church. He added that Mrs. Dodson had filed two sets of returns during the years in question: one for her congressional salary and the other a joint return with her husband (who was choirmaster of the church) for her salary from Abyssinian Baptist.

Nobody ever found out what happened to the more than $5000 a year Mrs. Dodson was receiving as a congressional secretary. At first she claimed she had spent the whole amount "mostly on clothes"—then later insisted she had stashed a lot of it in a safe deposit box as a "surprise" for her husband. Her husband would have been surprised indeed, since he told government agents he hadn't even known that his wife was holding down a second full-time job. Mrs. Dodson couldn't recall a single duty she had performed to earn her salary. Powell testified in her behalf, and reiterated her denial of the kickback charges. The prosecutor pointed out certain discrepancies in Mrs. Dodson's testimony, giving rise to the following exchange with Powell:

Mr. Bolan (prosecutor): On how many occasions do you have to be informed that Mrs. Dodson lied before you would change your opinion as to whether she was capable of lying?

Mr. Powell: I don't know. The Bible tells me seventy times seven.

Q. Seventy times seven?

A. That is what the Bible says. . . .

Q. That is 490 times, is that right?

A. That is what Jesus said, yes sir.

Q. . . . until Mrs. Dodson admits that she has lied on 490 occasions, you will stick to your opinion that she is not capable of telling a lie, is that right?

A. Yes it is, sir, yes it is.

Q. . . . did that passage refer to forgiveness, or did it refer to the capacity to do sin?

A. Forgiveness.

Q. . . . I didn't ask you whether you would forgive Mrs. Dodson if she lied 490 times. I asked you if your opinion would change as to her capacity for lying.

A. Her capacity to sin?

Q. Yes.

A. Okay, yes. I believe we all have it, a capacity to sin. Yes, sir.

Powell called Ford a man "who cannot be trusted, a man who indulged in sharp practices." The defense lawyer claimed: "The government is prosecuting my client because they don't have the guts to indict Congressman Powell. They want to send her to jail so they can brainwash her every day and beat her down to get her to give them information against Powell."

Mrs. Dodson was convicted, sentenced to seven months in prison and fined $1000. A grand jury subsequently investigated the kickback charges, but was unable to pin them down sufficiently to return an indictment. Powell charged that the kickback innuendoes were part of a drive to stop his fight against the White Citizens Councils. "There is some one or group trying to stop the fight I am making," he said, and added cryptically: "I'm accumulating evidence in both parties and the number is beginning to narrow. I think definitely that I will be able soon to put my finger on who it is." Assistant United States Attorney Thomas A. Bolan, who was in

charge of the case, complained that Mrs. Dodson had impeded
the government's investigation of Powell and had "lied repeatedly."

The government's pursuit of Powell was now out in the
open. United States Attorney Paul W. Williams said that the
indictments of all three Powell secretaries had grown out of
the investigation of the Congressman. The indictment against
Lennon charged the evasion of $4,210 in taxes for 1949
through 1954, the claiming of two non-existent sons as de-
pendents and the preparation of fraudulent returns for others.
The indictment against Hampton subsequently was dropped,
but the handwriting on the wall could not have been plainer:
the government was closing in on Powell.

Two weeks after Lennon's indictment, Powell departed for
a three-month tour of the continent, part of which time was
to be spent attending the World Conference of Parliamentarians. He thus avoided the Democratic National Convention
which nominated Governor Adlai E. Stevenson to run against
President Eisenhower for the second time. Upon his re-entry
into nearby coastal waters, he conducted a ship-to-shore telephone interview with the press in which he said he would
"come down the gangplank at New York with an open mind"
on whether or not he would support the Stevenson-Kefauver
ticket. It was the first inkling anybody had that Powell might
bolt.

As a condition of his support, said Powell, he wanted a
commitment from the ticket "against continued use of Federal funds in states that defy Federal law. And I don't want
that pledge confined to education." It was nothing less than
a demand for endorsement of the Powell Amendment, which
in the previous session of Congress had sabotaged Eisenhower's education bill. Without the pledge, said Powell, he
might "take a walk" and support the Republicans. But he

would demand a similar pledge from the GOP, whose platform plank on civil rights was "so little better than that of the
Democrats [as] to provide a Hobson's choice."

Asked if there were any significance to his absence from the
Democratic convention, he answered, "I wasn't invited." The
Democratic platform plank on civil rights was "wishy-washy,"
he said, and "definitely a retreat from the ideas of Truman
and Roosevelt . . . worse than four years ago and that was
pretty weak." Would he attend a Harlem street rally for
candidate Stevenson? He hadn't been invited to that either,
said Powell.

The Acy Lennon jury of seven men and five women was
chosen on October 5. Seven days later, Powell visited Eisenhower in the White House. After a thirty-minute meeting,
press secretary James Hagerty brought Powell before the
White House correspondents. Powell announced he was bolt-
ing the Democratic party to support Eisenhower in the forthcoming national election; that Adlai Stevenson (whom he had
supported in 1952) had twice refused to see him and had
similarly snubbed the nation's Negroes. Asked if he intended
to try to turn Harlem's traditionally Democratic vote to the
Republicans, he said: "I'm going to do my best to sway it." He
would form an independent Democrats-for-Eisenhower group,
he said, and enlist all "disillusioned liberal Democrats." The
switch, he insisted, was motivated by respect for the President's prestige abroad and his stand on civil rights.

The regular Democrats were enraged. Representative
Emanuel Celler of New York called Powell a "turncoat" and
recommended that—should the Harlem Congressman be re-
elected—he "be deprived of his seniority rights as a Democrat.
He was always unreliable, and furthermore ran out on his
own people when the Celler civil rights bill was called up for
debate and he went to Europe on a pleasure jaunt." Mrs.
Roosevelt, campaigning for Stevenson, said she "never had

any great respect" for Powell, and that his switch would have little effect "if the people of Harlem realize what Mr. Powell is doing." She accused him of "accepting promises of some kind, of benefit to him, but not to his people."

The whole Democratic machinery pounced on Powell's action as a sell-out and loudly proclaimed that Eisenhower was party to a craven deal to buy Powell's support in return for calling off the tax investigation of the Congressman. New York Democratic leaders met at the Biltmore Hotel in Manhattan and drafted a statement—signed by Borough President Hulan Jack, City Councilman Earl Brown (both Negroes) and a number of Assemblymen—denouncing the Harlemite:

"Adam Clayton Powell used to be a forceful spokesman for his people and for civil rights. As recently as March 2, he had the courage to accuse Eisenhower of dodging the civil rights issue, passing the buck, and trying to wash his hands, like Pilate, of the blood of innocent men and women in the Southland.

"He saw the problem clearly enough on June 23 last when he refused to capitulate to President Eisenhower's request that he support the Republican school bill.

"The people of Harlem regret that the White House was able to apply sufficient pressure upon Adam Clayton Powell— at the time of the trial of another of his personal staff now pending in Federal Court—to persuade him completely to change his convictions."

Powell's ire at the suggestion of a deal was edged with humor. "That is a complete lie," he said. "I didn't have any convictions to change." He called the signers of the document "rubber stamps and political stooges for the Democratic bosses downtown" and threatened that "if they open their mouths anymore, they are going to drive me to support [Republican State Attorney General] Jack Javits [against Demo-

cratic Mayor Robert Wagner] in the Senate race and I'll be
happy to do so." Subsequently, he did.

Willard Townsend, a vice-president of the AFL-CIO, called
Powell's action "a shocking betrayal of his race and party."
Press secretary Hagerty was moved to insist that no undue
pressure had been brought on Powell. The Congressman
made a gesture at explaining himself with an announcement
that three main points had helped him to the decision:

(1) President Eisenhower had agreed "not to oppose" a
federal school aid bill which Powell planned to introduce in
the new Congress. The bill, he said, would contain the Powell
Amendment as one of its provisions.

(2) President Eisenhower had agreed to give priority in the
new Congress to a bill protecting voting rights in federal elections.

(3) President Eisenhower had agreed on the procedure for
enforcing court integration orders through federal marshals,
arrests and trials for persons in contempt of court decisions.

But the Democrats would not let up on Powell. Governor
Averell Harriman of New York said he would not suggest a
"deal" had been made with Eisenhower, but that it was "sort
of strange that a man whose associates are known to be having
certain difficulties with the Department of Justice should
come out, as he left the White House, with a statement of this
kind."

Less than a month before the elections, the trial of Acy
Lennon with its revelations about the Tenants Protective
Association, got underway in New York. Called to testify,
Powell claimed complete ignorance of any tax investigation
of himself, but United States Attorney Williams said that the
scrutiny of Powell's finances which had started several years
earlier and which had thus far resulted in the indictment of
three of the Congressman's aides, was continuing.

Lennon was convicted on four counts and sentenced to a year in prison and a fine of $1000. (The maximum sentence was 20 years in prison and a $40,000 fine.) Powell called the Lennon judgment "the rawest deal a man ever got," thereby eliciting from Judge Archie O. Dawson the retort that his remark was "outrageous, completely irresponsible, and reckless, particularly coming from a man of such prominent position."

Powell continued to conduct his own campaign for re-election as a Democrat, in spite of his bolt to the Eisenhower-Nixon ticket. In newspaper ads, he declared: "I call on the Negro people and all democratic-loving Americans to repudiate Stevenson—and they do not have to leave their party to do so—unless he publicly repudiates the election to Congress of bigots like Eastland, Talmadge, Long, and Company, and takes an unequivocal position on the desegregation of public schools. . . . Join the Anti-Uncle Tom Freedom Crusade!" He continued to shout down accusations of collusion with Eisenhower over his tax situation. "No pressure from anybody except God and the voters of Harlem could force Adam Powell to do anything he did not want to, and I don't need any Tammany puppets to tell me what to do."

There were no surprises on election day. Eisenhower's vote cut deeply into the customary Democratic plurality in Harlem as well as everywhere else. Powell called it "the most important political trend in years," but said the vote did not necessarily mean a shift to the Republican Party by Negroes. "It does mean that the Negro people are standing up as American men and women, thinking for themselves and voting as independents." His own majority against Joseph A. Bailey, Republican regular, was 59,339 to 16,960 (77.8 percent of the major party vote) constituting another vote-of-confidence, another mandate for the man through whom so many Harlemites lived vicariously; the man who knew so intuitively how to lead them to a "gain in soul." If none of them could drop in on the President of the United States for a thirty-minute chat, their congressman could and, it was demonstrated, did.

A month after the elections, Federal Judge Sylvester Ryan was still at work on Powell's tax case, issuing directives for the Congressman to produce payroll records, cancelled checks, and other oddments of corroboration. But the investigation was already dying, and soon staggered to a complete halt. Assistant United States Attorney Thomas A. Bolan, who had argued the Dodson and Lennon cases, was given a temporary assignment elsewhere. The grand jury recessed. When Bolan returned in March from his interim assignment, ready to reconvene the grand jury, he reportedly was told to forget it because "Washington thought it was too hot to handle." Bolan resigned six months later and went into private practice. It was to be years before Powell's tax case came before judge and jury.

While Powell's energies were being sapped by litigation, the black revolution, which he had predicted twenty years earlier, had begun. Negroes had indeed started "marching up freedom road." Inside that one pregnant decade following World War II was sown the seed that blossomed into the spirit of the 1963 March on Washington and the great volume of mass action that accompanied it.

Near the beginning of this Pregnant Decade, in 1945, a number of men had sat down in a Manhattan apartment and wondered if it were possible to mount a frontal, legal attack on segregation: specifically, on the "separate-but-equal" doctrine arising from the 1896 *Plessy v. Ferguson* decision, which had concluded that "Legislation is powerless to eradicate racial instincts or to abolish distinctions based upon physical differences." The men present—Thurgood Marshall, Walter White, and William Hastie, among others—knew how tortuous and expensive would be such an undertaking and how inflammatory to the conscience of the whole American South, should they be successful. They were suggesting no less a mission than to establish in the courts that public facilities— schools, transportation, restaurants and so forth—no matter how "equal" did not afford equality of opportunity as guaranteed by the Constitution if they were "separate." The target of their sword was the very heart of segregation in the United States.

A few warm-up cases established that progress could be made through the courts. In a Texas case, *Sweatt v. Painter,* the court ruled that a Negro be admitted to the University of Texas because the Negro law school did not afford equal facilities. In *McLaurin v. Oklahoma,* the ruling indicated that discrimination existed when a Negro in a white university was forced to sit at a separate table in the library.

Finally, the NAACP Legal Defense and Education Fund found a test case with which to challenge segregation at the elementary and high school levels. The Reverend Oliver Brown of Topeka, Kansas, sued his local Board of Education on behalf of his 11-year-old daughter, seeking her admission to a non-segregated school. When the case reached the U. S. Supreme Court, Thurgood Marshall argued that slavery was perpetuated in separate-but-equal statutes and asked that they be banned in all public schools.

No small suspense—among both whites and blacks—attended the opinion. Shortly after noon on May 17, 1954, Chief Justice Earl Warren read a lengthy catalogue of background facts and arrived at the statement: "We come then to the question presented. Does segregation of children in public schools solely on the basis of race, even though the physical facilities and other 'tangible' factors may be equal, deprive the children of the minority group of equal educational opportunities? We believe that it does. . . . We cannot turn the clock back to 1868 when the [Fourteenth] amendment was adopted, or even to 1896, when *Plessy versus Ferguson* was written. . . . We conclude that in the field of public education the doctrine of 'separate but equal' has no place."

Reaction was varied: jubilation in the the Negro community, consternation among such legislators as Mississippi's Senator James Eastland, who said, "The people of the South will never accept this monstrous decision. I predict this decision will bring on a century of litigation."

"I don't believe you can change the hearts of men with laws or decisions," said President Dwight D. Eisenhower, the beneficiary of Adam Powell's political support.

White Citizens' Councils proliferated in the South to combat the decision's implementation. Resistance was bitter, with several Southern governors vowing to suffer imprisonment rather than succumb.

The following year, in Montgomery, Alabama, a Negro woman named Mrs. Rosa Parks said "No" to a bus driver who ordered her to surrender her seat to a white man. Her action was an end and a beginning. It ended the decade of flux and disjointed action that flowed out of World War II. It began the revolution which crystallized the new Negro leadership and organized the imagination of the American Negro community behind mass action for the first time in the nation's history. Someone asked Martin Luther King—whose prominence as a race leader dates from the Montgomery bus boycott—why Mrs. Parks had refused to move when so ordered by a bus driver. King answered: "She had been tracked down by the *Zeitgeist*—the spirit of the times."

It was King's destiny (he was then 27) to marshal the emotions of black men upon whom had been lost the subtleties of court victories; to engage the masses in such a way that they would become activists for the first time; to bring into the civil rights effort the folklore, the spirituals, the habits and ritual of the rural Negro, and to combine with Ghandian concepts of civil disobedience the powerful link that had been missing in American civil rights action—the Negro church. King believed that the time was past for fighting rear guard actions in the lower courts, that the Supreme Court had spoken and the Negro must move on to mass action. He was able to command the imagination of 50,000 Negro residents of Montgomery, Alabama, to the extent that they stayed off the buses for 13 months until the United States Supreme Court ruled that the buses be integrated.

King returned to his home town of Atlanta and formed the Southern Christian Leadership Conference, a confederation of Southern clergymen and their local protest groups which undertook to give succor to Negroes engaged in non-violent action. It conducted voter registration drives in many parts of the South, and supported the Student Non-Violent Coördinating Committee in its campaigns of sit-ins and freedom rides. A new and impatient Negro leadership was hardening in America, but one which would require another half-dozen years for its maturation. Nonetheless, the black revolution had begun.

Adam Powell, in his turn, could look back on a decade during which he had unquestionably been the pre-eminent voice in keeping Negro dissatisfaction before white America—a goad and an irritant to the conscience of whites; one which, fortunately, had had the ear of the Congress of the United States. He needed now only to read events correctly and apply to them his demonstrated energies and brilliance. Doing so, he could be assured a full share in the new leadership and the thanks of Negroes everywhere for the legendary insistence of his "New World A'coming" chorus, extending back to the middle 1930's. Both Powell and the "masses" he had been exhorting for so long, stood upon a threshold of breathtaking opportunity.

It also was a decade that claimed Adam Clayton Powell, Sr. The imposing and dignified retired pastor died on June 12, 1953, after two-thirds of a century's service to his church and community. Messages of condolence poured in from the city's high officials. Powell senior, by his benefactions and unremitting social action, had been among the most beloved and respected of Harlemites, and was the rock foundation over which his son's ambitions rose.

8. The Big Purge Attempt

Among the oddments of political life which Adam Clayton Powell could look back on by 1956 were an unsuccessful attempt to spark enthusiasm for his candidacy for Mayor of New York, a trip to Bandung, Indonesia, to attend a conference of emerging Asian and African nations, and a fist fight with Representative Cleveland M. Bailey, Democrat of West Virginia, in a House committee room.

In 1953, Powell had flirted with downtown Democrats in a test of his political appeal outside Harlem. "I know the town and I'll gladly run for the Mayoralty," he said. "If the Democrats want me, I'm available." They failed to take him seriously, and there is some question as to how seriously he was taking himself. In any case, the call never came. Far more auspicious was his participation as an unofficial observer in the 1955 Bandung Conference of 29 former colonial nations of Asia and Africa. They were meeting to discuss the spectrum of problems facing newly-emerging non-white countries. A danger existed that Communist China would attempt to propagandize the neutral conferees and turn them against the United States. The Eisenhower administration chose to ignore the conference officially.

Powell did not. He pointed out that the meeting was a

great milestone in the history of non-white nations and probably would be one of the most important of the century. He flew to Bandung in an unofficial capacity and, at the conference sessions, was an eloquent spokesman, pointing to the progress Negroes had made in the United States on many fronts. This defense, coming from a prominent American Negro, was impressive to the Asian and African neutrals, many of whom had been ready to accept the Communist version of race relations in the United States. It was a truly statesmanlike performance, and many United States diplomats and members of Congress applauded Powell's initiative. Senator Hubert H. Humphrey, for example, made a speech in the Senate, commending Powell's effectiveness.

Once back in the United States, however, Powell reverted to his customary abrasiveness, and appended the Powell Amendment to some favorite legislation of the Eisenhower Administration, thereby jeopardizing its passage. Liberals denounced his action as "irresponsible." When Eisenhower's school construction bill, which would authorize $1,600,000,-000 for federal aid to school construction over four years, came before the House Education and Labor Committee, Powell once again tacked on his rider which would exclude segregated schools from the aid. Representative Cleveland M. Bailey, a 69-year-old West Virginia Democrat, angrily accused Powell of insincerity and charged him with trying to wreck the public school system. Powell called Bailey a liar. The West Virginian threw a looping right hand punch that caught Powell on the jaw and sent him to the floor in a clatter of overturned chairs. Powell did not retaliate and chairman Graham A. Barden restored order with loud gavel-banging and an appeal to the combatants to "restrain your passions." Asked about the incident, Representative Bailey said: "It never happened."

Said Powell: "Cleve Bailey and I smoked cigars together and are old friends."

Adam Powell was standing on the brink of another kind of fight, the most bitter and significant of his career: a political campaign which is a classic study in minority politics; a "declaration of independence" from white control by Harlem's black voters and a historic break by a predominantly Negro congressional district from the shackles of political "Uncle Tomism." In all his election campaigns prior to 1958, Powell had been supported by the regular organization of New York County (Manhattan Borough) Democrats—known as Tammany Hall. As the Congressional elections of 1958 approached, however, it became apparent that Tammany—under the leadership of Carmine G. DeSapio, also the Democratic National Committeeman from New York State, and an archetype of the big-city political boss—had decided to purge Powell. On the surface, there was ample reason for doing so, especially from a white "party regular's" view. Powell had deserted the Democrats in 1956 to support Eisenhower; he was in continual income tax difficulty, and two of his aides had been convicted in tax trials; he had consistently ignored the wishes of House Democratic leaders in appending the Powell Amendment to important legislation; in 1957, he had voted on 36 percent of the major roll calls, compared to a House average of 88 percent (placing him third from the bottom); in the "on the record" tabulation—voting paired or expressing an opinion—he was at the bottom with 57 percent; also in 1957, on "party unity" roll calls, Powell voted with the Democrats only 47 percent of the time (the average House Democrat stayed with the majority on 70 percent of the roll calls). Many of his House colleagues viewed Powell's attitude toward his committee assignments—on Education and Labor, and Interior and Insular Affairs—as a trifle cavalier. He was easily bored and bridled at the normal congressional routine. He was, as well, the very opposite of the model "good Negro" as typified, in some legislators' minds, by Representative Dawson of Chicago, chairman of the powerful House Committee on Government Operations and a consistent opponent of the Powell Amendment. Powell regularly called Dawson an "Uncle Tom," a "house Negro," and a legislator acceptable to the Southerners.

All these reasons were valid enough for Tammany to tinker with the prospect of purging Powell. But there were other reasons more complex, which went deeper into the entrails of New York Democratic politics. Out of eight Democratic district leaders whose districts lay wholly or partly in the 16th Congressional District, six—of whom only one was white—voted to purge Powell, and one, Lloyd Dickens, backed him. One other white district leader, William Fitts Ryan, abstained. That the vote was influenced strongly by DeSapio's wishes is a necessary conclusion. But the district leaders themselves as well as Hulan Jack—the Negro Borough president of Manhattan and a DeSapio lieutenant—had their own strong feelings about Powell, who had been less than congenial to most of them, and had seldom taken part in their clubhouse politics. Hulan Jack, called "DeSapio's man uptown" and "Harlem's man downtown," and Powell had clashed publicly a number of times: once when Powell suggested that Jack, a Catholic, was siding with the Church and Mayor Wagner—also a Catholic, as was DeSapio—against the interests of Protestant Harlem in a particular municipal real estate deal. Both Jack and DeSapio strongly protested Powell's introduction of the religious issue. Powell had never made any secret of his contempt for the district leaders. "They're all slaves to the white folks who control them," he said.

DeSapio, in his turn, stood to make impressive political capital from a successful purge of Powell. He would have the gratitude of the white power structure "downtown," who had grown to despise Powell, as well as that of national party leaders who traditionally disapproved of mavericks—especially mavericks as intractable as the Harlem Congressman. DeSapio's own ambitions for national political stature thus would be served, and his solidarity with the Harlem leaders—who cast three of the 16 votes in any election for the leadership of Tammany Hall—would be enhanced. DeSapio was attempting a skillful power thrust at the Harlem Congressman at a time when Powell was the most vulnerable he had been at any time during his political career.

Plainly, Powell could choose to run in the general election as an independent or a Republican (which party subsequently gave him their nomination) and be reasonably confident of defeating almost any candidate Tammany and DeSapio could proffer. But in so doing, Powell would forfeit all the party seniority he had built up during fourteen years in the House. Committee chairmanships (he was next in line to chair the key Education and Labor Committee, pending the retirement or death of the aging Representative Barden) would be forever out of his reach. Powell needed the Democratic nomination if he wanted to continue in the House with any expectation of accession to power.

The problem over what to do about Powell's bolt to Eisenhower had come up in January, 1957, when the 85th Congress was organized under Democratic control. Inevitably, Democratic powers moved to punish Powell for his defection. He was about to vacation in Bermuda and the Virgin Islands as the House Patronage Committee chairman signed letters dismissing two Powell appointees. Other Democrats initiated moves to strip Powell of his seniority and bar him from committee assignments. In the House office building, a new office slated for Powell and his staff suddenly was assigned to another legislator.

These punitive gestures brought outcries from Harlem.

Negro leaders—many of whom had never been friendly with Powell—pointed out that the 1948 Dixiecrats had not been read out of the party; the proposed penalties against Powell were "racially motivated," they claimed. Roy Wilkins of the NAACP, never a Powell admirer, said it was "an inescapable conclusion that the Democratic Party is taking such punitive action because of Powell's race and also because of his efforts to secure passage of civil rights legislation." Washington's NAACP chief, Clarence Mitchell, charged Democrats with a grave blunder in attacking Powell instead of Senator Eastland of Mississippi. The New York State Baptist Convention sent wires to Speaker Sam Rayburn, Democratic National Chairman Paul Butler, and others, demanding that Powell's seniority be protected. Even Powell's old Republican opponent, Grant Reynolds, claimed that loss of the Harlem Congressman's seniority would set Harlem back 20 years: "The spineless politicians who felt obligated to drive their daggers into Adam's body because their downtown bosses ordered the same, should be advised that Harlem can ill-afford this kind of Uncle Tomism." A ministers' National Civil Rights Conference threatened to send a mission to Washington in Powell's behalf.

The House Democratic leaders decided at length not to strip Powell of his seniority. The *Amsterdam News* called the decision:

". . . A clean-cut victory for the New Negro who emerged on the scene in 1956. There is no doubt that the Democrats planned to chastise Mr. Powell and there is no doubt in our minds that they planned to do it simply because he was a Negro who 'ran off the reservation' and got out of 'his place.' A few years ago the Negro in this country would have sat idly by like a toad frog on a mushroom while the Democrats pulled off this dirty trick, but those days are gone forever. Instead of sitting by and letting the Democrats get away with it,

Negroes rallied around Congressman Powell as if he were their long-lost brother. Thousands of Negroes who have never agreed with Mr. Powell rallied to his defense. They did it not because they had suddenly fallen in love with Mr. Powell but because Mr. Powell was a Negro whom white people were trying to 'put in his place.' . . . The reasoning is simple. The leaders of the Democratic party weren't afraid of Mr. Powell himself. What they really became frightened over was the sound and the fury of the average Negro voter in the street who rose up in their election districts and said, 'You can try to put Powell in his place if you want to, but your name won't have a place on my ballot when you come up for re-election.' "

It seems incredible that, as the primary campaigns of 1958 got underway, the lesson of Powell's successful struggle in 1957 to retain his seniority should be lost on the New York City Democratic leadership. But lost it was. They proceeded with their plan to purge him.

The classic character of the 1958 purge attempt grew partly out of its nature as a confrontation between an entrenched leader of a minority group—which had not yet been assimilated—and a political organization whose power derived from the assimilation of minorities; partly out of the revelation that Negroes bitterly resented any attempt by the white power bloc to force a leadership upon them. When Powell first entered politics in 1941, Tammany Hall was in decline following the ouster of Mayor James Walker and the election of Fiorello LaGuardia on a Republican-Fusion ticket. Carmine DeSapio, an Italian from Greenwich Village, was elected leader of the Hall in 1949, thus ending the long control of Tammany by the Irish. He set out to modernize Tammany's image and discover new fonts of power in the wake of dwindling immigration from Europe, and the assumption by government of responsibility for many of the old social welfare practices—jobs, doles, and housing—from which the Eastern big-city political machines had always drawn their influence. After the election of Robert F. Wagner, Jr. as Mayor, in 1953, and that of Averell Harriman as Governor in 1954—both supported by DeSapio—the Greenwich Villager became the state's leading organization Democrat. He also was behind the successful bid of Hulan E. Jack, a West Indian Negro, for the borough presidency of Manhattan. (One reporter who followed that campaign described Jack as "an amiable mediocrity . . . [who] has made his way among politicians by hard application to the task at hand . . . and obedience to the party rule.")

DeSapio's decision to further extend his area of influence by disposing of Congressman Powell received unexpected support on May 8, 1958, when the United States Attorney announced Powell's indictment on charges of income tax evasion. Although two more years would pass before the case actually came to trial, the announcement of the indictment was dramatic enough to be used as another pretext for getting rid of him. Powell had a staunchly right-wing journal, the *National Review*, to thank for raking up this new trouble. William F. Buckley, its editor, had been conferring with Assistant United States Attorney Thomas Bolan, who had argued the Dodson and Lennon cases, and was angered by what he learned. In December, 1957, the *National Review* published an article entitled, "Death of an Investigation: The Wheels of Justice Stop for Adam Clayton Powell, Jr." The article quoted Bolan as saying he had uncovered enough evidence to indict Powell and had informed his superiors of the fact. It speculated that, in the arcane ways of high-level politics, word had gone out to stifle the investigation, either because of Powell's support of Eisenhower in the previous election, or because of some other, more subtle intimidation on the part of the Harlem Congressman:

"The Administration's decision to draw back its forces is most probably an act of political gratitude. Alternative explanations are not excluded. Adam Powell had intimidated people before by construing any opposition to him or what he wants as an attack on the Negro race and democracy. . . . It is naïve to suppose Adam Powell got direct from President Eisenhower a promise, or even a suggestion of a promise, that Powell would be forgiven any tax offense of which he was guilty in return for a political endorsement. Things do not happen that way in those circles and Powell, the operator, almost surely would not have affronted an essentially non-political President by any hint, however subtle, of his bill for political services rendered. Politicians have a way of exchanging vibrations and no doubt Adam Clayton Powell, Jr. felt things were understood—if not between him and Eisenhower, between him and the Republican Party—when he stepped out on the White House steps and told the reporters he would campaign for Eisenhower."

Copies of the magazine were mailed to members of the grand jury and both Bolan and Buckley met personally with the jury to describe the apparent dereliction. Their tactics worked. The jurors began pressuring United States Attorney Paul Williams for an answer as to why they had not been convened in Powell's case. They went so far as to threaten that they would convene themselves in rented space at the Commodore Hotel. Williams, a Republican with ambitions for the Senate, called the jury in to hear evidence against Powell.

Their indictment charged Powell with preparing a false return for his wife in 1951; of reporting a taxable income of $4,815 instead of $9,181, and with reporting a joint taxable income in 1952 of $5,252 instead of $8,952. The charges carried possible penalties of 15 years in prison and $30,000 in fines.

A week after the indictment was handed down, DeSapio called a press conference and announced that the Harlem district leaders—who were seated around him silently—had voted to withhold endorsement of Powell, and that Tammany had concurred in the decision. It was not the indictment that precipitated the purge, DeSapio insisted, but Powell's 1956 defection. "[The leaders] could not in good conscience support Mr. Powell because he is not a Democrat," DeSapio said. They had not settled on a candidate yet, but claimed confidence that Powell could be disposed of. Harlem braced itself for what the *New York Age* called "a nasty war."

Two days after the press conference, Hulan Jack and Powell shared a platform at an NAACP street rally celebrating the fourth anniversary of the Supreme Court decision on school segregation. When Jack rose to speak, he was booed loudly by what appeared to be a Powell claque, shouting, "Send that Uncle Tom back downtown!" The cry was taken up by most of the audience and continued until Powell himself stood and silenced the shouts with a wave of his arm, then magnanimously gestured Jack to the microphone. Jack was shaken by the unexpected vehemence of the demonstration and gave a half-hearted speech. Powell, in his turn, delivered an unvarnished appeal to racialism, condemning Jack as an Uncle Tom who was doing DeSapio's dirty work.

The next day, Powell followed up his attack by advising Jack and DeSapio to "stay off the streets of Harlem or we'll make it mighty uncomfortable," a warning which hinted at violence and thus drew the fire of the NAACP, through its Executive Secretary, Roy Wilkins. "The NAACP wishes to dissociate itself completely from the threats made by Mr. Powell. . . . We deplore . . . the banner of extreme racialism raised by Mr. Powell. . . . We cannot condemn racism in others while using it ourselves." But the NAACP had miscalculated seriously. They had failed to gauge Powell's success in dramatizing the election as a showdown between white America and the emergent independence of black voters. A volume of protest from Harlemites reached them and the NAACP backtracked, claiming that their statement had been "misconstrued' and that "we have not denounced Representative Powell . . . he has fought courageously and effectively for civil rights."

Tammany still had no candidate to oppose him, but Powell accelerated his own campaign. He inaugurated training courses to instruct volunteers in door-to-door electioneering. He sent out mailings advising Harlemites to scrutinize nominating petitions carefully before signing—and, coincidentally, to sign only those bearing Powell's name. He told Harlem that if elected he would disavow all the old party bosses, both black and white.

J. Raymond Jones joined Powell's campaign party a week after Tammany's announcement. His arrival in Powell's camp was significant. Jones had been a power in Harlem politics during the 1940's, but his career had lapsed after DeSapio gained control of Tammany. Since that time, he had held a $12,500-a-year patronage appointment (as secretary to a State Supreme Court Justice, and later as secretary to a General Sessions Judge), and was bereft of influence both in Harlem and downtown. Powell needed an unerring political hand to assure him a place on the Democratic ballot. So complex are New York's election laws that few are the lawyers who understand them. (Tammany was expert in manipulating them to its advantage.) Powell's own expert on the subject was Acy Lennon, but he was in jail—a circumstance Tammany found heartening. Jones, perceiving a chance for a return to leadership, let Powell know he was ready to help. Powell accepted, and Jones quit his job to become the Congressman's campaign manager.

The regular Democrats were having difficulty finding a

candidate to run against Powell. Thurgood Marshall declined, as did Hulan Jack. Governor Harriman reportedly favored the Reverend James H. Robinson, minister of the Protestant Church of the Master, who had run as a Liberal against Jack in 1953 for the office of Manhattan borough president. Robinson not only declined, but did so with a gratuitous swipe at the Tammany overlords:

"The Democratic leadership, both of Harlem and of the city, seems neither to have fully understood nor accurately gauged the basic political attitudes, unspoken but deep resentments and desires of the people of Harlem. . . . It seems also to have missed the very essential point that there is at least as much, if not more, anti-Hulan Jack feeling as pro-Powell sentiment."

As May was running out, the Democrats finally found a standard bearer. He was Earl Brown, 55, Harlem's representative in the City Council, who had defeated the Communist, Benjamin Davis. He was a Harvard graduate, associate editor of *Life* magazine, and a former editor of the *Amsterdam News*. Brown was, to say the least, a reluctant candidate. When informed by DeSapio that he was Tammany's choice for the nomination, Brown responded: "Why me!" He even left town briefly to avoid discussing the matter, but had to be back at his desk at *Life* on a particular Monday morning. Furtively, he returned to Manhattan around midnight on Sunday and was "captured" by Tammany men who had been waiting in a parked car opposite his apartment building. A discussion lasting until 4 a.m. ensued, during which Brown insisted that the Harlem district leaders were truly for Powell and that their better judgment was being suborned by DeSapio. But politics prevailed, and—worn down by the hours of early morning pressuring—Brown agreed to make the race.

Short and professorial, Brown was a loyal Democrat, but

had frequently criticized the Harlem district leaders in the past. He had a well-known dislike for Hulan Jack. He accepted Tammany's call on two conditions: that the Democratic organization pay all the bills, and that Jack stay out of the campaign.

Powell enforced at every opportunity the illusion that the real contest was between "black Harlem" and "white downtown"; between an outspoken advocate of Negro rights, and Southern Democrats eager to purge him. Having retained his seniority as a Democrat he was "only a heartbeat away" from being chairman of the important House Education and Labor Committee. Thus, he was able to claim, with some justification, that "a vote against Powell is a vote for Faubus." The lines of force were drawn clearly enough so that even the most unsophisticated Negro could conclude that this primary fight would be black against white; a seemingly persecuted black militant was tilting his lance at the massive white power bloc.

James Booker, an *Amsterdam News* columnist, said, "There is a feeling in the community that whenever a Negro in politics gets to a certain height he is a target for political bosses to try to bring him down or control him. Criticism of him from downtown is resented by the community—it rallies to support him." For the second time in little over a year, that is precisely what happened. Even A. Philip Randolph, the Congressman's frequent critic, lined up with Powell against the purgers and headed an independent citizens' committee for Powell's renomination. "I have never known in the history of Negroes," said Randolph, "when a Negro leader became the target of such a massive form of opposition and condemnation from the daily press, as well as from reactionary and some liberal politicians, as is now the lot of Powell. This is a distinct challenge to Negroes everywhere." Joe Louis became a Powell partisan with the announcement, "I like a man who's a fighter." One poll taker in Harlem elicited the response from a passerby: "I never voted for him before, but I'm going to this time."

Powell had found the proper string on his fiddle and he played it insistently: "I am being purged obviously because I am a Negro and a Negro should stay on the plantation." He invoked the plantation metaphor at every opportunity, calling DeSapio the "Mississippi plantation boss," and Hulan Jack the "house Negro" who curried favor with the plantation overlords at the expense of his fellow Negroes. It was a devastating bit of imagery—one carefully calculated to strike a responsive chord in Negroes of every caste. He called his opponent "Lookdown Brown," a three-cushion reference to Brown's habit of looking down when he spoke; an alleged, distant, ivory tower attitude on Brown's part to Harlem and its problems; and the subservient, Stepin Fetchit behavior of a "house Negro" in the presence of his masters.

"I ran away from the plantation in 1956 and now Carmine's trying to brand me," Powell told television interviewer John Wingate on June 6. On the same program, he threatened to desert the Democrats in the forthcoming gubernatorial elections:

"I spoke to Governor Harriman's private secretary, and I said, 'now the governor only won by 12,000 votes four years ago and I think it would be very disastrous if Tammany Hall dumped me now because it might, even though I might lose—although I don't think I will—it might be a difference of 12,-000 votes for his re-election.' [The secretary] said he would take it up with the governor. He wrote me, in a letter which I have in my files in Washington, 'the governor has instructed me that he does not take part in any primaries whatsoever.' So I took that on its face value. Jim Farley said that the other day when they asked him who he would support, myself or Brown: 'I don't take part in primaries.' But lo and behold,

James Robinson—the Reverend James Robinson of the Church of the Master—announced at his press conference that Governor Harriman brought him to his city mansion and begged him to run against me."

Harriman later denied he had asked Robinson to run and reaffirmed his neutrality. Powell insisted that DeSapio had never wanted him in the Democratic Party, but:

"He couldn't do anything about it—he didn't have leaders to control and he could not control the electorate. Now he felt that when I was being clobbered on all sides, it was an opportunity to hit me while I was down, but I'm not down as long as the people are up, and my people are up. And Carmine DeSapio's going to get the lesson—he's going to get a lesson in this—he's going to learn that the day of bossism is finished, not only for the Negro people of Harlem but all over town. People are sick and tired of bosses and Carmine DeSapio is going to learn the lesson of his life in Harlem and we hope that it is going to sweep all over this town and that people everywhere will throw off the shackles of bossism and we might have a Democratic Party that will be true to the best principles of days gone by."

Powell was asked to discuss his absentee record in the Congress:

"Well, my absentee record is—I'm glad you brought it up, it needs to be explained. In the first place, I carry too much of a load as compared with most of my other colleagues, because in addition to serving the 400,000 people of my district I frankly have to serve about 8,000,000 Negroes who are behind the color curtain in the South. I have more requests, more correspondence from Negro people outside of my district than those within. It keeps me overly busy; therefore, it has been my rule since I went to Congress not to answer quorum calls unless I happen to be in the area of the Congress."

The interviewer wanted to know why Powell had not shown up to vote on the 1957 civil rights bill:

"On June 1—now this is a matter of public record in TV, radio, and the papers—on June 1, I suffered a heart attack in the pulpit of my church. I was rushed to the New York Medical Center, then transferred to the U. S. Naval Hospital in Bethesda, Maryland. Doctors here—my personal doctor, Dr. Aaron Wells—doctors at the Bethesda Hospital . . . said stop all work and go away. And I did. And that civil rights bill that bore Celler's name was the civil rights bill that I got Mr. Eisenhower to promise me on October 11, 1956 [the date of his celebrated 30-minute conference with the President] that he would marshal all of his resources to push through Congress. [Powell, in fact, was in Washington on June 18 when the House adopted the Civil Rights Act; when the approved version returned from a Senate-House conference on August 27, he was in Europe.]"

J. Raymond Jones's chief task in Powell's organization was to guarantee that the Congressman would not be beaten on a technical knockout. The law surrounding nominating petitions is perverse and tortuous. A whole page of signatures can be invalidated by a single tiny error. Only 750 signatures are required for the placing of a candidate's name on the ballot, but Powell and Jones felt certain that Tammany would exert all its influence in the courts to invalidate Powell's petitions. Jones put together a team of 500 volunteers, trained them in the art of gathering petition signatures, and sent them out to Harlem's street corners. They were able to sign up 8,340 Harlemites (while Tammany's workers got 10,895 for Brown). Ray Jones's political expertise prevailed, and Powell ended up with far over the requisite 750 valid petitions (and, of course, so did Brown).

Tammany toyed briefly with the idea of having Powell's

Democratic registration set aside in court, but abandoned the plan as being bad public relations.

Powell still had to face the pitfalls of an election that would be conducted with paper ballots instead of voting machines. Any tiny defacement on a paper ballot can invalidate it. An unscrupulous election worker wearing a ring with a hidden sharp edge, for example, can invalidate hundreds of ballots in the process of "counting" them. Powell insisted that machines be used in the election, but the Board of Elections ruled finally that machines could not be used in Harlem while paper ballots were being used in other districts.

New York's white press demonstrated a peculiar insensitivity to the subtleties of the campaign. Repeatedly, they called Powell demagogic, racist, rabble-rousing, and irresponsible. Powell cheerfully read these attacks to Harlemites from a sound truck. They cheered and threatened the editorial writers with violence should they step north of 110th Street. Harlem did not intend to brook meddling in this campaign. As the attacks grew more virulent in the white press, Powell's support became more sturdy—not only among lower caste Negroes, but also, less predictably, among the middle class blacks of Strivers Row and Sugar Hill. Earl Brown's own organization workers were by no means immune to Powell's appeal, especially with the prospect facing them of Ray Jones returning to a position of high influence in Harlem. Brown was not the sort to inspire them to great activity in his behalf. Many workers, in fact, secretly held that Hulan Jack and the other leaders were not vocal enough in representing Harlem in Tammany. Brown wrote in the *Amsterdam News* that Negro leaders customarily fall into one of three categories: the Uncle Tom, the "loudmouth" whose demands and claims far outrun his results, and the more cerebral leader who works hard and unostentatiously for Negroes. Clearly, he intended

Marcus Garvey (1922). *(Underwood & Underwood)*

Adam Clayton Powell, Sr. and Adam Clayton Powell, Jr. *(Photo by Joe Covello from Black Star)*
Hazel Scott, Adam Clayton Powell III, and Adam Clayton Powell, Jr. (1956). *(Wide World Photo)*

Carmine DeSapio and J. Raymond Jones (1960). *(UPI Photo)*

Yvette Diago and Adam
Clayton Powell (1960).
(Wide World Photo)

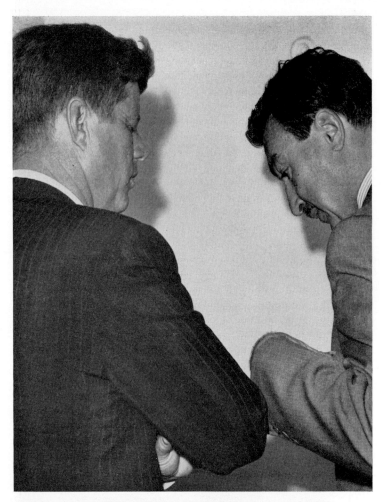

John F. Kennedy and
Adam Clayton Powell
(1963). *(AP Photo)*
Governor Luis Mu-
noz Marin (1962).
(UPI Photo)

it understood that Jack was the first, Powell the second, and himself the third.

Brown wisely eschewed debating Powell face to face. Mostly, he addressed small groups with the message that Powell's record was a "sorry" one. "Whenever a case of discrimination arises," he said, "Powell raises his voice in a dramatic howl. He rants and raves, stirs up people's emotion to fever pitch and then he quietly folds up and goes away. . . . He is never willing to work. . . . Powell spends so much time in Europe you would think he was a Roman Senator instead of a Harlem congressman." Addressing himself to Powell's reputation among senior Democrats in the House, Brown said, "Powell has no more chance than a hoot-owl of becoming head of any committee. . . . There is only one way to get any real seniority in any party—and that is to stay within your party, work hard and win the respect of its members."

Mrs. Eleanor Roosevelt backed Brown and called Powell a "demagogue." Powell, with brilliance and economy, replied only that "she has been an increasing opponent of mine since I introduced the Powell Amendment." The usually conservative *Amsterdam News* announced itself in favor of Brown with the statement: "We feel the time has come for deeds instead of words. And Mr. Powell . . . will never be able to deliver those deeds."

Powell had asked the Republican Party in Harlem for its nomination and gotten it. It was plainly a matter of Powell assuring himself a place on the ballot in the general election no matter what happened in the primary. The Republicans (who had 13,000 registered voters against 50,000 Democrats) saw a chance to make capital out of the Democrats' internal strife. They knew that if they fielded their own candidate in the general election, he would surely lose; but Powell's political appeal might rub off on some of their other candidates and carry them into office with him.

The Liberals, on the other hand, nominated Brown, thereby effecting the odd situation in which both Brown and Powell were assured places on the ballot in the November general election no matter what happened in the Democratic primary—Brown as a Liberal, Powell as a Republican. Increasingly, therefore, the prize was not only a seat in Congress, but the answers to two questions: Could Powell be emasculated as a Democrat and placed out of reach of a committee chairmanship? And could white America successfully penalize a militant and articulate Negro?

In the two weeks preceding the election, Powell toured Harlem nightly in his sound truck, making at least seven stops a night to deliver streetcorner addresses. Once, he even parked in front of Brown's headquarters hotel, the Theresa, and shouted "Come on out, Lookdown Brown!" But Brown was too smart for that. Powell also allowed his spokesmen to inject the religious issue subtly into the campaign: Italian-Irish-Catholic downtown versus Protestant Harlem. The ghetto had never gotten its share of jobs, the spokesmen said, because of favoritism shown white Catholic immigrants over black Protestants—many of whose lineage in the United States dated further back than that of the Irish and Italians.

At a climactic rally on August 9, Powell was at his charismatic best. Four thousand people milled about in front of the Hotel Theresa, surging and murmuring in an atmosphere of expectancy. The broad avenue was rimmed by police barriers to divert traffic. Powell, in shirtsleeves, sat on the speakers platform observing the tableau, as Dizzy Gillespie led his musicians in loud jazz choruses which echoed across the boulevard in the late afternoon sunlight.

A master-of-ceremonies introduced a buxom Negro singer. She approached the microphones, surveyed her audience and said, "Before I sing, I have a message for all you women—and I'll make it brief." She paused until the crowd was silent.

"We women are not allergic to masculine appeal," she said. Then her voice became more vibrant. She pointed to Powell and intoned, *"Send this she-wolf bait back to Washington!"*

The crowd applauded wildly. She sang and they cheered again when she was finished. Then Adam Powell was on his feet behind the microphones, his half-unbuttoned shirt revealing a chest shining with perspiration. He stood six-feet, three-inches tall, handsome, mustached, and athletic. He began to speak, inveighing against "Massa DeSapio" and the "Uncle Toms" downtown. The crowd quieted except for an occasional shout of "That's right!" He couched the issues as well as the invective in vivid metaphor: "We have been the backbone of the Democratic Party in Manhattan for many years, but our patronage has been so lean that our bellies have been rubbing against our backbones! It's been going on too long! *Harlem is on the march! The sleeping giant is awakened!"*

Again they roared. His voice became conversational, as he told them that race hatred was behind the scheme to purge him; that the attempt was supported by powerful Southerners fearful of his accession to the Chairmanship of the House Committee on Education and Labor. He told them that Harlem was a political force with which the downtown bosses would have to reckon.

"We know that a hundred and fifty thousand voters in New York State can and will swing elections after this one," he said. Already presuming victory in his own primary, he suffused his audience with a sense of their importance to the forthcoming gubernatorial election—and even to the Presidential race of 1960. For thirty minutes, Powell held them rapt. It was a strange and highly-charged scene. Powell was to the crowd not only the principal actor in a passion play— which few of the whites present could have been expected to understand—but also their confessor, their high priest, and their lover.

His words, gestures, intonations, and appearance were almost calculatedly sensual. At one instant, he roared his plaint so that it rumbled across the black faces; at the next he was silent, unbreathing, and tentative, until the next rush of passion tumesced in him. He worked over them with the attention and fastidiousness of an amorist. When the end came, they were ready for it, having been prepared skillfully. There was a pause, and then suddenly:

"I appeal to your manhood! *Harlem is on the march!*"

They met him like willing brides. A great swell of shouting and applause, mounting to a tumult, broke from them. Powell waved and smiled, then quickly departed the microphones, leaving the crowd relaxed and satisfied in the afterglow of his presence.

The next day, Powell told a church rally: "On Tuesday, we'll march to the polls; not as slaves, not as Uncle Toms, but as free men and women under God." The toughest campaign Powell ever waged was over.

On August 12, the polls opened at 3:00 p.m. In Powell's headquarters at Abyssinian Baptist, campaign workers stood by for "commands" to "defend" the polls in Harlem. Powell charged that Tammany-hired hoodlums planned to subvert the balloting. He ordered poll watchers to inspect the fingers of Tammany's men to prevent any invalidation of the paper ballots by sharp rings. Like a field general, Powell had organized his workers into numbered squads; when trouble was reported at a particular polling place, he ordered out "Squad Two" or "Squad Three" to deal with the matter. Actually, the voting was quite orderly.

By closing time, at 8:00 p.m., 23,343 of Harlem's 50,000 Democrats had voted—the biggest turnout for a Democratic primary in Harlem's history. Brown conceded a little before

1:00 a.m. Both DeSapio and Harriman sent telegrams of congratulations. At the Carver Ballroom, Powell, Ray Jones, and their advocates celebrated riotously.

Powell's vote on the Democratic side was 14,935 to 4,959, a plurality of three-to-one. He carried every election district (precinct) except a handful having mostly white voters. He even carried Sugar Hill, Strivers Row, and the other high-rent areas which had been expected to go to Brown. Hulan Jack's own 14th Assembly District went to Powell by 1,492 to 858 and the Congressman claimed to have carried Jack's own apartment building.

The "purge" had failed spectacularly.

DeSapio said he had gotten bad information from his informants in Harlem and that "emotion" had beaten the machine, not sound political practice. Powell's jubilation was boundless. "This is the end of Hulan Jack. . . . We will drive the Uncle Toms from Harlem," he trumpeted. "Carmine will have to pay the price. They'll have to treat us like the Irish and the Italians." Powell made one more trip around Harlem in his sound truck, thanking the ghetto-dwellers, then departed for a vacation in the West Indies.

Powell's victory symptomized historic changes in the character of Tammany Hall—and, to some extent, in the nature of machine politics in other large United States cities. District leaders were seeing less and less of their voters as social welfare processes became increasingly bureaucratized. In the case of Negro politics, a leader who went "downtown" for his orders was even less effective in his home precincts than a white leader who did the same—such was the resentment against white interference. So tenuous had become the ties between Hulan Jack and the rank-and-file that he was able to commit the massive error of informing DeSapio that Powell could be beaten. "I got the wrong analysis—no question about it," DeSapio said in retrospect. Powell said, "The white man just doesn't understand what the Negro is thinking. Everything they call me downtown—demagogue, racist—strengthens me uptown. My people want me to be a racist—we're all racists."

Journalist David Hapgood, reviewing the 1958 primary battle, concluded, "Civil rights, and the specific benefits offered by Brown's approach, do not offer the Negro full equality; he will still be considered a second class citizen in the culture in which he must live. It is to the Negro's desire for true equality, for escape from the prison of skin, that Powell's eloquence appeals"—which is yet another way of defining the "gain in soul," the illusion of an enlargement of self-esteem, which Powell held out to Negroes so tantalizingly.

9. Takeover in Harlem

The 1958 purge attempt established that—even as the black revolution was gathering momentum—white America did not know the mind of the Negro. Whites had been led into a historical debacle. Even the best-intentioned white integrationists were only beginning to discover the real depths of the Negro's dissatisfaction and the heights of his aspiration. Whites who had long prided themselves on being liberals were startled by the new urgency of the Negro demands. One political cartoonist had a white liberal complaining: "The civil rights movement was so much more *fun* before all these Negroes got mixed up in it." Negroes were announcing that they intended to settle for nothing less than full equality, and that neither paternalism nor gradualism was any longer viable. It would not be long before Martin Luther King's influence as a non-violent crusader would be eroded by the more caustic urgings of Malcolm X and other extremists. The Black Muslims were about to enter the white consciousness, with their paramilitary designs, implacability, and ancient appeal to the black man's self-esteem.

In Harlem, politics was still at center stage as the November congressional elections approached. These were of no interest to Powell, since his victory was assured and his House seat was now safe indefinitely. Brown, though still on the ballot as a Liberal, had withdrawn from the campaign wars. "I thought it best to be realistic about it," he said.

Of considerable interest to Powell, however, was the gubernatorial race between the incumbent, Averell Harriman, and newcomer Nelson A. Rockefeller. Should it be close, Manhattan's 200,000 Negro and Puerto Rican voters might easily make the difference. Most important, Powell was the nominee of both major parties and thus might reasonably endorse either man. Both Harriman and Rockefeller had aspirations to the Presidency of the United States. Both were multimillionaires. Ray Jones, with thinly-disguised glee, said, "It couldn't have been better if we'd written the script ourselves."

Powell and Jones sat back and waited for the bidding to start. Rumors persisted that Powell's terms included reimbursement for his expenditures in the primary, a figure that verged on $50,000. Powell denied this, but admitted he owed money for the campaign. Many Republicans expected Powell to support Rockefeller in retaliation for the treatment he had received at Democratic hands. Still, Powell had equally strong reasons to return to party regularity: protection of his jeopardized seniority in the House; access to patronage in New York City; his aspirations to dislodge all of the DeSapio district leaders in the elections the following year. From Jones's point of view, a return to the Democratic fold would strengthen his own leverage in seizing organizational power in Harlem.

Powell and Jones remained silent for two months. Then, on October 7, they convened a press conference at Abyssinian Baptist to announce their support of Harriman and the entire Democratic ticket. Harriman and DeSapio, Powell said, had assured him that Negroes would get better city and state jobs. The *New York Age,* supporting Rockefeller, trumpeted that

Powell was "back on DeSapio's plantation." Powell bitterly denied the charge, saying that DeSapio was merely a guest on *his* plantation. The Congressman became associate campaign director for Harriman and moved his headquarters into the Biltmore Hotel. Harriman and Powell were indeed strange bedfellows: the aristocratic scion of a railroad fortune, and the rough-and-tumble streetcorner politico. During the campaign, Powell frequently embarrassed Harriman by his methods. At a press conference in Harriman's New York townhouse, a reporter began a question:

"Governor, do you have any comment on Congressman Powell's charge that Rockefeller . . ."

Harriman interrupted snappishly and said, "He can say what he wants." The Governor studiously avoided recognizing that reporter for the rest of the press conference.

Powell was calling Rockefeller's campaign one of "duplicity and hypocrisy," and was contemptuous of the Rockefeller family's efforts in the area of Negro rights. The Republicans had offered him a campaign contribution of $50,000, Powell said, in return for his support of their ticket.

Powell's support was not enough to hand Harriman the election. On November 4, Rockefeller won the Governorship. (The liberal *New York Post,* in an eleventh-hour reversal, lifted its support of Harriman because of his supposed fealty to the New York state bosses, most notably DeSapio.) Powell won his own election easily, collecting 43,100 votes as a Democrat and 13,283 as a Republican, for a total of 56,383. Brown, still on the ballot as a Liberal, got only 5,705 protest votes.

In the new Congress, Powell set about mending old fences. He wanted his patronage rights restored and some assurance that he would succeed Barden as chairman of the Education and Labor Committee. He was handed the chairmanship of the Mining Subcommittee of the Interior Committee and performed well in the job, drawing the praise of congressmen from such mining states as Colorado and Pennsylvania. A move to split Education and Labor into two separate committees, however, met defeat because Powell would have been entitled to the chair of one of them.

Practical politics at the Manhattan street level now consumed Powell's interest. He dedicated himself, along with Ray Jones, to winning the complex but crucial Harlem district leadership elections of 1959. These leaderships in Manhattan are the theoretical base of political power. Harlem chooses ten leaders, constituting nearly one-fifth of the voting strength of Tammany Hall. "I'll name the next county leader," Powell said. He announced his intention of running for one of the leaderships himself and said Jones would run for another. He also hinted he intended to run for the presidency of the City Council—perhaps in 1961—as a "stepping-stone" to the job of Mayor of New York. He opened four insurgent clubhouses under the collective title of Independent Voters Association, and even began showing up in his own clubhouse on Monday evenings to meet supplicants.

His severest problem would be in arousing the ghetto and convincing Harlem's voters that this was no inconsequential election, that it would have immediate bearing on the lives of all of them. To do so, he once again took to the streets.

When weather is good in Harlem, tenementization pushes the ghetto dwellers out-of-doors. There is little to do there. Many gather on street corners and on doorsteps chatting about their near-misses in the numbers game. Dope-pushers, pimps, and prostitutes prowl the streets. Television sets blare in two-for-one barrooms. The curbstones are crowded with automobiles, many double-parked. Older ghetto-dwellers sit on folding chairs put down near their stoops, and talk indolently. These are Harlem's voters—beyond the mainstream of New York City life, human wastage in an economic cesspool stretching from Central Park to the Harlem River.

Powell needed to dramatize for them why their votes were desperately needed in a party primary traditionally bringing out only ten to fifteen percent of enrolled Democrats. The boredom in the streets worked in his favor, for Adam Powell is a show. Signs began appearing, set up below street lamps: "A. C. Powell to speak here." Sound trucks blared: "Congressman Powell will be here soon! He's now at another corner." Loud music would attract the attention of bystanders. Then Powell came into sight, riding in an old station wagon (not one of the sportscars for which he is better known) accompanied by three voluptuous girls and a male driver. Powell would get out, wave and mount the platform of the sound truck. He was going to be their "instructor" in political science, he told them, and he had a "lesson" for them right now. Negroes would sidle from their stoops and doorways into the streetlamp glare. Young couples held hands. Powell, in shirtsleeves, his collar open and sleeves rolled, "instructed" them:

"I like pigs' feet," he shouted. "I like them hot, I like them cold, I like them with the bones in, I like them sliced." He grinned, and indulged in a long pause. "But I want to reach up on those haunches! I want to get to those ribs where the choice cuts are! *Now I want to tell you about the Powell, formula for patronage!* A little lesson in political science. . . ."

He outlined his "two-to-one formula" which a few years later would be called the "quota system" for hiring. "Now for every two jobs given out, one of equal prestige and salary must be given to a Negro or a Puerto Rican until a plateau of democracy is reached in keeping with the population structure of New York. Is this racism? *Yes!* Racism has been played in this town for half a century."

He analyzed Tammany's 1:1:1 ratio in allocating jobs among Italians, Irish, and Jews. That formula should be junked, he told them, and reverted to only after Negroes and

Puerto Ricans had gotten their share of the jobs. (Reference to Puerto Ricans was appearing with growing frequency in Powell's public statements.) Then he shifted gears from job patronage to municipal contracts, many of which, he said, equalled a year's total job patronage salaries. It brought to mind another appetizing metaphor: "It's this big cream that's floating! It should be ours!"

Powell and Jones ran two entries for district leaders—one male and one female, as the law provides—in each of Harlem's five executive districts. On election day, they lost only one district, that of Borough President Hulan Jack (he was also a district leader) whom they had not seriously expected to defeat. Their victory now was complete. As a duumvirate, they ruled political Harlem, having virtually excluded white influence. Carmine DeSapio was in steep decline as a political boss, having demonstrated that he was neither as shrewd nor as invincible as earlier supposed. Two years later he would be defeated for leader in his home district in Greenwich Village —the ultimate humiliation.

Once again, while Powell's political fortunes were flourishing, his domestic ones were foundering. His "Utopian" marriage to Hazel Scott was about to dissolve. Their professional lives kept them apart a great deal: Hazel had her concert tours, and subsequently her engagements as a singer and dancer in such luxury night clubs as the Latin Quarter; Powell was immersed in politics, and surrounded by scores of aides and hangers-on. He was irascible at times as a result of the limitations placed on his actions by an unpredictable heart condition.

In 1958, Hazel had accepted a three-week engagement in Paris. She then remained to accept others in night clubs on the Continent, in the Middle East, and North Africa. At the end of a year, she sent for Skipper, their 12-year-old son. Powell, meanwhile, was experiencing renewed income tax problems, some of which arose out of his handling of Hazel's returns. He had also met, during the Harriman campaign, a pretty Puerto Rican divorcee named Yvette Marjorie Flores Diago, whose grandfather had been the last Republican elected mayor of San Juan. Mrs. Flores had become Powell's secretary and confidante, and was destined to be the third Mrs. Adam Clayton Powell, Jr.

Roy Wilkins, in an interview in 1959, said he knew nothing about the Black Muslims. Even so, the Muslims were already powerfully organized by that time, and their emergence as a voice—a bellicose and strident voice, to be sure—in the black revolution was charged with significance, not only for the masses, but for Adam Powell and his struggle to define himself as a leader inside the context of the revolt. The Muslims were the first black nationalists since Marcus Garvey to make an observable impression on the nation as a whole, and to attract Negroes in great numbers to their banners. They posited the thesis that Islam was the religion of the West African blacks before their uprooting and forced servitude, and that Christianity, "the white man's religion," has contributed to perpetuating that servitude. They resent the term, "Negro" —a white coinage, from the Spanish word for black—and forsake their surnames (in favor of the anonymous "X") which their ancestors had taken from slaveowner masters. Muslims are avowed separatists—as inimical to the concept of integration as is the Ku Klux Klan—and look forward to a mythical day when Afro-Americans have their own nation, economically and geographically distinct from the white man's realm. America's Black Muslim leaders claim ties with the spiritual leaders of Islam in North Africa and the Middle East. (Concomitantly, the Muslims are "anti-Zionist," and are fond of suggesting that the shopkeepers and landlords who hold economic sway over America's black ghettos are predominantly Jewish.) Elijah Muhammad, leader of the sect in the United States, and his principal lieutenant (until their estrangement in 1963), Malcolm X, made pilgrimages to Mecca, in spite of a historic divergence between Black Muslimism and orthodox Islam. The latter teaches universal brotherhood irrespective of race; the former claims that white men are devils and must be fought with the weapons of war.

American Muslimism derives from an obscure door-to-door salesman who operated in the Negro ghetto of Detroit in the early days of the Depression. His name may have been W. D. Fard—although he sometimes called himself Farrad Mohammad, or F. M. Ali—and he claimed to come from Mecca. He sold satins and silks which he claimed were similar to those worn by black chieftains in Africa. Around Detroit, he became known as The Prophet. In the evenings, he held meetings in private homes and rented halls, proselytizing and spreading the gospel of Islam. It appears he was highly persuasive in his attacks on the Negro church as a bastion of the status quo, and on all "white, blue-eyed devils" as natural enemies of Afro-Americans. He made converts rapidly and soon founded a University of Islam and a military-style task force called The Fruit of Islam, trained in judo and the use of firearms.

A Negro from Sandersville, Georgia, named Elijah Poole, was an early convert. Fard gave him the name "Muhammad" and made him the first Chief Minister of Islam, with the charge of opening Temple Number Two in Chicago. Around the same time—according to the best information—Fard and some of his followers got into trouble with the Detroit police on a charge of alleged sacrificial killing of human beings: a practice which was, indeed, part of the Muslims' teaching. Fard joined Muhammad in Chicago and the two of them returned to Detroit in 1933. Soon after that, Fard's public ap-

pearances grew less frequent and in 1934 he vanished altogether. The mystery of his disappearance has never been
solved. Speculation that he was a willing or unwilling human
sacrifice during an internal power struggle has never been
substantiated. Whatever the truth, Muhammad emerged as
the top Muslim and bestowed upon himself the title of Messenger of the Prophet of Allah.

The Black Muslims attracted little attention under
Muhammad's guidance, except for their leader's refusal to
register for the draft and his subsequent confinement in
prison for four years. After the war, a young Negro named
Malcolm Little joined the Muslims and, through him, the
sect found new life, drama, and sense of mission. Little—born
in Omaha, Nebraska, in 1925, the son of a Baptist minister
who had been a follower of Marcus Garvey—was the product
of a bitter and impoverished childhood. He fled to New York
in his teens and allied himself with the Harlem underworld
of dope-pushers, pimps, and policy racketeers, whose overlords
found in him an eager and ruthless lieutenant. He wore expensive suits and always had plenty of money to pay off the
police. In 1947, he went to prison for burglary.

At the maximum security prison in Concord, Massachusetts, Little met a Muslim inmate and was converted to the
teachings of Muhammad. After his release, he sought out
Muhammad, offered himself to the cause and became Malcolm X. He rose quickly to become Muhammad's right hand.
Malcolm X had what Muhammad lacked: youth, energy to
burn, the sort of raw conviction that breeds charisma, and an
oratorical flair to match that of Adam Powell and the soon-
to-emerge Martin Luther King. As the black revolution
burgeoned, Malcolm X trumpeted the Muslim position that
sit-ins, freedom rides and court battles were doomed to end in
bitter failure for the Negro because white America would
never honor its promise of integration; that the masses would

one day forsake King and Wilkins and Farmer and Randolph and the rest of the leadership dedicated to non-violence, and turn to the Muslims and the code of violence. "Martin Luther King is a chump, not a champ," Malcolm said. "Any man who puts his women and children on the front lines is a chump, not a champ."

At the Harvard Law School Forum in 1960, Malcolm said: "Just give us a portion of this country that we can call our own. Put us in it. Then give us everything we need to start our own civilization here . . . that is, support us for 20 to 25 years until we are able to go for ourselves. This is God's plan. This is God's solution. This is justice and compensation for our 310 years of free slave labor."

At a rally attended by 4000 people at Seventh Avenue and 125th Street in Harlem, Malcolm urged upon his listeners the Muslim code of clean living and family cooperation:

"The largest concentration of black people on earth is right here in Harlem, so we are gathered here today in Harlem Square to a Freedom Rally of black people, by black people and for the benefit of black people. . . . The Western World is filled with drunkenness, dope addiction, lying, stealing, gambling, adultery, fornication, prostitution and hosts of other evils. These evils must be removed if the world is to have peace. . . . The American so-called Negroes must recognize each other as brothers and sisters . . . stop drinking whiskey, taking dope, reefers and even cigarettes. No more gambling! Save your money. Stop fornication, adultery and prostitution. Elevate the black woman; respect her and protect her. Let us rid ourselves of immoral habits and God will be with us to protect us and guide us."

He threatened Negro politicians with voter retaliation if they did not free themselves from white control:

"A big election is coming up this year. What kind of leaders do we want in office? Which ones will the black masses get

behind? Mr. Muhammad has thousands of followers and millions of sympathizers. He will place his weight behind any
fearless black leaders who will stand up and help the so-called
American Negroes get complete and immediate freedom. If
these black leaders are afraid that to be identified with us they
will irk the white man or lose the white man's favor or support, then they can no longer expect the support of the black
masses. . . ."

In speeches at various universities in the South, Malcolm
adopted a more didactic attack:

"Messenger Muhammad has taught us how we so-called
Negroes were kidnapped from the East by the white Christian slavemasters, brought to America in chains, and robbed
of our own God, His religion, our language, culture, names,
flag, and even our own nationality. . . . We are now able
to speak only the slave master's tongue, and are still being
called the same 'slave names' . . . such as Jones, Smith, Powell,
King, Bunche, Diggs, Dawson, et cetera. . . . We really have
been robbed.

". . . Only three million of the eleven million Negroes
who are qualified to vote take an active part. . . . The three
million voters are the so-called middle- (or high-) class Negroes . . . who have been educated to think as patriotic indi-
vidualists, with no racial pride . . . who believe in and look
forward to the future 'integrated-intermarried' society promised them by the Negro politicians. . . . The eight million
non-voting Negroes are . . . the downtrodden black masses.
They have refused to vote or to take part in politics, because
they reject the Uncle Tom approach of the 'clergy-politician'
leadership that has been handpicked for the American Negroes by the white man himself."

In an interview with author Louis Lomax, Malcolm X discussed non-violence in civil disobedience: "The white man
supports Reverend Martin Luther King, subsidizes Reverend
Martin Luther King, so that Reverend Martin Luther King

can continue to teach the Negroes to be defenseless in the face of one of the most cruel beasts that has ever taken people into captivity."

Lomax said, "There are rumors that you may run against Adam Clayton Powell."

Malcolm answered, "Why must I run against a Negro? We have had enough of Negroes running against and fighting each other. The better bet is that we would put a Muslim candidate in the field against a devil, somebody who is against all we stand for." In May of 1964—after his split with the Muslims, and nine months before being murdered while addressing 500 of his followers in Harlem—Malcolm, in a private conversation, had this to say about the Harlem Congressman: "Powell is more independent of political machinery than any other politician of national stature, principally because he's from Harlem. Harlem is not as brainwashed as other areas of the country. When the press maligns Powell, it isn't taken seriously in Harlem. I would never make any statement criticizing Powell. I don't let myself be used to make statements against anybody who is fighting for the same thing I am."

The time was not far off when Powell—unable to penetrate the inner sanctum of power among the emerging united Negro leadership—would find companionship with Malcolm X and other hard-nosed and "extreme" civil rights fighters. They were to be a haven for him when he badly needed a home.

10. Beach Head at Cerro Gordo

A Negro woman, who had been standing in line for three hours outside the courtroom where Adam Powell's long-awaited tax trial was scheduled to begin, told a reporter, "I'm here because Adam is a militant leader and we need him. We must stand solid like this and let him know it." Passing down the line in the crowded corridor, the reporter drew other comments from Harlemites who had traveled downtown in the hope of attending the trial:

"I'm standing here praying for him. I know God will answer my prayers. He champions the underprivileged and is a leader of people in all walks of life."

"I love Reverend Powell. He began helping us workers years ago. I know this day he's being persecuted for helping us. I intend to stand for him until the end of this unfair trial."

"Adam has been tried in the white newspapers and not been given fair coverage. I came to see him tried so I can see for myself if there is any difference between Mississippi courts and those here."

"Reverend Powell is the greatest living Negro we have. It's a downright shame he has to suffer for this."

"I feel that because he has been so outspoken in representing us is the very reason he's in there."

"I'm for Adam because he can't be bought. He fights hard out there for me and I know it."

Once again, the ranks were closing around Powell in a time of beleaguerment by white America. Days before the trial began, Hazel Scott returned to New York from France for the first time in three years, and said, "I have absolutely no comment regarding my private life, the tax case, or Mr. Powell, except to say that Mr. Powell is still my husband." The *Amsterdam News* claimed that "a highly-placed anti-Negro Southern Congressman with powerful influence over federal officials" had called upon the Department of Justice to press the case against Powell. Whether such intervention had occurred or not, it was a fact that the South now had a great stake in Congressman Powell's future, because Representative Graham Barden, chairman of the House Education and Labor Committee, had announced his retirement the previous January. The following January, Powell presumably would assume the chairmanship—the culmination and prize of his 15-year tenure as the black ghetto's representative in Washington.

To conduct his defense, Powell chose Edward Bennett Williams, the youthful firebrand from Washington who already had achieved celebrity for his handling of cases involving Senator Joseph McCarthy, teamsters Dave Beck and James Hoffa, gambler Frank Costello, and *Confidential* magazine. The trial got underway in New York on March 8, 1960. Williams began by challenging the selection methods which had produced a panel of 125 prospective jurors, only five of whom were Negroes. He also challenged the validity of the 1958 indictment because of the pressure applied to the grand jury by William Buckley of *National Review*.

Powell's jury of nine women and three men was all white— "lily white," said the Negro press. The Congressman, if convicted on all three counts of the indictment, could be sentenced to 15 years in prison and fined $30,000. The three counts—two of which subsequently were set aside by Judge Frederick Van Pelt Bryan—charged that Powell had falsified his wife's earnings for 1951; taken exorbitant deductions for his own professional activities in the same year; and failed to report portions of his income in 1952. He had deducted many thousands of dollars "in a flagrant manner for imaginary and personal expenses," said assistant United States Attorney Morton S. Robson, who was directing the government's case.

According to the government, Powell had deducted such "professional expenses" as restaurant checks, primarily at Sardi's and "21"; his annual liquor bill of more than $500; the cost of his son's tuition in a private school; the cost of two TV sets and maintenance of two boats at Westhampton, Long Island; his insurance bills; 40 percent of his laundry bills; 40 percent of his fuel and light bills; all phone bills; theater tickets; and virtually every department store and clothing purchase, including $237 for clerical garb.

In 1951, when Powell and Hazel had a joint income of $70,000, Powell's figures indicated a joint indebtedness to the government of less than $1000. In 1952, when their combined income was around $90,000, their return showed a tax liability of $700. The prosecutor cleared Miss Scott of complicity in Powell's arithmetic. In describing the Congressman's tax return for 1951—a year in which he accompanied his wife on a concert tour of Europe and Israel—Robson said, "He claimed $2,500 for living expenses in Washington for four days each week during a ten-month period. But he was only in the United States for eight months. The evidence will show that he spent less than $300. He deducted $2,535 in fares between New York and Washington that year. As a Congressman, he was entitled to take off transportation. But it must be remembered he was in Europe four months of the year. The round trip ticket to Washington was $23. At that rate, he would have had 100 round trips, which in itself is incredible." But, Robson added, Powell had a clerical pass entitling him to buy tickets at half fare, reducing the cost per trip to a little over $11. At that rate, Robson concluded, Powell would have had to make 200 round trips to spend the amount he deducted.

In 1952, read one of the indictment counts, the Congressman had overlooked $3000 in income from his church and a $300 check received for a newspaper article. "All of this was done wilfully, knowingly and fraudulently and by him alone," the prosecutor charged, thus minimizing the role of Powell's tax adviser, a lawyer and one-time tax collector named James W. Johnson.

Each day the courtroom was crowded with Powell's well-wishers and with curiosity-seekers who had the patience to stand in line for hours for the chance to observe the impressive Edward Bennett Williams in action. The combination of Powell and Williams was a powerful magnet. For seven weeks, the trial was, by any standard, the best show in town. Harlem ministers and civic leaders crowded in to demonstrate their sympathy for Powell in his moment of "persecution." Baseball player Jackie Robinson posed proudly for news photographers with the Congressmen. A regular, but unobtrusive, backbench observer—unrecognized by and, in fact, unknown to most of the newsmen present—was Malcolm X, whose interest in the law dated to his own unfortunate involvement with it, and who also had a continuing fascination with the Congressman's career. Williams and Powell did not disappoint their gallery. When Powell took the stand in his own defense, he and Williams staged a dialogue which held the courtroom taut and attentive.

Powell denied in booming tones that he ever tried to cheat the government out of taxes. Williams, working at two blackboards, performed the not inconsiderable task of demonstrating how the government's own figures could be used to prove that Powell had overstated—not understated, as the prosecution alleged—his wife's 1951 income. So unprepared was the government for this resourceful bit of bookkeeping, that their own tax expert, who had been working for four years on Powell's case, was led to the admission that—depending on how one looked at it—either set of figures could be correct. Judge Bryan threw out two counts of the indictment, leaving only Powell's alleged fraudulent preparation of Hazel Scott's 1951 tax return.

During the last four months of 1951, Powell had accompanied his wife on a concert tour of Europe and Israel and, according to his testimony, used the travel time to study "the relationships between Church and State in the field of education." Powell's committee chairman, Representative Barden, had declined to authorize funds to cover expenses on the trip, said Powell, so he paid for it "out of my own pocket, as I did to the Bandung conference in 1955." He added: "I was working all the time!" Two main points interested the prosecution: first, the Powells appeared to have spent a good deal more on their European tour than there was any record of their having had with them, or received there; and second, the government claimed, not all of Hazel's European income was listed on the return.

Powell attempted to absolve the first mystery by revealing the existence of a "little box" in which he customarily kept $12,000 to $15,000 in cash. Most of that money came from a $3000 annual holiday gift which his late father was in the habit of giving him, Powell said, and the rest from "grateful parishioners" at Abyssinian Baptist.

"Gratitude for what?" Robson wanted to know.

"For the services I have been rendering to the cause of fighting for democracy in this country," Powell said.

The "little box"—in actuality, a two and one-half foot

square safe—was in the Westchester residence he had shared with Hazel Scott, Powell said, and no longer contained any money. Powell vigorously denied Robson's suggestion that the fund of money had come from Mrs. Hattie Freeman Dodson—his secretary who had been convicted of tax evasion —in the form of kickbacks. Keeping ready cash at hand was "a habit I learned from my father," the Congressman said. "That's the way he operated." In 1951, as he and Hazel were about to leave for Europe, Powell testified, his father gave him not only the usual $3000 gift, but an additional $4,500 so that he wouldn't run out of pocket money. (Powell claimed that the $4,500 was a loan which he later repaid.)

He then went to Abercrombie & Fitch and bought a money belt, Powell said. Into it he put about $5000, and wore the belt to Europe.

As for the second point, Powell testified that, after suffering a mild heart attack in 1952, he had given Mrs. Dodson the task of drawing up a work sheet on his and Hazel's earnings and expenditures. She was to hand the figures over to James W. Johnson, the Congressman's tax expert who was paid $500 for preparing the actual return. Powell said that he had read the tax report, "but not in detail" before signing it. Robson pressed the point:

Q. Did you believe it was accurate?
A. I had to. I did not have the knowledge to prepare it. I took the expert opinion of the man I had retained and hired.
Q. You expected him to go over the figures in detail?
A. That's what I expected. That's what I paid him for and I was shocked in this courtroom to find he had not done that.

A month and ten days after the trial began, the prosecution and defense attorneys rested their cases. Crowds jammed the courtroom and overflowed far down the corridor as Edward Bennett Williams prepared to deliver his summation. Powell's indictment grew out of "a maelstrom of misinformation," Williams said. He accused the Justice Department of "conduct unworthy of agents of the United States government." Williams then baldly threw down the accusation he had hinted at many times during the trial: "Were they conducting a grand jury investigation—or were they conducting a political vendetta designed to destroy the defendant . . . ? Was he the victim of the worst political vendetta ever engineered by an agency of this government in modern history?"

Prosecutor Robson, red with anger, rose and shouted, "There is not the slightest bit of evidence to sustain these charges before this jury and it is a reflection on myself and my entire staff. I say that they are lies!" Judge Bryan studied the prosecutor silently, then returned his gaze to Williams.

"I stand on my statement," the defense counsel said. He proceeded:

"I know that he [Powell] has spoken from the frustrations of a soul who stands in the ministry and is qualified for the well of Congress, but is denied meals and lodgings in some parts of this country. I suppose he has made enemies. I suppose they are strong and powerful."

Williams's summation continued for four hours. Near the end of it, he said: "I ask you to consider whether you believe, really and truly, that there is behind this trial simply the charge, recklessly and carelessly put together in this indictment, or whether he is on trial for political liquidation. I say that if you believe the latter, you should give thundering notice through the corridors of this courthouse that there is no room for political trials in this land, that an indictment is not a substitute for the ballot." Every man, said Williams, "whomsoever he may be, whatever his heritage, whatever his background, whatever his color" was entitled to equal justice under the law. "I ask no more for this man," Williams said.

He stood a moment, surveying the jurors' faces, then walked slowly back to the counsel table.

In his charge to the jury (which now included one Negro woman—a male juror having withdrawn for reasons of health), Judge Bryan used two hours and twenty minutes to instruct them that three basic questions remained for them to decide: had the defendant aided and assisted in the preparation of his wife's return for 1951? Did the return "substantially" understate her net income for that year? If so, was it done "wilfully, fraudulently and with intent" to deceive? Bryan emphasized that Miss Scott was an established star and could therefore be expected to have high professional expenses for clothing, music, arrangements, books, maids, and so forth, and that deliberate intent to defraud the government must be proved in this, a criminal action. He spoke sympathetically of the defense contention that Powell was the victim of errors made by his secretary and tax lawyer. "I think it can be stated in all fairness," said Bryan, "that Johnson did a sloppy job of preparing this return for the $500 he was paid."

The jury retired to deliberate. In the corridor, a court reporter said, "I've never seen a jury so beaten over the head to bring back an acquittal." Negroes stood around in clusters discussing the case. One Harlemite, his enthusiasm for Powell conditioned by days of listening to the trial's legalisms, said, "The government wilfully prepared a fraudulent indictment with deliberate intent to prosecute." A reporter eavesdropped on another conversation among waiting Negroes:

"The judge gave the jury a chance to be honest."

"This trial has made Adam a martyr. No matter what they do, he's a bigger man."

"Adam says what he thinks. That's why they're out for him."

"Nobody can hate Adam. They may not like him, but they can't hate him."

"No. They hate him. They can't control him. They're out to get him."

The jury was out for 26 hours during which time 20 ballots were taken. The sounds of shouting and recrimination filtered through the door of the jury room. One juror became hysterical; another had a gall bladder attack. On the second day, the jurors returned to the courtroom and informed Judge Bryan that "it will be impossible to reach a verdict with this jury." The vote was ten to two for acquittal and the two dissident jurors would not be budged. Bryan declared a mistrial and dismissed the jury "with the thanks and appreciation of the court."

Powell and his supporters were jubilant. The Congressman declared that a "prayer meeting in thanksgiving" would be held at Abyssinian Baptist later on and that everybody was welcome. "All I am really happy about is that I will be able to get back to work. . . . In this hour of complete vindication I shall go forward to see that what happened to me shall not happen to any other person."

One juror who voted for acquittal said: "Judge Bryan left us with nothing to decide." The one Negro juror said later: "I think quite a few jurors felt there was something else besides the tax situation behind Mr. Powell's troubles. I personally felt the case was a hoax after listening to all of the evidence the government presented. Most of us felt the judge leaned heavily in favor of Mr. Powell and that he wanted an acquittal, especially after his charge to the jury." A Powell aide said the Congressman had spent close to $70,000 defending himself against the indictment.

Although the trial ended indecisively, Powell was, for the moment, victorious. Seven months later, Hazel Scott divorced him. The government announced it would press for a retrial and seek to enlist the testimony of Miss Scott to impugn the validity of deductions taken by Powell on her tax return. But in the eyes of great numbers of Negroes, he had succeeded for the hundredth time in vanquishing those elements of white America which were intent on silencing him.

In the spring of that same year, 43-year old Senator John F. Kennedy of Massachusetts came to New York seeking support for his aspiration to the Presidency of the United States. At the time, Powell was in an extremely strong position. He had three aims: to be recognized as a national party leader by the Presidential nominee; to clinch the chairmanship to which his seniority entitled him; and to convince the Department of Justice to forego a retrial on his tax case. He supposed that his aims could be made complementary with those of the Democratic Presidential nominee—whoever he turned out to be.

After Representative Barden announced his retirement, pressures began to build to deny Powell the chairmanship. Powell insisted publicly that "Mr. Sam promised me" the post. At his first mass meeting appearance since Barden's announcement—which happened to be a Salute to A. Philip Randolph in Carnegie Hall—Powell told the audience of the Speaker's pledge, thereby putting Rayburn in the position of having to take that stand on the matter or invite a charge of racism.

But Powell's real leverage came from the politicking he could accomplish in regard to the Presidential nomination. Behind the scenes, he ingratiated himself with Senate majority leader Lyndon B. Johnson, as well as with Speaker Rayburn. He spoke highly of Johnson as Presidential timber and disparagingly of Kennedy. The Massachusetts Senator had had a well-publicized "breakfast meeting" with Governor John Patterson of Alabama and Sam Englehardt, Alabama's Democratic State Chairman and a White Citizen's Council leader. Powell taunted Kennedy about the meeting, repeatedly demanding that he repudiate any arrangements springing from it, and finally insisted that Kennedy was soft on civil rights and therefore "unacceptable." He knew Kennedy could not repudiate his Alabama endorsers without jeopardizing other Southern support. At a news conference in the National Democratic Club in New York, Kennedy was asked:

"Senator, the Powell people say that you are unacceptable because of your civil rights position. What about that?" Kennedy observed the reporter coldly, and said: "What's your question?"

The reporter said: "Powell demands that you repudiate the Patterson-Englehardt breakfast understanding."

Senator Kennedy then embarked on a bit of pressmanship, responding lengthily and reviewing his entire Senate civil rights record. After several minutes of discourse, he turned to another reporter without having mentioned the meeting with the Alabamans. But reaction to the breakfast session bothered him. Subsequently, he sent an emissary to Powell in an attempt to reconcile the issue. A Negro politician close to Powell said that Robert Kennedy had described the breakfast as a "tactical error," but that position was never conceded publicly.

If Powell chided Kennedy, he was careful to indicate that religion was not a factor. He encouraged Roman Catholic good will by insisting that the vice-presidential nominee be a Catholic and spoke highly of both Governor Edmund (Pat) Brown of California and Senator Eugene McCarthy of Minnesota. "We'll break the Catholic barrier," he said, "and then the Jews and later the Negroes will have a chance."

In January, 1960, Powell privately named Senators Stuart Symington of Missouri and Hubert Humphrey of Minnesota as the strongest candidates and spoke favorably of Governor G. Mennen Williams of Michigan. He called Senator Johnson "not the worst candidate" available to the Democrats and indicated his willingness to view the Texan as a westerner rather than a southerner. But at the Democratic convention in Los Angeles, Powell announced himself in favor of Symington. The Missouri legislator was viewed variously as a compromise candidate and a stalking horse for Lyndon Johnson. Johnson, as majority leader, held to the stratagem of not disclosing his availability because of "demands of party leadership" in the Senate. Any delegate strength which Symington could muster could be swung to Johnson at the proper time and withheld from Kennedy in the meantime. Powell's political partner, Ray Jones, became a drumbeater for Johnson and was, in fact, one of four New York delegates casting his vote for Johnson rather than Kennedy. Powell was careful to make it clear that he would support the Democratic ticket no matter which of the principal contenders got the nomination. He would not bolt, as he had in 1956. But the question was "how actively will I campaign?" That was the weapon Adam Powell wielded so conspicuously in an election year when Vice-President Richard Nixon was the early betting favorite to hold the Presidency for the GOP for another four years.

Even after Kennedy won the Democratic nomination, Powell remained silent and refused to make any public display of enthusiasm for Kennedy's candidacy. Just as the Harlem Congressman had forced Averell Harriman to negotiate for his services in 1958, he was doing the same to Kennedy in 1960. And just as Harriman had come to Powell, so did Kennedy, after he became the nominee. Such a power play required steel nerves of both Powell and Jones. Powell desperately needed to have himself publicly declared a valued member of the team—not only Democratically respectable, but a true-blue professional in whom one might confidently invest responsibility.

Powell called a news conference in September in Sardi's restaurant, the actors' hangout in the heart of Manhattan's theater district. He announced he was going to "sacrifice" his own campaign for re-election to Congress and spend the time stumping for the national ticket. He would tour ten states for Kennedy and Johnson, he said, while also serving as consultant to them on urban affairs.

In the ensuing month Powell did indeed work hard for the ticket, traveling to Negro communities and declaiming to ghetto dwellers that their best chance for improving their lot was to hew to the Democrats. When Kennedy and Johnson won the election by seventeen one-hundredths of one percent of the total vote, a Negro tactician working nationally for the Democrats said of Powell, "We needed him." Later, he added: "He played a decisive role. He was sort of a brand name. But he also knew that he had to project himself as a more responsible leader than he had done before. He's made the fight of his life to overcome [his past image]. I think he's overcoming it. But I would be less than honest if I said all had been forgotten." Powell gathered 74 percent of the Harlem vote in his Congressional election.

Five months later, a federal judge dismissed the tax fraud indictment against Powell at the government's request. The Justice Department said it "could not obtain a conviction in a second trial" and there was thus no reason to press the matter further. Powell jubilantly expressed the view that he had achieved "complete vindication" and praised Attorney General Robert F. Kennedy for his "fair play." He reiterated his displeasure that "not a single" Puerto Rican and "only three Negroes" were on the panel from which his jury was picked.

"If this kind of treatment happened to me, what could happen to an ordinary John Doe?" Powell asked. "God help the rest of America if they can do this to me. That's why I'm going to fight for the protection of everybody." Morton Robson said that the case was being dropped because Hazel Scott refused to testify against her ex-husband and that Mrs. Hattie

Freeman Dodson, who had been "an extremely uncooperative and hostile witness" during the trial, probably would behave similarly in a re-trial. There was just no use, said Robson.

When the new Congress convened, Powell assumed the chairmanship of the House Education and Labor Committee. Powell announced that he was instituting a voluntary ban on his own use of the Powell Amendment. It had served well in the past, he said, but times had changed and he was eager not to jeopardize any of the legislation of value to Negroes which the New Frontier had in prospect. Inevitably, capital old-timers suggested that Powell had felt some more of the same "vibrations" with Kennedy in 1960 that he had with Eisenhower in 1956. And the ghetto Congressman would have been the last to deny that his sensitivity to such vibrations was less keen than that of any politician worthy of the name.

In 1960, Powell was asked in an interview: "Is there anti-Puerto Rican prejudice among Negroes to any extent?" He said there was. "It's just like the anti-West Indian feelings among American Negroes. . . . I know I can subdue and scrub this out personally. In the past year or year and a half I have done a good deal. . . . They're where the Negro was 30 years ago, not only economically, but in their own squabbling and bickering." He described how he maintained contact with many Puerto Ricans through their baseball league, which was "very important, with 5000 registered voters." He said they were politically-oriented, but "they're ignored by the politicians." He opposed the New York voters' literacy law, which defined literacy as the ability to work with English. "Some of the Puerto Ricans don't speak very good English. But one of them came up to me and said, 'You know what's wrong with us? We always fight each other. What we need is a dictator. You be our dictator!' " Powell laughed. "Can you imagine that—*me*, their dictator!"

Adam Clayton Powell at rally in Englewood, N.J. (1963). *(Wide World Photo)*

The Big Six. From left to right: John Lewis (SNCC); Whitney Young (Urban League); A. Philip Randolph (Negro American Labor Council); Martin Luther King, Jr. (Southern Christian Leadership Conference); James Farmer (CORE); Roy Wilkins (NAACP) (1963). *(Wide World Photo)*

Adam Clayton Powell at rally in Harlem (1964). *(Wide World Photo)*

From left to right: Adam Clayton Powell; Milton Galamison; Jesse Gray; Malcolm X (1964). *(Wide World Photo)*

March on Washington (1963). *(Paris Match Photo)*

Dr. Kenneth Clark
(1964). *(UPI Photo)*

Adam Clayton Powell and Corrine Huff in Hawaii (1964). *(UPI Photo)*

Since the late 1950's, he had spent progressively more time in Puerto Rico. In the early 1960's, he appealed time and again to Puerto Ricans in New York City to follow his political leadership. It was obvious that he dreamed of an amalgamated Negro-Puerto Rican voting bloc. A study of Manhattan school population statistics indicated that within a few years such an alliance would comprise the largest single voting bloc in the borough—exceeding Italian, Jewish, and Irish factional strength. While the ten Democratic district leaders in Harlem had less than decisive influence in Tammany Hall, a united Negro-Puerto Rican front might one day name the County leader.

Powell's first wife had been a native-born American. During the period when he was trying to unify native-born and West Indian-born Negroes, he romanced and married Hazel Scott, a Haitian. Only the most unchivalrous of his critics has pointed out that his marriage in San Juan in 1960 to Mrs. Yvette Marjorie Flores Diago—an attractive 29-year-old divorcee and member of an influential and well-connected Puerto Rican family—came at a time when the island commonwealth was about to review its status vis-à-vis the United States. Powell subsequently testified before a meeting of the House Interior Subcommittee on Territorial and Insular Affairs to advocate a referendum on statehood for Puerto Rico. He was quoted as saying: "There are people who say to me that I would be a fine successor to Governor Muñoz Marín, or that if statehood should come to Puerto Rico, I could be the best United States Senator for them."

Powell met Mrs. Flores when she was working with the minorities division of Averell Harriman's campaign organization. ("You ought to see the kook I'm working for," she told a co-worker, after meeting Powell for the first time.) He took her to Washington as a member of his congressional office staff at a salary of $3,074. After their marriage, he raised her

salary to $12,974, and—after he built his dream house, called
Villa Reposa, at Cerro Gordo in Puerto Rico—he shifted her
base of activities to the luxurious ocean-front retreat, claiming that she earned her salary by handling his voluminous
correspondence with Puerto Rican constituents.

Villa Reposa is a showplace—not far from the Rockefeller-
built Dorado Beach Hotel—which Mrs. Powell's uncle, a contractor, built for the newly-married couple at a reported cost
of $42,000. (Its resale value is almost twice that amount.) The
house has two bedrooms, a library, a three-car garage, several
patios and well-landscaped yards with fruit trees and bright
flowers. The ocean rolls up to within a few dozen yards of the
house. Powell sails, surf fishes, swims, and plays badminton
while his wife and four servants run the household in such a
way as to assure him maximum ease and privacy. The whole
scene is, in brief, as far removed from both the experience
and imagination of Harlem's tenemented blacks as to be
largely incomprehensible to them. It is a shiny fragment in
the mosaic of a lifestyle to which they could only dimly aspire.
Early in his Puerto Rican period, Powell began investing in
local business, most notably an insurance company—Seaboard
Life—administered by his in-laws. He moved furniture and
family heirlooms from Harlem to the Cerro Gordo villa and
undertook a schedule of sustained commutation that would
have withered a less energetic man: from San Juan to Harlem
—where he conducted services on Sunday at Abyssinian Baptist—thence to Washington, and back to San Juan. One irrev-
erent Harlemite suggested that the reason Powell spent so
much time in the Caribbean was to keep up his tan so as not to
be mistaken for a white man. But Powell's real intentions in
the Caribbean were apparent enough: the nurturing of an entente with Spanish-speaking peoples that would crystallize in a
power bloc strong enough to hand Powell political control of
all Manhattan; or—given statehood for Puerto Rico—the

added dignity of a Senatorship or even Governorship of a grateful Puerto Rican people.

In 1959, Powell had even made a journey to visit Fidel Castro in Havana. According to a Powell aide, the Cuban leader kept Powell waiting in an anteroom while he read poetry to a dark-haired and shapely Fidelista. When he emerged from those duties to meet with the Harlemite, a palpable lack of rapport prevented any arrangement that would operate to the benefit of either. When Castro's association with the Soviet Union became more apparent, Powell drew back rather than invite the suspicion that his own youthful flirtation with the Communist Party was anything more than a summer romance.

11. The Politico and the Tammany Tiger

"For six years, Barden was intentionally rude to me in public," Powell told a reporter for *Ebony* magazine in 1963. "The chairman presides over committee meetings flanked by the ranking Democrat and the ranking Republican. When the chairman finishes, he yields to the next ranking Democrat and so on down the line. I was the ranking Democrat, but Barden used to look right through me and ask the third-ranking Democrat, 'Got anything to say, Mr. Bailey?' Then after every one of the thirty members, Democrats and Republicans, had spoken, I would say, 'Can I say something, Mr. Barden?' and he would say, 'Yes, briefly.' "

When Powell heard the news that Barden was retiring, he is reported to have said, "I got down on my knees and thanked God!" Barden had indeed gone out of his way to put Powell "in his place," not only through gratuitous rudeness in committee hearings, but also through the extraordinary measure of denying Powell subcommittee chairmanships to which his seniority entitled him. Barden was, in fact, supported in this by liberals on the committee who could not forgive Powell's "grandstanding" to his Harlem constituency through his consistent use of the Powell Amendment—thereby retarding much liberal legislation. But even in the best of circumstances, Powell and Barden were worlds apart—Northern black liberal versus Southern white conservative—and their mutual animosity was a pervasive and omnipresent thing.

Labor might have been expected to rejoice at the passing of Barden from the scene. As a key figure in the Southern Democratic-Republican coalition, he had opposed and systematically undermined every piece of pro-labor legislation that came under his eye. He had been a firm supporter, on the other hand, of such measures as the Landrum-Griffin bill. Labor, however, was less than jubilant at the prospect of Powell acceding to the chairmanship. Asked how he felt about it, George Meany, president of the AFL-CIO, said: "Terrible."

The trouble with Powell as chairman, labor leaders declared, was that he could not be depended upon to roll up his sleeves and go to bat for the unions; also, that he had a low boredom threshold. Moreover, George Meany viewed Powell as being as racist in his way as the southerner Barden. It was a demonstrable fact that many craft unions were highly discriminatory toward Negroes in their membership requirements—a situation which Powell had decried vociferously and repeatedly throughout his eight terms in Congress. At this time, the issue of union jim crowism was being sharply debated within the "house of labor." A. Philip Randolph had founded the Negro American Labor Council, which was financed and controlled by Negroes, thus incurring Meany's wrath. The two labor leaders engaged in sharp verbal duelling within the AFL-CIO executive council. Meany saw the NALC as a splinter movement, weakening labor's thrust. "Who in hell appointed you spokesman for all American Negroes?" Meany had shouted at Randolph. And, in the same session: "If you put [jim crow] in a class with corruption and Communism, that's where you and I part company, Phil." Despite this intemperate outburst on the part of Meany in 1960, the two powerful men held each other in mutual respect as labor leaders. Publicly, Randolph went out of his way to assure the Negro community that Meany was no racist, and Meany never suggested that Randolph was a power-seeker. Therein lay the distinction between Meany's hostility toward Powell, and his opposition to an organizational effort by Randolph; he saw Powell as self-serving and unreliable.

Barely a month after the new (86th) Congress convened, Powell addressed a meeting of Randolph's Negro American Labor Council in Washington. His remarks, not generally reported, announced to American labor—if they did not know already—that he intended to needle them mercilessly about the conduct of their own house. Introduced as "one of God's angry young men," Powell claimed that labor had an implied contract with the Federal government—growing out of legislation guaranteeing the right to organize, the right to strike and picket, and so forth—to insure that *all* workers were given equal job opportunity. ". . . To the extent that labor fails to clearly represent all workers, its argument for relief from alleged oppressive legislation and its demand for greater powers fall short of persuasiveness," said the Congressman. "Now labor cannot escape this affirmative obligation to wipe out all vestiges of discrimination within its own ranks by pious declarations such as: 'It takes time to change,' or 'Progress is being made.' Such declarations would never have been accepted by labor during its rise to recognition and power." Powell's tone at the meeting waxed loud and contemptuous. The session was taking on a revival meeting atmosphere as the audience greeted his assertions with fervent exclamations of "Hear, hear!" White observers from the Civil Rights Commission reported later that Powell had created what seemed to them a "circus tent atmosphere."

He warned that black labor faced "dark days" because "the

Frankenstein of automation is upon us." Twenty-five thousand elevator operators had lost their jobs in New York during the previous nine years, he claimed. Twenty-five percent of white males worked in professional and managerial jobs, but only seven percent of Negroes. Powell paused and, in a near-shout, declared: "In the skilled crafts we find that there is not a single craft where the number of Negro workers reaches two percent of the total employed. In Mr. George Meany's own union—the plumbers and pipefitters—out of 11,000 undergoing apprenticeship training, only 90 are Negroes—or less than one percent. I say, as chairman of the House Labor and Education Committee, this must be changed now!" Another pause, and a change of mood. "Randolph, you're right," said Powell. "You can't move prejudices with faint, half-hearted efforts. The trouble with labor is that it has become soft, has degenerated into the cocktail, black tie, Milquetoast diplomats. It's time for labor to get calluses back on its hands and fight this battle with all its strength."

Only the day before his address to the NALC, a group of black nationalists had staged a near riot in the balcony of the United Nations. Powell extemporized a reference to it, calling it "symbolic of the frustrations of the black man. . . . It's time for the New Frontier to include black men as well as white. Black faces must be seen sitting by Mr. Stevenson at the United Nations. The calcification of our State Department must be broken. Our embassies and consulates across the earth's breast must have black and brown and yellow and Latin. It is no longer, and never was, a white man's world. This is God's world. . . . This is the moment when all of God's children will have the same rights." The Negro labor leaders gave Powell a standing ovation. If the AFL-CIO had had any vestigial expectations that Powell would deal with their interests without reference to the race question, they had been summarily disabused.

Powell was indeed in a state of high elation over his new power and prominence; and the Kennedy administration went to extraordinary lengths to confirm the impression that Powell was, on his own terms, a member in good standing of the Democratic Establishment. In February, some Powell supporters gave him a testimonial dinner at the Commodore Hotel in New York. Among those who came to pay their respects to the Congressman—who was still under indictment for tax fraud—were Abraham Ribicoff, Secretary of Health, Education and Welfare; Arthur Goldberg, Secretary of Labor; and Carmine DeSapio. Altogether at ease in such company, Powell flippantly referred to himself as "the flamboyant Mr. Powell," and made certain that the significance of Ribicoff's and Goldberg's presence was not lost on the Harlemites who had trekked downtown in black tie to attend the affair. Powell pointed out that on that very evening, President Kennedy was holding his first cabinet reception in Washington, but had excused Ribicoff and Goldberg for the supposedly more important duty of attending the New York dinner. Powell introduced members of his family: his new wife, Yvette; his son from the marriage with Hazel Scott, Adam Clayton (Skipper) Powell III, and some in-laws, whose family name was Kelly. He glanced around the room mischievously, and said: "I don't know how I get mixed up with all these Puerto Ricans and Irish." Then, addressing his words to Carmine DeSapio, seated on the dais, he said, "You know, Carmine, if the Democratic party here could get together the way my family has, we wouldn't have any problems."

Not only did Adam Clayton Powell stand on a pinnacle of influence and power as the first session of the 87th Congress began, but he appeared to have nowhere to go but up. Most importantly, he had achieved that happy state on his own terms, which were those both of black race leader and political professional. His Congressional seat was forever safe—as safe, ironically, as those of the entrenched Deep South congressmen who hated him. He held control at the party executive district —or ward—level of the Democratic machinery in Harlem, which, under certain conditions, might give him a balance of power in both city and state politics. In addition to these twin power bases, he held the chairmanship of a key House committee which was, in itself, quite safe, barring some extraordinary punitive action. His opportunity for achievement was almost boundless. It would not be Adam Powell, the Negro, who could enlarge his historic niche. He could now accomplish the dream of every black man and woman: to escape from the bondage of skin color without denying or defiling his Negroism. He would never need to be a "house Negro" or an Uncle Tom as he moved ahead as legislator and national party leader. And Powell did, in fact, make an excellent beginning.

In a matter of months, his conduct as chairman began receiving increasing—if, in some quarters, begrudging—commendation. Democrats and Republican agreed that he had hired a better qualified staff than his predecessor. His request for $633,000 to operate the committee for two years passed the House easily. The committee—composed of 19 Democrats, including the chairman, and 12 Republicans—got down to business amid high good hopes that the New Frontier's first hundred days would be memorable and productive.

During his campaign, Kennedy had promised a $1.25 minimum wage law and it fell to Powell to see that he got it. Powell gave Representative James Roosevelt, Democrat of California, the job of conducting hearings on the bill and fashioning a draft. So eager was Powell to serve Kennedy's interests in the matter, that he agreed to exclude from the bill's provisions certain low-wage employees such as laundry workers, hotel workers, and waiters in restaurants, in spite of the fact that many of those jobs were held by Negroes. He agreed to further compromises after the bill came back from the Senate, and the measure passed by such an impressive majority that Kennedy was able to claim his first major Congressional victory.

Less successful was Kennedy's school aid bill, in spite of the fact that Powell had by that time announced suspension of his use of the Powell Amendment. The Catholic Church hierarchy claimed that Kennedy's school bill was inimical to their interests, a controversy which raged in the press and in Congress for months. Powell's committee approved Kennedy's bill—which excluded church schools from aid—and sent it to the Rules Committee where it went aground on the shoals of the church-state controversy.

But Powell had demonstrated both skill and energy in his maneuvering on the school aid bill. His performance was a cheerful revelation to party managers, confronted by the realities of his power. Kennedy strategists subsequently decided to use Powell and the investigative powers of his committee to try to torpedo Nelson Rockefeller in New York. (Kennedy could not rely on the New York State Democratic Party, which was fragmented, to deliver the state in 1964, should Rockefeller be the Republican nominee. Rockefeller would be standing for re-election in 1962 and Kennedy's men were eager to hold down his margin. Thus, Powell set up an investigative task force to examine the farm labor situation and "discovered" that the New York State Industrial Commission had recruited Puerto Ricans living in New York for virtual peonage labor on a Virginia farm owned by a New Jerseyite. The revelation shocked the Puerto Rican community, in which Rockefeller had shown popularity in his 1958 campaign. The Governor's Industrial Commissioner was called to testify, and Powell chaired the hearings in Manhattan's Foley Square federal court house. His penetrating questions and often humorous but barbed observations made the state administrator appear out of control of a poorly organized operation. Rockefeller cried "politics" and Powell denied it. The Governor won re-election easily the following year, but Kennedy's forces—through Powell's exertion of influence in his home precincts—had won an early moral victory which could be resurrected and enlarged in any Kennedy-Rockefeller confrontation.

Mrs. Eleanor Roosevelt, in private correspondence in June 1961, conceded, "I have to own that Mr. Powell is proving a good chairman of his committee."

The same month, a highly-placed Negro Democrat discussed Powell in Washington: "Jack and Bobby [Kennedy] have given him rope. Adam will listen to them and they still hold the other end of the rope. . . . Adam is really trying to win their respect. . . . We ought to build leaders committed to rationalism, like [Roy] Wilkins and [Martin Luther] King— and even Powell. He's essentially rational, despite what he does sometimes. . . . Very seldom [is] he found on the wrong side of a liberal issue. . . . Unless his foot slips he's going to be a bigger man than ever. . . . Now he's on the track. But I'm not saying he won't get off the track. . . . When Adam is on the spot, he'll really go to work and he's a crafty operator. He's like FDR; when he spills his milk, he never looks back."

Also in June 1961, the ranking Republican member of Education and Labor, Carroll D. Kearns of Pennsylvania, spoke of a "very fine association" with Powell and said that the other committee members had "trust and confidence" in the chairman. "He's on the job the first thing Monday morning and stays to Friday night," Kearns said, thus exempting Powell from membership in what Congressmen call the "Tuesday-Thursday" club—legislators who live relatively close to Washington and come to the Hill only Tuesdays through Thursdays, spending the rest of their time at home politicking and attending to private business interests. "His maneuvering on the floor has been very good," Kearns added. "We're getting our legislation on the floor. What more can you ask of a chairman?"

The ultimate benediction came in the form of expressions of good will from both the *Wall Street Journal* and the *New York Times,* the latter of which had been among Powell's most consistent detractors. On April 14—the day after the Justice Department dismissed the income tax evasion charges against Powell—the nation's press reported the Harlem Congressman's proposed moratorium on his use of the Powell Amendment. On April 30, Powell appeared on a local New York television interview program called *New York Forum* and had the following exchange with a group of New York lawyers:

Q. Mr. Congressman, the Powell Amendment, which bears your name, is an amendment which would deny Federal funds to any school district operating segregated schools and you have introduced this amendment for many years. [Now you promise] to withhold [it] . . . and that if anyone else offered an anti-segregation amendment . . . you'd lead the opposition to it. Now, can you explain your apparent switch on the Powell Amendment?

A. In the first place, that is not correct. I said if anyone offered the Powell Amendment who was an enemy of Federal aid to education, I would lead the opposition to that amendment, as I did last year. The Powell Amendment was introduced by the enemies of public housing and I defeated the amendment. In other word, I will not allow the Powell Amendment to be used as a political device to kill legislation. Now as regards my switch, I have not switched so much as the climate of Washington has switched and I now have faith in the administration there, under Mr. Kennedy, that there will be proper protection of the Supreme Court decision by the executive branch. Attorney General Robert Kennedy, as you gentlemen know, took an unusual step two days ago when the Department of Justice became a complainant rather than a friend of the court in the case of segregated schools in Virginia. This was the Powell Amendment being enacted by . . . the judicial branch of the government and, therefore, I don't think it is needed in this kind of climate that we have now . . . my correct statement to the press was, not that I would not introduce it, because one of the members of the press asked me if this was definite and I said ninety-nine percent definite, and I still hold that one percent as my escape hatch in case the executive branch does change, but I don't think the executive branch will change.

In May, 1961, even as Powell was luxuriating in the perquisites of his new respectability, a group of Freedom Riders stepped from a bus in Anniston, Alabama, and faced angry crowds determined to contest their attempted use of all-white facilities in the bus terminal. Similar confrontations occurred in other bus stations in Alabama, Georgia, and Mississippi. The Congress of Racial Equality and the Student Non-Violent Coördinating Committee mobilized students as the school year ended and sent them off to demonstrate at beaches, restaurants, parks, and playgrounds. Another summer of protest in the American South was forecast, as history was hastening over the eddies and chicanes of white resistance.

Adam Powell's preoccupation with his own circumstances precluded his taking an active part in those events. Besides maintaining and enlarging his own niche in the Capitol, he had to hold in mind the complexities of New York City politics—a jungle of power factions and personalities. But to Powell it was home and, as the Mayoralty and district leadership elections of 1961 approached, he understood the importance of keeping in good repair those ramparts which guarded his rear, and which allowed him to move with such confidence in the national sector.

Reform had been in the political atmosphere of New York City since the later 1950's. Democratic insurgents, representing a younger generation inspired by Adlai Stevenson, were eager to wrest control of the Manhattan machinery from the oldtimers, led by Carmine DeSapio. The New York press was having a field day unearthing scandals in the administration of Mayor Robert F. Wagner, son of a distinguished New Deal Senator. Wagner had reached the Mayoralty, after a bruising primary in 1953, with the assistance of DeSapio. At the time, the Greenwich Village boss had been Tammany leader for only four years, but his impressive masterminding of Harriman's drive for the Governorship and Wagner's for the Mayoralty gave him pre-eminence among state Democrats. He was, in addition, New York State's National Committeeman and State Secretary of State in Harriman's administration. Now in 1961 DeSapio was, for the reform Democracts, the embodiment of all that was going wrong in New York City. He and Wagner—who was viewed at the time as an honest, well-intentioned, but bumbling administrator—were the targets of sharp criticism from such reform-minded locals as former Governor Herbert Lehman and Mrs. Roosevelt.

When the myth of DeSapio's invincibility was punctured in 1958 with his spectacular failure to purge Powell (and the subsequent general election losses of both the Governorship and a United States Senate seat), and as anger mounted over his increasingly heavy-handed use of his power, reform Democrats were encouraged about the chances for a fusion candidate for Mayor in 1961. Powell, Ray Jones, Mark T. Southall, and Lloyd Everett Dickens had captured four of Harlem's five leadership districts, losing only the district of DeSapio's man, Hulan Jack. Nostalgia for LaGuardia's success as a "fusion" Mayor was strong in Manhattan. The reformers began casting about for a white knight to unhorse Wagner and bring a new order of scandal-free government to the city.

Among the possible contenders in the lists were: William Fitts Ryan, the first New York reformer in Congress; Republican Senator Jacob Javits, a liberal and a vote-getter of demonstrated prowess; the handsome and popular young Republican Congressman from Manhattan's "silk-stocking" 17th Congressional District, John V. Lindsay; Republican State Attorney General Louis Lefkowitz; and a number of other prominent Democracts and Republicans who had declared themselves dedicated to city government "clean as a hound's tooth."

Powell and Ray Jones sat in Harlem and surveyed the downtown maneuvering. They concluded that advantage to each of them could accrue from the developing situation. It was simply a matter, as usual, of reading events correctly, assaying one's position vis-à-vis the shifting power factions and deciding how much one could purchase with the resources in one's political poke. The resources of the Powell-Jones duumvirate were impressive. They needed only to present a solid front and to keep their legions in neat and formidable array behind them. Jones's ambition was no less than accession to the leadership of Tammany Hall, with all the power and patronage perquisites of that office. For public consumption, he stated his goals differently: "A basic re-organization of the rules of the county committee," and a "decentralization of power."

Shortly after the 1959 primary, Powell and Jones had organized their district leaders into what they called the United Democratic Leadership Team with the aim of demonstrating an unprecedented unity in a community which—like other big-city ghettos and slum districts—is more often a political maelstrom. Their biggest gain came on March 22, 1960, when Hulan Jack, the lone Tammany survivor of Powell's 1959 sweep, defected to the United Democratic Leadership Team. It was big news in Harlem. One Harlem newspaper ran an

eight-column bannerline which read: "THEY SAID IT COULDN'T
BE DONE, BUT NEGROES ARE UNITED!" The *Amsterdam News*
reported: "Unity was the keynote and action was the watch-
word Wednesday as Harlem awakened to find that Negroes in
New York had been welded together under Hulan Jack and
Adam Clayton Powell into one of the most united, power-
packed political packages in the entire nation." The unity
shown by the Negro leaders surprised political circles all over
the state. The move was virtually unprecedented in Negro
political circles. Everyone downtown and uptown agreed that
if the unity were maintained it could lead to unprecedented
gains for the Negro. As one veteran Harlem leader put it,
"White people kept kicking us around and now they have
done for us what we couldn't do for ourselves—they have
united us."

Actually, Hulan Jack's sudden urge toward unity was not
entirely altruistic. Like Powell (whose income tax trial had
been in progress at that moment), Jack found himself in
trouble with the law, caught up in conflict-of-interest charges
over a $5,500 painting job on his apartment which allegedly
was paid for by a New York slumlord who was in occasional
difficulty with the city housing authority. Jack was in danger
of losing (and subsequently did lose) his $25,000-a-year job as
borough president of Manhattan as a result of the disclosures.
He was thus one of the crosses which Mayor Wagner had to
bear on his trip to the Golgotha of a third term past grum-
bling reformers. He was, in addition, an embarrassment to
DeSapio.

So Jack took refuge in the new Harlem team. Powell
privately was contemptuous of Jack's handling of the conflict-of-interest disclosures, but publicly embraced him. Just
as Powell had claimed that the federal government tax case
against him was racially-motivated, he invoked the same accusation on Jack's behalf. At a joint press conference to an-

nounce the merger, staged in the borough president's office, Powell said that his group "had been working toward this end" for some time, and that there had been "no ultimatum and no capitulation." Any acrimonious exchanges between the two men in the hot primaries of 1958 and 1959 had been "wiped out of our thinking and our minds," said Powell. Included in the merger, although not announced at the press conference, was an arrangement as to whom the team would back for judgeships. It resolved a dilemma for Wagner and DeSapio, who had not reached agreement on whether to work out judgeship nominations with Powell or with Jack.

Confident now that he was advancing from a position of even greater strength, Powell threw down loud complaints about the status of Negro patronage in New York. Negroes supplied 20 percent of the Democratic vote in Manhattan, he said, but got only five percent of the jobs. So confident was he, in fact, that he included in his catalogue of economic miscarriages a complaint that no other politician in the state and, perhaps, the nation, would have dared to mention: Negroes were not getting their fair share of the illegal numbers racket "handle" in Harlem. Police were driving out Negro "bankers" and "runners" in the policy racket, he insisted, while protecting Italians (presumably Mafiosi) who paid high fees for protection. From the pulpit of Abyssinian Baptist, Powell declared: "Until the day when numbers is wiped out in Harlem, I am going to fight for the Negro having the same chance as an Italian." He said that the white policy bankers were "pauperizing Harlem" by taking $50 million a year out of the community. Powell claimed that Harlem ought to be allowed to retain within its boundaries a larger share of the profits.

Similarly, he charged that Wagner was not enforcing laws banning discrimination on work done by city contractors. "The building trades union and the craft unions in general are the largest group of employment discriminators in America," he said; ". . . the employment picture of New York's 850,000 Negroes is but little different from what it was in January, 1950."

By his conspicuous discontent, Powell announced to the New York Democrats that in the all-important primaries of 1961 he would be the man to treat with; that he would entertain suggestions from all comers—be they regular or reform—about how to get more jobs for Negroes; that if any bargains for Negro betterment happened to coincide with advantage for himself, the coincidence would not be held against the bargain. There was always the background possibility that enough of DeSapio's district leaders might be defeated by reformers to give Powell's team a balance of power in the Hall, at least on some issues.

Peculiar mathematics is involved in calculating factional strength in Tammany. Each of Manhattan's 16 Assembly Districts provides the Hall with one vote, but the party has divided the Assembly Districts into executive districts comprising variously a whole, a half, or a third of an Assembly District. As a result, there are 33 executive districts, each of which elects two leaders. Each leader has a fractional vote depending on how his Assembly District has been carved up, if at all. If an Assembly District is not fractionalized into two or more executive districts, then the party voters go to a primary to choose two leaders, one male and one female, to represent the entire Assembly District as a single executive district. The two leaders, together, then have one vote. If the Assembly District is subdivided into *two* executive districts, four leaders are chosen, each with one-fourth vote. And, if the Assembly District is subdivided into three executive districts, then the local voters elect six leaders, each with a one-sixth vote. This incredible system is not designed to help the rank-and-file voter understand how his party makes decisions. Rather, it abets the professional politician in manipulation of party control. In New York, the relatively few Democrats who bother to involve themselves in clubhouse politics are the only ones who know what a district leader primary election is all about. Prior to the reform challenge to Tammany and prior also to Powell's battle to unite and control the Harlem district leaders, a normal turnout for a district leader primary was 15 percent of enrolled Democrats; subsequently, it often exceeded 50 percent. United Harlem had three votes in Tammany Hall; DeSapio still held a majority of the votes and the reformers had the rest.

Powell and Jones began the tricky business of dealing with the several factions to discover where their own best interests lay. Jones—"The Fox" of many backroom manipulations— went to work on the reformers to convince them he was not a political bad guy. Powell was anathema to them, and Jones was never able to win them to the belief that the Congressman ought to have a role in their plans for the city. Some reformers, however, did look kindly upon Jones. He customarily came up with highly-qualified names for the major patronage plums of judgeship nominations, and his expertise and knowledgeability in city politics was well known. "I have a flair for publicity," Adam Powell had once said, "and Ray Jones is a genius at organization."

But there was an undercurrent of trouble in Harlem. For as long as their interests coincided, Powell and Jones constituted a formidable duumvirate; but, as spring wore into summer, it became increasingly apparent that in the forthcoming elections, their interests would subtly diverge. Powell had little to lose and much to gain by picking a winner, but Jones absolutely needed to be on the winning side if his ambitions in Tammany were to prosper. More crucial than this incipient divergence of their political interests, however, was a more elemental dispute—involving money—the seeds of which had been planted as far back as 1958.

On November 11 of that year, the real estate firm of Brooks, Hampton, Levy and Walker, Inc. (William Hampton was a close aide of Powell) filed an application for sponsorship of a proposed $40,000,000 housing project to be called Esplanade Gardens. Aimed at alleviating a tiny portion of Harlem's housing problems, the project was to be built with the help of a 90 percent city mortgage at four percent and a 50-year tax abatement. On September 21, 1960, a second real estate firm named Balaban-Gordon Company, Inc., filed for the right to develop the same project. Balaban-Gordon then brought into the picture a construction corporation formed to handle the building, one of the directors of which was the wife of Ray Jones's attorney. Another was a former president of Jones's Carver Democratic Club. On December 15, 1958, a member of the City Controller's engineering staff had reported favorably on the application of Brooks, Hampton, Levy and Walker. However, on April 14, 1959, the Brooks group received a letter from one Milton H. Frankfurt, who was director of housing projects in the Controller's office: "In view of existing municipal requirement for property," it said, "we are unable to give present consideration to the location. Should the situation change at some future date, we stand ready to reopen the file." Balaban-Gordon then filed its application and was awarded the sponsorship.

At that point, accusations began to fly that "two powerful political factions" were trying to "reap a harvest" of "consultant" and legal fees in Harlem. The Brooks group charged, and subsequently brought suit to the effect, that Jones had used confidential information and had, in fact, conspired with city officials to get sponsorship of the $40,000,000 project for his friends. All the complex details of the Powell-Jones involvement in city real estate did not become public information for another two years, when the legal skirmishing between the two Harlem giants broke into the open after the March on Washington. But in the summer of 1961, the backstairs wrangling was sufficient to effect schism in the duumvirate—with far-ranging political consequences in New York.

The reformers—led by Mrs. Roosevelt, Governor Lehman, and former Air Force Secretary, Thomas K. Finletter—had still not found their white knight to lance the Wagner-DeSapio axis. Most of the men named as strong possibilities to relieve Wagner of the Mayoralty—the second biggest administrative job in the nation, after the Presidency of the United States—simply pointed out to the reformers that the post was the most thankless, bone-wearying one in all politics, and most often turned out to be a political *cul de sac*. Privately, they admitted that rank-and-file New York City voters were rarely sufficiently shocked at run-of-the-mill scandal to overthrow the regular Democratic nominee; a Seabury investigation—which deposed Mayor James Walker in the early 1930's and produced Fiorello LaGuardia—would be required to fuse the forces of reform. Things just weren't that bad in the city.

The reformers agreed, but were able to circumvent that logic in peculiar fashion. They simply drove a wedge between Wagner and DeSapio. Wagner, with aspirations to the United States Senate—to follow in his illustrious father's footsteps—gave an attentive ear to Mrs. Roosevelt and her colleagues in reform. He knew, as well as they, what had happened to Harriman: DeSapio had been the millstone around his neck and Nelson Rockefeller might one day be President of the United States as a result. Wagner's response was, in effect, to quicken to righteous wrath, and cry, "Throw the rascals out!" Mrs. Roosevelt and her colleagues applauded the "new Wagner" and set about fashioning a campaign based on clean government and anti-machine orientation.

Ray Jones assessed the situation hurriedly and decided to join Wagner and the reformers. That act effectively widened the gap between Powell and Jones, since the reformers would have nothing to do with the Congressman. Still, for bargaining purposes, Powell was maintaining a conspicuous neutrality as late as April 30, when he appeared on a local WCBS-TV program, *New York Forum:*

Q. Do you intend to support Mayor Wagner for re-election?

A. If he runs, yes, I do.

Q. What about the factional dispute between the Mayor and DeSapio?

A. Well, that's their dispute. I have nothing to do with that at all.

Q. You were quoted in the papers also, Congressman, as saying that your decision about backing Mayor Wagner would depend on who was opposing him in the primary.

A. That's true.

Q. . . . before, you stated that you probably would back Mr. DeSapio [for county leader] and, in the same series of questions, you indicated that you would probably back Mr. Wagner. Now, aren't these two gentlemen in conflict, or doesn't it make any difference?

A. It doesn't make any difference to me at all. Wagner is the mayor. If he can't get along with Mr. DeSapio, that's too bad. I get along with him all right. . . .

Q. Are you aligning yourself with Mr. DeSapio?

A. Mr. DeSapio doesn't elect me. I am aligning myself with the people who elect me to get the maximum possible benefit for the people who elect me as district leader.

Q. Congressman, you were reported in the papers as saying that you had settled your differences with Mr. DeSapio. Does this mean as district leader you would be in favor of his reelection as New York County leader [Tammany Hall]?

A. No, it does not, but I haven't seen any other candidate

that captures my imagination and so, until I do see another candidate, why, my candidate is the man that I would support.

Q. Would Mr. [Joseph] Zaretski [then State Senate Minority Leader, and a district leader in Manhattan's Washington Heights] be an appropriate candidate?

A. I think Zaretski would be a very fine candidate. I could think of many people in this town. . . . There are some in my own area, such as Ray Jones or Lloyd Dickens.

Q. Would you prefer any one of these gentlemen to Mr. DeSapio?

A. . . . after all, you know a county leader is someone to bargain with. I would have to see just what the promise would be and what the conditions that they would operate under after they were elected. . . .

Q. Mr. Powell, would you, if a vote were taken today in the executive committee of New York County, would you vote to retain Mr. DeSapio as leader of the executive committee?

A. Oh, yes, I would, very definitely, because the primary is in September. There is no point in switching County leaders now with just a few months left 'til the primary.

Powell continued that sort of backing-and-filling through most of the summer. DeSapio named as the "regular" Democratic candidate, to oppose the incumbent—and insurgent—Mayor, the State Comptroller, Arthur Levitt. Levitt, the only Democrat to survive the Rockefeller landslide of 1958, was reported to be a reluctant candidate. In July, Powell was heard to say, "I'm still uncommitted on the Mayoralty. At present, I'm a neutralist." Nonetheless, he was occasionally contemptuous toward the reform movement, saying that "there is just as much bossism on their part as they charge on the part of others." He did announce his endorsement of Lloyd Dickens—a member of the Harlem United Leadership Team—for the Manhattan Borough Presidency over Edward R. Dudley, a Negro who was then serving out the unfinished term of Hulan Jack following Jack's resignation as a result of the conflict-of-interest charges.

On July 27, Powell showed his hand. He called a press conference in Washington and announced that his man was Levitt. He had settled on Levitt, he declared, "not because Mayor Wagner is not a fine gentleman, but because our city is in grave danger [and needs] a man of more character." There was a "scandal a week" in the city administration, he said. Wagner "can't project his own moral character into the administration of the city," Powell insisted. "I feel Wagner got where he is because of his father, a great man." Describing the Mayor as a "chip off the old block," he added, "I'm confident that this election will be 'goodbye, Mr. Chips.'" Powell discerned a "consistent policy" in the Wagner administration of refusing to make sufficient use of New York's 2,000,000 Negroes and Puerto Ricans in city jobs. Acknowledging that there was "a token commissioner here, a token deputy commissioner there," he added, "There are over a dozen departments in the city of New York without a single Negro or Puerto Rican at a policy-making level." He suggested that he might convene an investigating subcommittee of his House Education and Labor Committee to hear complaints against Wagner's regime on September 5—two days before the primary.

Actually, Powell was one of 17 New York City Congressmen endorsing Levitt as the "regular" Democratic candidate (with only the reform Congressman William Fitts Ryan dissenting). But only the Harlemite's announcement made big headlines, as speculation mounted over the terms of Powell's entente with the DeSapio-Levitt axis. Rumors of great sums of money in the form of contributions to his campaign fund were denied by Powell. No one bothered to deny that should Levitt prevail, Powell would be handed a vast amount of high-echelon patronage in the city.

Asked by a reporter about the schism between him and Ray Jones, Powell said, "Ray and I are friends. He's just picked the wrong candidate. . . . For the time being, he's not on the team."

Besides the Mayoralty, the district leaderships were up once again. In Harlem, Powell, Jones, Southall, Dickens, and Jack would be running against tepid opposition for their old seats (Jones was supporting Dudley for the borough presidency over his "teammate," Lloyd Dickens) and in Greenwich Village, a reformer named James Lanigan was opposing DeSapio for leadership of the Tammanyite's home district. Exuberantly, Powell predicted a two-to-one sweep for Arthur Levitt and, as the election approached, he foresaw similar good fortune for "regular" Democrats all over New York City.

The magnitude of Powell's miscalculation began to be apparent early in the evening on September 7 as the vote returns rolled in. Harlem was going heavily to Wagner. Unable to believe that his influence and persuasiveness had been so totally ineffective, Powell telephoned the NBC News tabulation center and asked for a breakdown of the vote, district by district. What he learned left him uncharacteristically speechless. Harlem had gone to Wagner four-to-one. In addition, DeSapio had lost in his home district, thereby forfeiting the Tammany chieftainship he had held since 1949. Ray Jones's candidate for the borough presidency, Edward Dudley, defeated Lloyd Dickens. The reformers were claiming a "sweep," having won the leaderships in all but one district in which they contested. The Harlem leaders reclaimed their districts easily. When the smoke had cleared, Tammany had a new profile: Harlem, three votes; the reformers six and one-sixth votes; oldline Tammanyites, six and five-sixths votes.

Powell had not only backed the wrong Mayoralty candidate, but was now cut off from his organization ally, Carmine

DeSapio. Ray Jones, on the other hand, was now the most important party organization leader in Manhattan, and the most experienced professional on Wagner's team.

New York City Negroes—knowing that Jones had been the principal strategist in Wagner's impressive victory—demanded that he be given the fruits of his labor, the job he had coveted for so long. The *Amsterdam News* said, "The only thing standing between J. Raymond Jones and the leadership of Tammany Hall is the color of his skin—and we don't think that should be used to bar him from the job he has so richly earned!" Jones himself said, "I believe that I deserve consideration because of my service in the campaign for the Mayor and my record of forty years of service to the party."

In spite of their differences during the campaign, Adam Powell was professional politician enough to agree: "If Ray Jones were a white man, he would be county leader by now, whether he was from the regular or reform clubs." Should Wagner fail to name Jones as his choice for the post, said Powell, it would be a "lynching, Northern style. What is happening in New York County today is bossism worse than Carmine DeSapio ever dared to try."

Wagner showed obvious reluctance to hand Jones the leadership of Tammany Hall. Jones, after all, did not convey the proper reform image: he was too professional, too knowing, too burdened with past associations and causes to satisfy the reformers' notion of a leader. In addition, the Negro press speculated that Wagner was unwilling to have both the borough presidency and the County leadership in the hands of Negroes. He tested Jones's mood by offering him a specially-created liaison post which would give "The Fox" a private avenue of influence between Harlem and City Hall. Jones refused.

Other influential Negroes rallied to Jones's cause. Roy Wilkins said, "It is regrettable that ethnic considerations have

entered into the discussions. In a political structure, it is inevitable that certain factors will have weight in a party decision. Race and religion should not be among these." Dr.
Kenneth Clark was more outspoken. "This is incredible," he
said. "It is sheer racism under the guise of expediency and I
call upon the Mayor and all so-called liberals and reform
Democrats to repudiate this immediately." Church and civic
groups in Harlem bombarded Wagner with telegrams demanding he publicly support Jones. But to no avail.

"The Fox" simply was not acceptable to the new breed of
Democrats. An East Side early reformer named Edward Cos-
tikyan *was* acceptable, and to him went the prize—although
the Tammany leadership would not soon, if ever again, con-
fer on its owner the sort of power it had symbolized in De-
Sapio's hands, and in the hands of every old-fashioned big city
boss before him. It appeared that those days were over.

Like the good soldier he was, Jones bowed to the dictates
of his party. He accepted the special liaison assignment which
Wagner described to him in a letter: "Without prejudicing
the privilege of organization leaders to have direct access to
me, you will be the ordinary channel of communications between me and that leadership on citywide matters. In addition, you will be my representative and chief planner for such
city-wide organizational activities as registration, petition-
gathering, etc., and, of course, you will perform such other
duties as I may assign or request." Wagner also assured Jones
that Negroes and Puerto Ricans—who now comprised one-
quarter of the city's population and voter strength—would be
hired for city jobs in increasing numbers.

A few months later, the New York Democrats staged for
Jones one of the most awesome testimonial dinners the city
had seen in years. A reporter arriving at the Waldorf-Astoria's
grand ballroom that evening was astonished at the array of
political "big muscle" on the dais.

"Why all the horsepower?" he inquired of a colleague.

"It's Ray's consolation prize," he was told.

Honorary chairman of the affair was Mayor Wagner himself (who had cruised to victory in the general election over Republican State Attorney General Louis Lefkowitz). The honorary co-chairmen included such people as Mrs. Roosevelt, James Farley, Herbert Lehman, Deputy Mayor Edward F. Cavanagh, Jr., and City Council President Paul Screvane. The speakers were Dr. Kenneth Clark, Ralph M. Paiewonsky (Governor of the Virgin Islands, Jones's birthplace); Mayor Wagner; and the principal speaker, no less a figure than John M. Bailey, chairman of the Democratic National Committee. Powell was listed among the speakers, but sent a congratulatory telegram instead. The program quoted Theodore H. White's estimate of Jones as a political leader: "Ray Jones is a man of distinguished mind and great learning. He can play it tough, or way up high where men speak of America's ultimate purpose. How he uses the power of the Negro in American politics may determine our culture for years to come." President Kennedy sent two close aides to represent him—associate press secretary Andrew Hatcher, and Louis Martin, Deputy Democratic Chairman, both Negroes—and followed up with a telegram which claimed that Jones's "political skills and energy have helped open the gates of opportunity to all men."

Ray Jones demurely accepted this gift of good will and political camaraderie. It all comprised in subtle fashion a promissory note which would be paid in full after the 1964 Presidential elections, when Jones achieved his vaunted ambition to be the leader of Tammany Hall. His old sidekick, Adam Powell, was still—in those palmy days of early 1962—the most powerful Negro politician on the national scene, while Jones was New York State's top Negro Democrat. But

Jones suspected in his heart of hearts that Harlem was not big enough for both of them. As usual, he was right.

As the New York Democrats were going about their house-keeping, the cauldron of Birmingham—with its police dogs, firehoses, and the bomb-killing of four Negro school children —was barely twelve months away. After it, no politician engaged in the struggle for Negro rights would ever be quite the same.

12. Fallen Archangel

"Take a Congressman with a record of tax troubles with Uncle Sam, frequent absenteeism from his Capital post, uncompromising fixation on a single cause, one-time desertion of his party, and a reputation for playboy high-jinks," wrote the *Wall Street Journal* on April 4, 1961, during Powell's period of high good grace with the New Frontier. "Propel this gentleman into a position of high responsibility among his party's legislative leaders, where the White House must count heavily on his ability and willingness to buckle down to hard work as a team player. What's to be expected—'statesmanship' or sabotage?"

The *Wall Street Journal* had to conclude that Congressman Powell was delivering a sizable amount of the former and no discernible quantity of the latter, and added that "while it's too early to tell just how the drama will turn out, there are signs that a new, more responsible Powell may be replacing the old model, with results pleasing indeed to the New Frontiersman."

There was a consensus that Powell was now in possession of the chance he had been waiting for all his life, and that he was determined to prove that—given a task and the confidence of his party leaders—he could be as responsible as any man.

He was meeting now regularly with House Speaker Rayburn and his aides, with cabinet officers Goldberg and Ribicoff on problems of labor and education, and, occasionally, with the President. His natural liberal tendencies promised to produce for the administration better bargains than had Congressman Barden. A Rayburn lieutenant said privately that he considered Powell "one of the dozen smartest men in the House. He's the type you don't tangle with until you've done your homework." George Meany, however, in spite of Powell's impeccable pro-labor voting record, remained implacable, and pointedly stayed away from Powell's minimum wage hearings. He was still feeling "terrible" over the Harlemite's accession to the chairmanship of Education and Labor.

Kennedy's strategists in the civil rights area were careful to keep Powell informed of their plans. Even the Congressman's social life among Washington officialdom was improving; he found himself on a growing number of invitation lists. One hostess said: "Adam is one of the most delightful men to be around you'll ever meet." And another remarked, "He could charm a band of Ku Klux Klanners."

Even as this Era of Good Feeling was in progress, Powell continued to shuttle to Puerto Rico when his work load allowed. Rumors persisted that he was growing increasingly attached to the idea of becoming Governor of Puerto Rico, or—assuming the Commonwealth attained statehood in the foreseeable future—one of its two United States Senators. Such an aspiration would not have been uncharacteristic; he had been in the House for 17 years at the time, and that sort of tenure for a man of his demonstrated restlessness was considered remarkable in itself.

Puerto Rico was a "perfumed colony," he said, and deserved to be upgraded from a "colonial" appendage to more equal status, particularly since its residents were American citizens. In February, 1962—at the same time he was processing important New Frontier legislation, such as the Man-power Training and Development bill—Powell introduced a resolution in favor of giving Puerto Ricans the right to vote in Presidential elections. It was a gesture calculated to earn him good will on the island, since enfranchisement would require nothing less than a constitutional amendment. At about the same time, Powell announced that, while he would stand for re-election in the fall of 1962, he expected it would be his last term in Congress; he would not run in 1964, he insisted. During the same press conference, he let it be known that a new entity, the Adam Clayton Powell Foundation, had been established "for the benefit of needy Puerto Ricans in New York." All these elements combined to create the illusion of a shift in Powell's traditional concerns, bringing the problems of Puerto Rico and the Puerto Ricans in his own constituency well into the foreground.

To Governor Luis Muñoz Marín of Puerto Rico, who was involved in delicate maneuverings to improve Puerto Rico's "commonwealth" status vis-a-vis the United States, Powell's intrusion was an unwanted complication of his own plans for the island. Muñoz felt that Puerto Rico was not yet ready for the financial burdens of statehood, and would in fact, never be ready, since its per capita income was less than a third that of Mississippi, despite impressive gains resulting from his "Operation Bootstrap." Nonetheless, a statehood movement had been gaining popularity on the island, and its partisans—who comprised the island's statehood party, which is allied to the mainland's Republican party—had polled one-third of the vote in 1960 against Muñoz. It was with the Republican Statehood Party of Puerto Rico that Powell aligned himself.

Relations between Powell and Muñoz had never been good. This grew, originally, out of Powell's rather heavy-handed requests for the use of an official Puerto Rican Commonwealth car; Muñoz never complained publicly about Powell's request, but privately expressed displeasure on the matter to his staff. Subsequent disagreements were caused by real estate squabbles. An angered Powell began sniping at Muñoz—but always from good cover, since Muñoz's personal popularity in Puerto Rico was enormous. The Harlemite could not have chosen a more formidable adversary: son of Luis Muñoz Rivera, the "George Washington" of Puerto Rico; four-time Governor of the island; and architect of the much acclaimed "Operation Bootstrap," which was bringing the island out of the depths of economic despair. In the period between the two world wars, Puerto Rico was considered the social cesspool of the Caribbean. As a United States "possession" since its acquisition from Spain after the Spanish-American War, it was little more than a 19th Century-style colony with all the abuses which that status suggests. Historically, the island was treated somewhat better as a Spanish colony than as an American possession. The Spaniards granted the island a Charter of Autonomy in 1897 —negotiated by Muñoz's father—which gave Puerto Ricans parliamentary control over internal and some external affairs. The subsequent civil government instituted by the Americans failed to provide anything but the most elemental programs and services. It was a long step backward from the Spanish Charter of Autonomy, Muñoz Marín said later.

Muñoz Marín was 20 years old in 1917 when Puerto Ricans were granted citizenship. Later, he ran for the Puerto Rican Senate and became its president in 1942. He created the Popular Democratic Party and campaigned on the slogan, "Bread, Land, and Liberty." But, as Muñoz matured and attained an economic sophistication to match his political expertise, he realized that independence for his homeland would carry serious disadvantages. He determined to structure a new kind of relationship with the United States—one which would assure islanders their self-government, but which also would exploit many of the advantages of statehood, while incurring few of its disadvantages, such as federal tax burdens. After Muñoz became the first elected Governor in 1948, he worked out a unique "commonwealth" arrangement which was passed in Washington as Public Law 600 in 1950, and ratified by a plebiscite of Puerto Ricans in 1951. In the succeeding decade, he brought Puerto Rico out of its stricken, near-desperate state to a condition of solvency. "Today, Puerto Rico is a land transformed," say reports prepared by the First National City Bank of New York. "Puerto Rico has today one of the fastest growing economies in the world, with a real growth rate running well ahead of those currently reported by the European Common Market countries. . . . The island's standard of living . . . [is now] exceeded in the Western Hemisphere only by the United States and Canada. . . ."

Muñoz achieved outstanding international repute as a result of these gains. He was one of a community of rising Democratic leaders in the Caribbean and the southern hemisphere—men like Rómulo Betancourt of Venezuela and José Figueres of Costa Rica.

Now, Adam Powell, with his luxurious ocean-front villa at Cerro Gordo and his marital connections with rich and influential islanders, was insinuating himself into the life of Puerto Rico. Just as he was an irritant—often a valuable one— in mainland interracial affairs, he was now undertaking a similar role in the inter-relationships of San Juan and Washington, D. C. But there was a difference. He was now not tilting at white controllers who were discriminating against him as a symbol of Negro discontent. He was instead sallying forth against a man who had himself known economic and social discrimination as the spokesman of a downtrodden citizenry—a man who similarly was an eloquent leader of a mass of impoverished people.

By May, 1962, Muñoz and Powell were in public disagreement over the question of a plebiscite to determine Puerto Rico's legal status. Powell was stumping for a vote between simple alternatives—statehood and independence. Muñoz strongly favored a plebiscite offering three choices: statehood, independence, and improved commonwealth status. Powell's objective was clear: in any vote between statehood and independence, statehood inevitably would win. But Muñoz was firm in his resolve—and his position did, in fact, mirror the consensus on the island—that Puerto Rico would not request statehood until its standard of living more closely approached that of the United States.

Powell was insistent. In New York on July 14, he demanded statehood as soon as possible. "Now, not in ten years, nor in one year, nor tomorrow, but now." He importuned Puerto Ricans: "Arise with all the dignity and strength that God has given you as a people and proclaim: We begin to battle for statehood, right now. . . . Without any doubt, statehood is the only solution. . . . The sentiment for statehood for Puerto Rico has gained ground among members of the Congress of the United States. . . ." He referred again to his resolution calling for presidential voting rights for islanders as a "first step."

While Powell and Muñoz were locked in public combat over their respective goals, the *Independistas*—fewer in number than either of the other two activist elements on the island —also chose the Harlemite as a target. On July 19, Juan Mari-Bras, leader of the *Independistas*, declared, "The fight of the [*Independistas*] of Puerto Rico against Congressman Adam Clayton Powell will continue without letup." At this time, the group was picketing Powell's residence at Cerro Gordo, against the opposition of the Puerto Rican Department of Justice, some of whose functionaries felt that the picketing of a private residence was illegal.

On July 16, a small group of dissidents marched on Powell's home, which was occupied at the time only by his wife and new son, Adam Clayton Powell Diago, who had been born a few months earlier. They threw stones and fruit at the house and shouted demands that he depart the island. In Washington, Powell angrily charged that the attackers were the same group of nationalist-terrorists who had fired shots across the floor of the House of Representatives in 1950 and whose followers had tried to assassinate President Truman—and succeeded in killing one of his White House guards—at Blair House on November 1, 1950. He appealed to President Kennedy for protection. "But I have also taken steps of my own to protect my family," said the Congressman. "I have dispatched a private detective there from New York and he will remain with my family until I can go there a week from Friday. Yvette, whom I wished to come here immediately, has instead applied for a gun permit. She was calm during the whole thing. She felt she had little to fear from a 'courageous' group of hoodlums who would attack a defenseless woman and her infant son under the darkness of early morning."

The dissidents also phoned San Juan newspapers with the message, "We have a bullet for Powell—in New York, Washington or Puerto Rico." On August 5, La Prensa of New York received a cable dispatch from San Juan describing a bitter "war of nerves" that was in progress on the island, with regard to the prospective changes in Puerto Rico's legal status. Nationalists exploded bombs and distributed threatening letters, one of which said, "Death to Congressman Adam Clayton Powell. . . . The bullet that is going to kill him is already in the gun."

The civil unrest and the continuing threats on his life failed to mute Powell's insistence that statehood was the only path for the island to follow. He was probably right in his assertion that at least some of the nationalist activity was Communist-inspired and that "Puerto Rico could become another Cuba" should those extremists prevail. He called the three-choice plebiscite "useless" and a "waste of money." It would be "absolutely absurd" to expand the commonwealth concept, he said. "Whoever, including Governor Muñoz Marín, tries to tell the people that Puerto Rico would have more independence and the Congress less to say, would be saying words of deceit and hypocrisy, and lacking honesty."

Powell also involved himself, purposefully, in a language-teaching controversy on the island. He took the position that teaching of Spanish well—with English often taught poorly in the form of Puerto Rican dialect—in the island schools was contributing to a rising anti-Americanism and to the erosion of loyalty to the United States. Powell invoked his position as Chairman of Education and Labor in the dispute. He suggested that Congress might hold back federal funds for school aid on grounds that the language methods represented a trend away from Americanization.

The *San Juan Star* criticized Powell for his position and also viewed dimly a report he had prepared for the Interior and Insular Affairs Committee recommending English instruction courses as a means of insuring "loyalty" to the mainland. The *Star* defended the island's educational system and took that occasion to chastise Powell: "It is highly improper . . . for the chairman of a congressional committee to use his position to influence and impose methods, standards and guidelines upon education in Puerto Rico. Education is purely a local affair, in which Mr. Powell and Congress have no place. They should assume a role of non-intervention, telling the people of Puerto Rico to decide their own wishes with respect to the education of their children. . . . As to the question of 'loyalty' of the residents of Puerto Rico to the nation of their citizenship, Mr. Powell ought to examine the record of Puerto Ricans in the last two wars."

Powell did not give up his fight over the teaching of English, however. As late as December 16, 1963, *El Diario-La*

Prensa was editorializing: "On the island, polemics over the advisability of making obligatory the use and instruction of English in public schools is a topic which has turned many political leaders against Muñoz Marín. However, within the government itself are heard voices opposed to making the use and teaching of English obligatory in public education." So, once again, Powell had chosen a sensitive spot in the political armor of the great and powerful Muñoz. *El Diario-La Prensa* concluded: "At the root of all this action, observers of insular politics have not overlooked the fact that Powell was searching for a defect in the administration of the program by local authorities, in order to convert his investigation into a political argument against Muñoz Marín."

But no action on the plebiscite seemed likely in 1962. So Powell turned his attention to matters closer to home. There was the effort being made by himself and other Harlem district leaders to head off a redistricting attempt by the county committee which would include more Negro and Puerto Rican voters in the "silk stocking" 17th Congressional District, contiguous to Harlem on the south. There was also an investigation of the International Ladies Garment Workers Union, which the House Education and Labor Committee hoped to convene. In Washington, an important vote would be taken soon on the poll tax, a subject of vital concern to the nation's Negroes. At a press conference on August 8, at which he discussed some of these matters, a reporter asked Powell if by chance he had any plans to sail for Europe later that morning on the *Queen Mary,* which at that moment was poised at a Hudson River pier. Not at all, said Powell. He *had* a reservation earlier, but had cancelled it because of the press of important business.

One hour and fifteen minutes later, the *Queen Mary* sailed for Europe and Powell was on it. Asked for an explanation, Powell's lawyer said that the Congressman had misled the press out of fear for his personal safety arising from the Puerto Rican nationalist attack on his villa at Cerro Gordo. A hurried investigation by reporters turned up the fact that Powell was not alone on the luxury liner. Accompanying him were two members of his Washington staff, each of whom happened to be young, attractive, and female: Corrine Huff, 21, his $95-a-week receptionist who had been Miss Ohio of 1960, and a runner-up in the Miss Universe contest; and Mrs. Tamara J. Wall, 31, a brunette divorcee who was employed at $194 a week as an associate labor counsel for Education and Labor. The three of them would return six weeks later, around September 21, said a Powell spokesman, after studying equal employment opportunities for women in the Common Market countries.

Powell's life had been filled with more controversy, perhaps, than any other senator or congressman then on the scene; but the storm that was to erupt around him as a result of his European junket with the two pretty aides was more severe by far than any previous imbroglio. It effectively changed the course of his public life. To Powell, it was just another respite—one of many he had always managed to fit in among periods of professional exertion. But this time higher issues asserted themselves—issues such as the dignity and good reputation of the House of Representatives as a deliberative institution; the image of President Kennedy's New Frontier and its resolve to establish an early and impressive legislative record; recent disclosures of nepotism which had sensitized the House to tendentious accusations about its integrity. Powell, on the high seas, could not have imagined the virulence of the reaction to this tour. He was enjoying a good press at that moment, after all, and might reasonably expect the residue of good feeling flowing from his 18-month-old period of industry to carry him through the mere six weeks of his sojourn. The State Department had coöperated in arranging the junket and sent a cable to its embassies in London, Paris, Rome, Athens and Venice:

"Congressman Adam Clayton Powell, Chairman Committee Education and Labor, accompanied by Mrs. Tamara J. Wall and Miss Corrine Huff staff members traveling Western Europe accordance following itinerary: August 8 sailing *Queen Mary* arriving Southhampton 8/13; Paris 8/16; Venice 8/20; Rome 8/23; Athens 8/27; Delphi 8/30; sailing *Leonardo da Vinci* 9/15 from Gibraltar. Arrival times and flights forwarded when firm. Provisions handbook congressional travel apply. Codel [cable abbreviation for congressional delegation] authorized use local currencies 19FT561 [counterpart] funds. Meet assist appoint control officers. London request three tickets 8/14, 15 best shows playing, except Broadway plays [Powell had already seen all the Broadway offerings]. Paris-Codel desires use U. S. Army car and chauffeur. Reserve three for first show and dinner best table Lido 8/16. Venice—if the film festival going on request three tickets 8/20 or 21. Codel also requests use consulate's motorboat [for the Grand Canal]. Delphi-Codel inquires whether boat trip about six days around islands possibility. Possible visit Rhodes." (Counterpart funds represent an economic novelty arising out of the United States foreign aid program. Countries receiving certain forms of American aid—especially the large-scale distribution of surplus agricultural commodities—make payment in their own currency. These payments are accumulated to the credit of the United States for reinvestment in improvement projects inside those countries. Five to ten percent of counterpart money in each country is available to the United States for support of its various missions there and, under an amendment to the Mutual Security Act of 1953, members of Congress may draw on this portion of the account for official travel within each of the countries. The State Department manages all this, but has nothing to say about whether or not a congressman will get the funds, or how he will spend them. The accounting for counterpart funds is haphazard at best and the "club rules" of Congress preclude any legislator being challenged on his use of them.)

In London, the Powell party checked into the Cumberland Hotel for a nine-day stay and went to the theater each evening in a limousine provided by the American Embassy. Pushing on to Paris, they stopped at the Hotel Crillon in the Place de la Concorde and included in their three-day stay a visit to the famous Lido night club—known for its nude showgirls—on the Champs Elysées. In Venice, the trio attended the film festival and toured the Grand Canal in a gondola. An Embassy official met them at the Rome airport and escorted them to the Hotel Excelsior on the Via Veneto. Three days later they were en route to Greece, where they visited Athens, the ruins at Adelphi, and embarked on a six-day cruise of the Aegean Islands. Then Powell and Miss Huff flew to Madrid, after arranging to rendezvous with Mrs. Wall in Gibraltar in time for the September 15 sailing of the *Leonardo da Vinci*.

By that time, news of his idyll was circulating in the United States, and his colleagues in Congress were honing their wrath to a keen edge in expectation of his return. The newspaper-reading public, which was following his progress through Europe's luxury retreats with a mixture of bemusement and indignation, discussed the episode over their dinner tables and, for the first time in his professional life, Powell found himself the subject of a great national colloquy. *The New York Times* lost its legendary equipoise in considering the Powell journey. An editorial on September 6 entitled "Powell's Shameless Junket," complained:

"In the midst of the important closing period of the Congressional session, when a record of accomplishment vs. do-nothingism is in the balance, the chairman of a major com-

mittee of the House is traveling about Europe on a frivolous
junket. Almost needless to say, this is Adam Clayton Powell
. . . who annually vies with [Congressman Charles] Buckley
of the Bronx for the dishonor of being among the most absent
members of Congress.

"The reckless, irresponsible conduct of Mr. Powell is a
disgrace to the people of his district, to the United States
Congress and to the Kennedy administration, which to its
discredit sent Secretaries Ribicoff and Goldberg to New York
last year to attend a Powell glorification dinner.

"We say it is time for the people of Harlem to wake up,
quit making a hero out of this man who holds in such contempt his obligations in public office. . . . As for the House
of Representatives and the Kennedy administration, have
they no discipline for a member, and especially a committee
chairman, who runs away to Europe for six weeks on idle
whimsy like this 'inquiry' just at a time when Congress is
(belatedly) trying to get down to serious business."

Powell—whose imperviousness to criticism of his personal
behavior was well-known—was stunned by the vigor of the
outcry at home. In an uncharacteristic gesture, he cut short
his trip by two weeks, left Miss Huff in Madrid, and flew
home to Puerto Rico on September 6. His wife, whom reporters described as looking "tired and distraught," met him
at the airport in San Juan and they went into seclusion immediately at Cerro Gordo with their infant son. (The villa
still was under 24-hour guard following the extremists' attacks.)

Powell remained in Puerto Rico for two weeks before returning quietly to Washington.

A New York Congressman recalled Powell's first appearance on the floor of the House after the trip: "We didn't
know he was back. He was standing over at the door, where
the Speaker sometimes stands. There was a quorum call and

he stepped forward to answer. There was a ripple of laughter —yes, snickers. The laughing was spontaneous and yes—it was derisive. It was a punishment."

A few days later, Representative Omar Burleson, Democrat of Texas, and chairman of the House Administration Committee, gratuitously criticized some of Powell's committee consultants on Education and Labor and suggested he was ready to block the funding that kept them on staff. Powell rightly perceived it as the first lash of the whip.

Instinctively, he turned to the source of his power for succor: the Negro community which had closed ranks around him so often in the past in moments of beleaguerment from white America. He called a meeting of ministers and civic leaders at Abyssinian Baptist and told them that his plight was an observable result of racist tendencies in Washington, D. C.; that most other congressmen regularly did as much and were never flagellated in public for their actions; that an unwritten double standard existed in American politics which decreed that Negro leaders be "purer than Caesar's wife" while no such burden lay upon whites. The ministers—and all of Harlem, indeed—were predisposed to agree with Powell's conclusions. The reaction of black America to the Congressman's grand tour of Europe—a tour which wooed many whites to the belief that, at last, the Negro community would have to agree that Adam Powell was wholly irresponsible and deserving of the ultimate chastisement—found its most concise expression in a page-one editorial in the *Amsterdam News,* an essentially conservative and serious journal: "We do not agree with everything Congressman Adam Clayton Powell does . . . but we do agree . . . that he is entitled to all the privileges and rights that pertain to other Congressmen." The editorial denounced the House Administration Committee for singling out Powell's committee payroll for scrutiny, while not taking similar action against other chairmen.

"We would like to know why? Why Adam Powell?" the editorial asked. "We suspect we know the answer!" Powell, in taking a trip abroad with two members of his staff, had not done any more than many other Congressmen, said the *Amsterdam News,* and as long as he was Harlem's man in the House of Representatives, he had a claim on its perquisites.

Once again, the great wagon train of Negro loyalty to Powell, as a symbol of the most vital and personal aspirations of so many of them, was drawn in a circle around him—to the dismay and bewilderment of white America.

As Powell well knew, the root of his predicament was not so much in racism as in the fact that he had cast a strong public light on certain well-guarded congressional privileges. House members were, and are, intensely protective of their institution's reputation and rituals. This proprietary sense in a congressman increases directly with his seniority and is best observed in many Southern conservatives who prosper and age in the House because of the familial loyalty and stability of their constituencies. When one of them finally becomes a committee chairman, this proprietary sense is at its most intense; he is now, in a literal sense, a keystone in the American political system—invested with influence and perhaps power, but always with the rewards of his constancy. Privilege is accessible to him in various guises—lobbyists with their formidable expense accounts; the many jobs which are his to dispense; access to counterpart funds for travel abroad, and scarcely any inhibition to his use of them except his own conscience. Happily, the House is almost infinitely forgiving; it displays an avuncular understanding of the foibles of its members. It is understood, for example, that congressmen—including chairmen—sometimes yield to their temptations, but that it is bad manners for other members to carp about it; that the offense lies in public displays of privilege—or public abuses of privilege. Powell had not only committed

the unforgivable sin, but did so in a manner so flagrant that
the House's capacity for infinite forgiveness could not be invoked in his behalf.

Thus, Powell's action transcended considerations of race—
which is not to say that many Southern legislators were not
secretly jubilant at the prospect of cutting down this "up-
pity Negro" whose abrasiveness had discomfited them for so
long.

For a brief time, certain congressmen discussed the possibility of an official censure vote against Powell, but wisely
gave it up at the realization that it would generate a torrent
of protest inside black America. The fact that Powell was a
Negro almost certainly preserved him from such an indignity
—a peculiar and ironic working-out of what he himself had
often called "the advantages of the disadvantages."

At all events, the House's worst fears were realized: Powell's dereliction set off a flurry of journalistic probes into the
habits of congressmen. *The New York Times* found that the
House Committee on Foreign Affairs had sent no fewer than
thirty of its members and staff employees to Europe and
South and Central America in 1962 alone. "Surprisingly,"
said the *Times,* "none seems to have visited any part of Asia,
the Far East, or Africa, despite the many problems that face
the United States there." The whole question of nepotism
was raked up again, and the most oft-cited "horrible example" was Powell's own employment of his Puerto Rican wife
at an annual government salary of $12,974.

Adding to his woes, a new Commissioner of Internal Revenue, Mortimer Caplin, charged Powell with "deficient payments" on his income tax for the years 1949 through 1955.
The deficiency was $26,005, said the IRS, and the total debt—
including penalties—was $40,981. ("HO HUM," a Harlem news-
paper headlined the story. "THEY'RE PROBING ADAM POWELL'S
TAXES AGAIN!") It was a civil suit this time, not a criminal

one, and the IRS reported they had been seeking a settlement with Powell since the previous April, but with no success. The IRS petition for payment along with Powell's denial that any deficiency existed were placed on the docket of the United States Tax Court in Washington.

In the midst of these travails, Powell ran for his ninth term in the House—although he conducted no formal campaign—and polled almost 70 percent of the vote. The election took place barely two months after his return from the European junket.

Then, on February 5, 1963, in an unprecedented attack by a member of one chamber of the Congress on a member of the other, Senator John J. Williams, Republican of Delaware, denounced Powell by name on the Senate floor—and the Kennedy administration by association with him. "Today I wish to call to the attention of the Senate the loose manner in which the administration has been shoveling the taxpayers' money out to Congressman Adam Clayton Powell," Williams said. "During the past five months various agencies of the Government have been scrambling around to see who could give Mr. Powell the most favorable deal. Last summer on the front page of every newspaper were accounts of Mr. Powell's European vacation with his lady friends, where he attended all the night spots of the European capitals on a tax-paid junket that was financed through the State Department."

Williams went on to complain that other agencies seemed determined not to be outdone. "For example, on August 1, 1962—just four months prior to the election—the Department of Health, Education and Welfare made an outright grant of $250,000 to Mr. Powell and his associates . . . allegedly . . . for the purpose of developing the nucleus of a domestic peace corps. The fact that a domestic peace corps, as yet, has not been approved by Congress did in no way deter the Department from financing such a project." The Health, Education, and Welfare Department, Williams pointed out, had tapped an appropriation which had been approved under Public Law 87-274 for the study of juvenile delinquency. For the New Frontier to authorize such a grant was an "insult to the intelligence" of America's taxpayers, the Senator said.

Williams did not shrink from driving home his sword. "Mr. Powell, whose escapades have been on the front page of every newspaper for several months, could well be recognized as an authority on 'adult delinquency,' but most certainly he is not the caliber of man who the American people would want to set an example for the youth of the country." He then launched on a carefully-detailed itemization of Powell's involvement with federally-supported housing. "I cite an example of Mr. Powell's influence with this administration under the Housing and Home Finance Agency. Long-term loans totalling nearly $11,000,000 at interest rates as low as three and one-eighth percent have been approved to Mr. Powell and his associates. Three loans totalling $10,836,000 have been approved for the construction of a housing development and the purchase of hotels, the total cost of which, based on the administration's own records, was to be only $8,588,000. Not only were these loans sufficient to cover one hundred percent of the acquisition cost of the properties in question, but, in one instance, the loan approved was for exactly double the acquisition price. . . ."

As he spoke, Williams put into the record copies of letters from the Housing and Home Finance Agency which denied that final approval had been given to federal insurance on the loans. "In addition to approving these loans," he went on, "the Administration gave its support to H. R. 12752, introduced on August 1, 1962, the sole purpose of which was to exempt from all District of Columbia real estate taxes one of the properties listed above—Hotel 2400 in Washington, D. C."

The hotel Williams named was one for which he claimed Powell would get double the acquisition price. The Senator inserted in the record the House Resolution he had cited, one part of which read: "[It] is hereby exempt from all real property taxation so long as the same is owned by and used to carry out the purposes of the Adam Clayton Powell Foundation, Inc., and is not used for commercial purposes."

Williams then turned his guns on Powell's recently-aggravated tax problems: ". . . while these three agencies [State Department; Health, Education and Welfare; and the Housing and Home Finance Agency] were shoveling out the taxpayers' dollars to Mr. Powell and his numerous operations, we find that the Treasury Department, over on the other side of the street, was still carrying Mr. Powell on its books as delinquent in his Federal income taxes for the years [1949 through 1955]. While the Treasury Department states that as yet it has not accepted a compromise for settling of these taxes, I find no evidence where the Department is really trying to collect the money."

The skirmishing resumed on the Senate floor the following day. This time a Democrat—one noted for his conservatism—Senator Frank Lausche of Ohio, articulated some of his own fears about the New Frontier's budgetary schemes, specifically in their relation to Powell's own newly-forged Associated Community Teams (ACT), which was charged with coördinating the Congressman's efforts and interests in two main areas: the proposed domestic peace corps, which would bring money and volunteer workers to Harlem and other depressed communities; and low-income housing projects, including those initiated by the Adam Clayton Powell Foundation. "Signs are already appearing of extravagance in the project," said Lausche. He had in mind, he said, the $250,000 granted to ACT in 1962 for the development of the nucleus of a domestic peace corps. He listed proposed salaries for

ACT directors, ranging from $14,000 for the project director on down; three other posts were in five figures. "The salaries . . . if followed in other domestic peace corps units throughout the country, will work havoc with local and state salary schedules," he said.

He pointed out that in Harlem, $17,000 was budgeted for space rental. The space was in Abyssinian Baptist Church.

Senator Wayne Morse then took the floor and asked that, in the interests of decorum, Williams's remarks about Powell be expunged from the record. No Senator was allowed to impugn personally another Senator, Morse pointed out, and that courtesy ought to be extended to members of the other chamber. He suggested that Senate Rule XIX be expanded to include the House ("No Senator in debate shall, directly or indirectly, by any form of words, impute to another Senator or to other Senators any conduct or motive unworthy or unbecoming a Senator"). "This is not a question of black or white," said Morse. "It is traditional. . . ."

Williams not only refused to allow his remarks on Powell to be expunged, but resorted to a debater's trick in his counterattack. He had not called attention to Powell's "relatives on the payroll who are not working," he insisted. "I am not calling attention to it today. . . . I will not mention the fact that his wife is on the payroll, nor will I raise any question as to whether she does any work. Neither will I say that he is not fulfilling his duties and is guilty of a great deal of absenteeism. I will not call attention to that fact. I did not say it yesterday. . . . I will not say that my remarks refer to the administration's expenditures and its allocation of money to Powell . . . . I was criticizing the administration. Perhaps I could refer to him as the administration's sacred cow, but that perhaps would not be proper. Maybe I should refer to him as a sacred bull of this administration. . . ."

Powell was in Puerto Rico and unavailable for comment

on Williams' attack. He had departed suddenly, the day before the Williams speech, after opening an announced two
weeks of hearings on President Kennedy's education bill. His
sudden decision to leave Washington gave rise to suspicion
that he had been warned of Williams' intentions.

Returning to the Capitol, apparently refreshed and determined to confront Williams' charges, Powell called a press
conference in the Caucus Room of the Old House Office
building. Scores of reporters and television newsmen crowded
into the room as Powell took his place at a head table and
began handing out mimeographed pages which listed Senator
Williams' votes on civil rights legislation. The tabulation
indicated that Senator Williams had supported a bare few of
the pro-Negro measures. Asked why the Delaware Senator
had attacked him, Powell said: "I say unequivocally it was
because I am a Negro."

One reporter wanted to know if Negro leaders should not
"lean over backwards" to avoid the sort of criticism Powell
had attracted in the preceding months. The Congressman
said: "I take the view that equality is equality . . . and that
I am a member of Congress as good as anybody else. As long
as it is within the law, it's not wrong. . . . If the law is wrong,
change the law."

He announced that he had changed his mind about not
running for Congress in 1964, because "If I didn't run again,
it would look as though I was running out." He bore down
heavily on his charge that Williams had been racially motivated: the Senator was "a man who is one hundred percent
opposed to civil rights," said Powell.

In an interview with the *Amsterdam News,* Powell was
even more vigorous in his counterattack. He called Senator
Williams "stupid," and a "liar," and challenged the entire
United States Senate to reveal whether "any or all" Senate
wives were on their husbands' payrolls. "I do not do any more

than any other member of the Congress," he said, "but by the Grace of God, I'll not do less!" He added: "The Senate is so dishonest that it won't publish its payroll list so I don't know what Senate wives, including Mrs. Williams, are on their husbands' payrolls."

Powell said he had learned from the Library of Congress that in 1961 the average Senator spent $2000 for trips to Europe, and the average among Representatives was $900. "The night I was in the Lido Club, Senator Estes Kefauver was there with ten guests. Senator Kefauver's reservations were made by the United States Embassy and the Embassy gave him the money to pay his bill." Powell named other Senators he had run across in various *boîtes* on the continent. Many of his colleagues in the House felt that this indiscriminate tattling, while justifying his own behavior, was driving the wedge between them too deeply to be retrieved. On the housing matters, Powell said: "Williams lied when he said the FHA loaned me $11,000,000. The FHA doesn't loan money. It guarantees mortgages."

Williams had indeed shaded his attack on the side of hyperbole, but that fact merely underlined the truth that his real target was not Powell but the Kennedy administration. Williams, a dedicated fiscal sleuth, would not have wasted his fervor on a playboy congressman. He was after bigger game, such as Kennedy's Youth Employment Opportunities Act, and the proposed Urban Service Corps, a domestic application of the Peace Corps. His allies in this cause were the National Association of Manufacturers, the Republican National Committee, and the Chamber of Commerce of the United States, which was declaring in a news release: "The President's recommendations for a Youth Conservation Corps and a Local Area Youth Employment Program are an unrealistic palliative more appropriate to the unemployment problems of the 1930's."

But Powell could not gracefully admit that Williams viewed him as the most vulnerable patch in Kennedy's armor. To do so would be self-demeaning. So he invoked the all-purpose defense which had served him well in the past: racism.

At Kennedy's first press conference after the Williams speech, the President had this exchange with a reporter:

Q. Mr. President, Congressman Adam Clayton Powell has been in the news quite a bit recently. Much of the publicity has been evoked by an attack upon him by Senator Williams. . . . There have also been published reports that his activities are embarrassing the White House. Number one, since you are a former member of the Senate, what do you think of the propriety of Senator Williams' attack on Mr. Powell? Number two, are the activities of Mr. Powell embarrassing to the White House; and number three, as President of the United States, what is your assessment of him as a Congressman and as a Negro Leader?

A. I would not comment on the dispute between Senator Williams and Congressman Powell. Congressman Powell has proved in his life that he is well able to take care of himself. Number two, I have not been embarrassed by Mr. Powell. Number three, I would not attempt to rank congressmen. What I am most interested in is the passage of legislation which is of benefit to the people. I thought last year that committee members did a good job in the House Education and Labor committee in passing out bills which were very useful—minimum wage, the education bill. I would hope that we would have the same kind of record this year. I think that is the best answer to any attacks. I would hope the chairman holds the same view.

With his usual understatement, Kennedy had laid down the guidelines by which Powell might salvage some modicum of trust from his leaders, and suggested a foundation upon which he might construct a return to grace. But other Democrats were more implacable. Their goal was to humble Powell without enraging the Negro community. Such Negro leaders as A. Philip Randolph already had let it be known that they would interpret any move to relieve Powell of his chairmanship—or split Education and Labor into two separate committees—as being motivated by racial prejudice.

So the Democrats called upon reserves of ingenuity to get their man. Powell had requested $697,000 to operate the Education and Labor Committee for the ensuing two years. At hearings before the House Administration Committee, Representative James Roosevelt of California spoke for Powell, claiming that the chairman could not attend the meetings personally because of an attack of Asian flu. The other House members erupted into laughter. They decided that Powell would receive only $200,000 for one year's operations and would have to come back, hat in hand, to request his second year's funds. More importantly, they stripped him of the committee chairman's privilege of handling the money. Instead, they doled it out in $25,000 portions to six subcommittee chairmen, leaving Powell only $50,000 with which to work. After the hearing, one committeeman said, "I think the cuts were too deep; but let's face it, he asked for it."

In Puerto Rico, Powell heard the news and repeated his regret that he had not been able to attend the hearings due to his "Asian flu—I mean Afro-Asian flu."

Days later, he was back in Washington testifying before the House Rules Committee, which was considering a resolution by Representative Phil M. Landrum, Democrat of Georgia, to divide Education and Labor into two committees. Dressed in a fawn-colored suit and pale blue shirt, Powell puffed his pipe and was chatty and confident. "You came here to split the Adam," he told the House members.

The commiteemen pointedly did not cavil about Powell's

junketing habits. The closest anyone came to mentioning them was a remark made by Representative Clarence J. Brown, Republican of Ohio, "You are very liberal with other people's money," he said.

"Yes, I believe I am," Powell replied.

There was nothing personal in their entertainment of Representative Landrum's resolution, they assured Powell. It was simply that "the delicate and important, and sensitive" subjects of labor and education were unable to get proper attention from one overworked committee. Powell nodded, and puffed his pipe. But, as all of them expected, the resolution died in infancy. There was simply no graceful way to hand Powell that unprecedented a penalty.

Nonetheless, the Harlemite's political life was in an impoverished state and he knew it. The only road back to grace was the one suggested by President Kennedy in his news conference and that involved the sort of pick-and-shovel work— the grinding day-to-day bargaining—which Powell had never enjoyed. He hoped instead for some expression of confidence both from high adminstration officials and such Negro leadership groups as the NAACP and Martin Luther King's Southern Christian Leadership Conference.

The thoughts of these and other civil rights activist groups, however, were almost totally involved with the sweep of events in the American South. A young Negro named James Meredith, assisted by the NAACP Legal Defense and Educational Fund, a bodyguard of deputy United States marshals, and 10,000 army troops and federalized National Guardsmen, had managed to enroll in the University of Mississippi after savage rioting on the campus in which two men were killed and 375 injured. It had been the most significant confrontation between states' rights interests and the Federal government since the Civil War. Governor Ross Barnett of Mississippi had defied a Federal court order to allow Meredith to register, calling him "unqualified morally and mentally" to attend the university. He invited all Mississippians to "join me in the determination that we shall, in the end, attain victory." In spite of the continuing resistance to his presence and the need for a bodyguard of deputy United States marshals, Meredith remained registered at the University of Mississippi. It was a massive victory for the black revolution in the heart of the resistant Deep South, and encouraged the Negro activists to quicken their efforts for the approaching summer of 1963—the summer which would see Negro hopes travel the long road from Birmingham, Alabama, to the steps of the Lincoln Memorial.

In Washington, Adam Clayton Powell's preoccupations were more personal and parochial. A Negro Democrat, upon whom Kennedy relied for advice on civil rights matters, conferred with the Congressman on some ways and mean by which the Harlemite might regain the confidence of his party leaders.

Kennedy's man told a reporter later, "We're going to save Adam if we can." In Harlem, Ray Jones said, "The impression we get in New York is that the White House and Attorney General are solidly behind him."

A few days later, in an act so inexplicable as to bewilder even his most complaisant partisans, Powell placed himself beyond easy salvation.

13. Prophet at Bay

On March 23, 1963, Adam Powell stood on a platform at Seventh Avenue and 125th Street outside the black nationalist bookstore and told 3000 Negroes that Malcolm X— who was seated behind him on the platform—was his "friend," and that "we Negroes are not going to get anything more in this life except that which we fight for and fight for with all our power." He added: "This may sound like black nationalism. If it is, then what is wrong with it? Why is it that racism and nationalism are only dirty words when applied to Negro people? What the white man fears is the coming together of Negroes."

The heart of his message on that chill spring day was this: ". . . one of the things I am very close to agreeing [on] almost completely with Malcolm X is his analysis of our present national Negro organizations. Unless we can seize completely the administration and policy-making of our national Negro organizations, then we must say there is no hope there for us. And I include the NAACP, Urban League, CORE, and Southern Christian Leadership Conference under Martin Luther King." Powell said that the civil rights struggle would be won only by those groups "that are totally owned, controlled and maintained by Negro people." He included, in his bitter complaint about white control, the Negro colleges and universities.

His words, delivered with typical Powell gusto, struck his audience, and the entire Negro community, like a thunderbolt. He was aligning himself unequivocally with the hard Muslim line of excluding whites from any strategy-making participation in the civil rights struggle. Such exclusion had been the subject of a debate inside the black revolution for some time, but most Negro leaders were committed to full coöperation with sympathetic whites who conscientiously offered aid to the cause. Distrust of white motives found its most complete expression among the Muslims.

The March 23rd speech was no typical Powell plaint, despite the fact that he had struck at white paternalism in many earlier speeches. The Negro press was quick to recognize that Powell's repudiation of the moderate Negro leadership—the leadership dedicated to non-violence—was a premeditated departure for the Congressman, and one of the most significant acts of his political life.

The response to his attack was swift and similarly unequivocal. A. Philip Randolph said, "I am unalterably committed to the program of the NAACP. . . . Negroes can't solve the problem except with the aid of white people committed to its solution, morally and spiritually. It is unfortunate that Congressman Powell made the attack that he did. I was quite shocked that [he] called on Negroes to boycott [the civil rights organizations]. . . . It's almost incredible. If we didn't have white people committed to the problem, we'd never solve it."

An aide to the Reverend Martin Luther King said: "Powell doesn't know what it is to fight in the slit trenches day after day."

Whitney M. Young, Jr. of the Urban League said, "at a time when the whole world is crying for and working toward unity, it comes as a terrible shock to hear the voice of a person of Congressman Powell's stature sowing the seeds of racial discord."

Former Negro baseball star Jackie Robinson in an open letter to Powell, said: "[It is my] sincere belief that you have grievously set back the cause of the Negro, let your race down and failed miserably in the role which our people justly expect you to play as an important national leader of the Negro. . . . I refer to your vicious attacks upon the NAACP, your intemperate . . . suggestion that Negro people boycott the NAACP because of the participation in its affairs of white people and your rallying call to the Negro people to support Malcolm X and the Black Muslims."

Privately, Ray Jones said: "We've worked hard for unity. In one movement, [Powell] has split the community down the center. . . . We concentrated this great power in his hands. He proceeded to dissipate it. Isn't he just another congressman now? . . . Now for him to throw himself in opposition to these organizations or to side with the black nationalists [is another act of dissipation]. . . . I can foresee trouble on 125th Street . . . and when it comes, Powell will be in Puerto Rico or Europe or someplace." Still later, Jones remarked privately, "Everything he's doing is planned. Nothing is spontaneous. . . . Let's see what is the public's capacity to accept. I don't think he's got the thing right at all. . . . This steady contempt is directed against those whom he portrays as enemies of the people."

Publicly, Jones announced he was taking out a lifetime membership in the NAACP for his grandson. At the same time, the Carver Democratic Club, of which Jones was leader, passed a strongly-worded resolution in support of the NAACP: "This is a problem which was created, and continues to be nurtured, by white people who have an obligation to work for a just solution of this issue. . . . We cannot call for integration while advocating segregation." Jones was not yet publicly attacking Powell. Formally, they were still the duumvirate in control of Harlem. But Jones's action announced unmistakably that he was totally opposed to Powell's new separatist logic.

The unanswered question in the minds of many whites was just why Powell had embarked on so desperate and unpopular a course; why had he chosen to leave the main roads of Negro protest for the byways of separatism and racism. The answers were not long in coming. *The Courier,* a nationally circulated Negro newspaper, pointed the way: "It is known that [Powell] has long been rankled by what he considers the desertion of Negro leaders when he has gotten into trouble. Habitually in and out of hot water, Powell has often decried the lack of support and assistance from Negro leadership. He steadfastly maintains, however, that this does not bother him." The mass leaders—King, Wilkins, Farmer, Randolph, and Young—rarely sought Powell's advice, in fact, nor invited him into their strategy-making sessions. This purposeful slight angered Powell deeply, especially since he espied the unfolding of a great historic drama and was, at this juncture, uncertain of his own role in it. The black revolution—which he had predicted decades earlier and for which he had kept hopes alive like an erratic John the Baptist—had begun, and it was in other hands than his. His wrath led him to the belief that by the force of his public self he could turn aside the black revolution into a byway of his own choosing. If the moderate black leadership would not have him, he would find companionship among the extremists. He was astute enough, at the same time, to sense a growing impatience—especially among young, urban Negroes—with the path of non-violence and the religio-mystical leadership of Martin Luther King, whom pollsters were finding "the most popular Negro in the United States." Powell's assessment of the Negro mood helped him to the conclusion that the Muslim mystique would enjoy broader and broader acceptance as civil rights forays in the South met mounting resistance and violence.

In succeeding weeks, Powell renewed his attack. On March 31, at the Upper Park Avenue Baptist Church, he said, "We are prisoners. How can we expect our jail keeper to give us freedom?" He pointed to the fact that in the NAACP white persons held the positions of president, secretary-treasurer, head of the life membership campaign, head of the legal defense fund, and the two senior memberships on the board of directors. He advised the NAACP to start taking part in sit-ins and economic boycotts and "stop the nit-picking process of racial advancement by confining its activities to the courts."

That same week, in Washington's Metropolitan Baptist Church, he began a speech by quoting from Emmet John Hughes's book, *The Ordeal of Power:* ". . . the art of politics . . . [is not] to close some tiny gap . . . but to define and to advance . . . policies for a thousand tomorrows." In pursuit of the Negro's tomorrows, he suggested, the major civil rights groups might have to be abandoned in favor of all-Negro organizations. He also advised Negroes to spend their money only with their own race. "This is one thing the white man does not want to happen, for money means power."

At the Shiloh Baptist Church in Washington, a few weeks later, he warned that the capital was in for a race riot unless "sassiety" Negroes spent more time with their own people and less time trying to act like whites. He told the 5000 people in the audience that "the great mistake of the white man throughout the centuries has been his claim . . . that he 'knew' the Negro. The picture has been further complicated by a very small group of the black bourgeois elite who, in this day and hour, in order to obtain token employment and token social life, ape Uncle Tom with a Harvard accent, and tell the 1963 white liberal that he is correct in thinking that he, too, 'knows the Negro.' " He condemned the "ivory tower, 'sassiety,' bandanna Negroes" in official Washington, and said "even those who occupy high positions do not represent the Negro community. . . . The trouble with Washington is that it has hated the word 'black' from the day that Negro 'sassiety' was born, and while the Negroes of this nation are beginning to think black and talk black, Washington 'sassiety' is still wrapped up in the ante-bellum dreams of a mulatto society."

Powell's most powerful and emotional speech during this period was one he delivered at an outdoor integration rally in Englewood, New Jersey. He said, in part:

"We now stand in the middle of the black man's revolution. Make no mistake about it, this is a revolution. No black man should be anything but a fighter. I am a fighter and I'm proud of it. The greatest enemy of the black man are those black Uncle Toms that are against you. . . . Don't let anybody, including my friend [Attorney General] Bobby Kennedy, tell you it's the wrong time. I say the time is now! . . . The dollar is our power! God the Father, God the Son and God the Holy Dollar. . . . Nobody can tell you how to vote, and with those things, we have America by the throat. . . . It is as ridiculous for a white man to lead the Negroes' fight, as it would have been for a British officer to lead the American Revolutionary troops. . . . A black man should be a fighter from the moment he leaves the womb. . . ."

Powell's hands trembled visibly as he half-shouted his extemporaneous remarks, punctuating them with an intermittent pounding of his foot on the platform. He had many targets in mind that day. Adlai Stevenson, Powell charged, had requested three light-skinned Negroes to work as clerk-typists on his United Nations staff. "He didn't want them as full secretaries and he didn't want them black." (A spokes-

man for Stevenson angrily denied the charge the same day.)
The speech was studded with such expressions as "racial muscle," "fighter," "black man," and "revolution." He flaunted
his famous European junket by telling the audience he was
returning to Europe on the following Sunday to attend the
World Labor Conference in Geneva. (He did attend the conference, on a brief, and apparently businesslike, trip.)

"They tried to stop me," he shouted at the audience, which
by now was under the spell of his performance. "But I'm going again . . . *the luxury flight to Paris* . . . with lots of relatives . . . *at the government's expense . . . !*"

"First class!" somebody in the audience yelled.

"Yes!" shouted Powell. *"First class!"*

He built to an emotional denouement as he told them that
white people were afraid of the new, militant black. "He's
not afraid of the physical black man," Powell added. "He's
afraid of his conscience. He's afraid when he dies and goes
before the Lord, God will say, 'Go to hell, damn you!' "

On a WNBC-TV interview program, *Open Mind,* Powell
was introduced as being at "the center of volcanic explosions
not only in the white but the Negro community." He listened
as the moderator, Dr. Eric Goldman, quoted a *New York
Times* editorial which called his recent pronouncements "a
philosophy of a fundamental and irreconcilable antagonism
between whites and Negroes." Powell answered:

First I want to make a correction and say that I do not
advocate the ousting of whites from the NAACP. I advocate
that the national board of the NAACP shall be more representative of the Negro community. . . . In other words, the
men and women who represent the black masses are not on
the board. I say they should be there . . . we need a national
organization, just as any other ethnic group in this country
has—the American Jewish Congress, the Federation of Italian
Societies, the Poles, the Irish, etc. We need a new national

board. . . . Now if we can't capture the NAACP in the name of the black masses . . . then maybe we should have an agonizing reappraisal. . . .

Q. Does all this imply that in the subsequent battle for civil rights . . . that the white man has no important role at all?

A. No, he has a role of being a volunteer, a role of being helpful, but cannot have a role of being a leader of black people.

Q. And he cannot hope to understand either the Negro or what the Negro wants?

A. Only the English understood the Blitz, only the Polish Jews understood the ghetto of Warsaw, and only the black man understands black men.

Powell restated his personal ethic when asked by Goldman if he had a special responsibility, as a prominent leader of a minority people, to be particularly above reproach:

A. I have a special responsibility of being the equal of every white man in the House and in the Senate.

Q. Equal in evil as well as in good?

A. It's not evil if it's legal.

Q. Anything that's legal is okay?

A. Of course. Naturally. . . . And if the law is wrong, then the law should be changed.

By the time Powell returned from his labor conference in Geneva, practically everything had changed. Birmingham had happened.

> *Send me a letter, send it by mail*
> *Send it in care of the Birmingham jail.*

A letter, not to, but from the Birmingham jail, written by Martin Luther King, became the *J'accuse* of civil rights fighters in the violent summer of 1963. King had gone to Birmingham from Atlanta with the stated purpose of mounting the most massive assault on the barricades of segregation that had been attempted up to that time. Birmingham was the citadel of die-hard segregation. In the previous 22 months prior to King's arrival, the city had seen 24 bombings of Negro homes and churches. It had, in addition, a demonstrable record of police brutality toward Negroes. Two other reasons motivated King to choose Birmingham as the battleground for his summer campaign. First his organization, the Southern Christian Leadership Conference, had its strongest affiliate in Birmingham: the Alabama Christian Movement for Human Rights, led by the Reverend Fred Shuttlesworth. Second, Birmingham had recently suffered the loss of vital industry and was economically vulnerable to Negro boycotts of its merchants. As King was later to write, "If Birmingham could be cracked, the direction of the entire non-violent movement in the South could take a significant turn."

King arrived in Birmingham in the first week in April. He recruited 200 Negroes who were willing to go to jail for the cause, and planned his strategy in a series of meetings with local Negro leaders. Awaiting King in Birmingham and planning strategy of his own, was Public Safety Commissioner Theophilus Eugene ("Bull") Connor, a man who was to become a symbol of police brutality and Southern white resistance. Connor sent spies into the Negro community to seek information. Fearing that their phones were tapped, King and his colleagues took code names—"JFK," "Dean Rusk," "Pope John"—and referred to prospective demonstrators as "baptismal candidates." The whole operation was labeled "Project C"—for confrontation.

King's forces came into the open late in April. Day after day, Negroes—dressed in the best clothes they owned—paraded the downtown streets singing freedom songs and chanting slogans. "Bull" Connor's men arrested scores of them at lunch counters, in the streets, wherever they gathered. Soon the

Birmingham jail was overflowing with singing, non-violent Negroes. But the Negro ranks were constantly replenished with newcomers. The protests went on unabated. Finally, on Tuesday, May 7, 2,500 Negroes poured out of their churches, surged through police lines, and paraded into the downtown area chanting and clapping. "Bull" Connor furiously ordered fire hoses turned on them and sent policemen into their midst swinging clubs. Police dogs leaped at the demonstrators and an armored truck moved into the throng, herding them along the street. News photographers shot pictures of the fighting: a police dog flying at the abdomen of a demonstrator; a Negro woman pinned to the street under the knee of a policeman; Negroes cowering on the sidewalks under the brutal force of the city's firehoses.

Hundreds were arrested—bringing the total to around 3,300 —including Martin Luther King. The Negroes had created their crisis. "Bull" Connor had made it a success. (President Kennedy said later, "The civil rights movement owes 'Bull' Connor as much as it owes Abraham Lincoln.") News photos of the violence were broadcast to the nation's front pages, films of the violence were seen in millions of homes, and the European press gave the story prominent display. The nation's outrage over Birmingham was palpable. Roy Wilkins, usually the most self-contained of the civil rights leaders, said, "My objectivity went out the window when I saw the picture of those cops sitting on that woman and holding her down by the throat." Reaction was similar throughout the Negro community and among large segments of the white population. Suddenly, a pervasive unanimity gripped the Negroes consciousness. Middle-class Negroes who had been spending their energies trying to win acceptance from whites found a powerful identity with poor rural Negroes whose status precluded their entertaining any such aspirations. Many wealthy Negroes, who had been unwilling to identify with the black revolution, forgot their inhibitions and joined in for the first time.

In the Birmingham jail, Martin Luther King sat among his fellow demonstrators and pondered the fruits of his efforts. A group of eight white clergymen had written a letter to him expressing sympathy with his aims, but deploring the violence and public disturbance that accompanied his methods which they called "unwise and untimely." King, who in the course of his civil rights activities had been stabbed in the chest once, physically attacked three times, whose home had been bombed three times, and who had been in jail 13 times, wrote a reply on the only bits of paper he could find—margins of newspapers, the backs of envelopes, pieces of toilet tissue— and smuggled it to the outside. It read, in part:

"Basically, I am in Birmingham because injustice exists here. . . . The purpose of our direct action program is to create a situation so crisis-packed that it will inevitably open the door to negotiation. . . . The nations of Asia and Africa are moving with jet-like speed toward gaining political independence, but we still creep at horse-and-buggy pace toward gaining a cup of coffee at a lunch counter. . . . When you see the vast majority of your 20 million Negro brothers smothering in an air-tight cage of poverty in the midst of an affluent society . . . when you are harried by day and haunted by night by the fact that you are a Negro, never quite knowing what to expect next, and are plagued with inner fears and outer resentments; when you are forever fighting a degenerating sense of 'nobodiness'—then you will understand why we find it difficult to wait. . . .

"I . . . stand in the middle of two opposing forces in the Negro community. One is a force of complacency made up of Negroes who, as a result of long years of oppression, are so completely drained of self-respect and a sense of 'somebodiness' that they have adjusted to segregation, and of a few middle-class Negroes who, because of a degree of academic and economic security and because in some ways they profit by segregation, have unconsciously become insensitive to the problems of the masses. The other force is one of bitterness and hatred and it comes perilously close to advocating violence. It is expressed in the various black nationalist groups that are springing up across the nation, the largest and best known being Elijah Muhammad's Muslim movement. . . .

"I have tried to stand between these two forces, saying that we need emulate neither the 'do-nothingism' of the complacent nor the hatred of the black nationalist. For there is the more excellent way of love and non-violent protest. . . . If this philosophy had not emerged, by now many streets of the South would, I am convinced, be flowing with blood. . . ."

In the months following Birmingham, Negroes fought civil rights battles in 800 cities and towns in the United States. Walter Lippmann assayed the historical moment: ". . . Experience shows that there is . . . a point of no return in a movement for the redress of grievances. That point is where gradual reform and token appeasement become suddenly not only insufficient but irritating. The long-standing grievances, which have been patiently endured, are suddenly felt to be intolerable. Then, instead of putting up with a little done slowly, there is a demand that much be done suddenly. For us the point of no return was marked and symbolized in Birmingham."

President Kennedy, who had been proceeding cautiously in the writing of civil rights legislation, now moved swiftly and made a nationwide television-radio address on June 11:

". . . The events in Birmingham and elsewhere have so increased the cries for equality that no city or state or legislative body can prudently choose to ignore them.

"The fires of frustration and discord are burning in every city, North and South, where legal remedies are not at hand.

"We face, therefore, a moral crisis as a country and as a

people. It cannot be met by repressive police action. It cannot be left to increased demonstrations in the streets. It cannot be quieted by token moves or talk. It is a time to act. . . . Next week I shall ask the Congress of the United States to make a commitment it has not fully made in this century to the proposition that race has no place in American life or law. . . ."

Kennedy produced a tough bill aimed particularly at voter rights, employment, and the desegregation of public facilities.

Adam Powell was speaking in the West at about the time the President delivered his historic civil rights speech. When Powell was queried about it, he said he thought the speech was great; that he had stayed up half a night helping with its writing and that, indeed, he had written more than half of it for the President. Kennedy was perplexed when he read the Powell quotes in newspapers. A Kennedy confidant called Powell to relay JFK's puzzlement. The conversation, as re-created in congressional corridors, went like this:

Aide: About that statement . . .

Powell: What statement?

Aide: (Explains the wire-service report read by the President.)

Powell: Oh no, I said over half of the President's legislation would go through my committee.

Aide: But newsmen have a tape recording of what you actually said, and it corresponds to what was published.

Powell: Well, you know those tape recorders. They have all those knobs that you turn on and off. . . . They put other things in other places. . . . That's what happened.

By far the most significant effect of the Birmingham crisis —one that would change the whole course of Negro rights action in the United States—was the determination it forged among the Big Six leaders to unite truly for the first time, and to work in harmony to solidify old victories and plan new ones. On July 2, a few weeks after the Birmingham eruption, the Negro Big Six met in New York: Martin Luther King, representing his Southern Christian Leadership Conference; Roy Wilkins of the NAACP; Whitney Young of the National Urban League; James Farmer of the Congress of Racial Equality; A. Philip Randolph of the Negro American Labor Council; and John Lewis, of the Student Non-Violent Coördinating Committee. After a two-hour conference in the Hotel Roosevelt, they emerged to tell the press that the newly-reinforced coalition would dramatize its demands by staging a March on Washington eight weeks later on August 28. It would be, they hinted, the most impressive display, both of Negro unity and Negro demands for justice, that the nation had yet seen.

If the Birmingham confrontation was a debacle for the Southern white resister, it was nothing less than that for Adam Clayton Powell. The magnitude of his miscalculation could scarcely be underestimated. He could not have foreseen the effects of Birmingham in terms of its powerful unifying influence on the whole Negro community, nor the guilt and outrage it instilled in wholesale numbers of whites.

In most elemental fashion, he had simply guessed wrong: black nationalism was not the mood of his people, not the source of moral fervor behind 20,000,000 marching blacks who were awakening to the "New World A'coming" which he had been predicting for decades. Like a faltering chess master whose massive pride depends upon his discovering some brilliant and crushing continuation to see him through to victory, Powell had deliberated, less with patience than with invincible confidence in his own powers. Then he made his move—only to recognize, almost instantly—that he had blundered into a trap. The civil rights groups he had been condemning by name were in possession of the black revolution and intended to advance it by non-violent means through the courts and in the streets. They were staunchly integrationist and opposed to all such alternatives as offered by the Black Muslims. Bayard Rustin, whom the Big Six named to master-mind the complex planning for the March on Washington, was able to describe the mood of the new leadership this way:

". . . The problem of involvement means bringing Ne-groes and whites, North and South, together. All over New York and other parts of the North, many of my Negro friends are advocating the extremist forms of violence. . . . Now the problem of allies is an important one because if we do not attract allies, the civil rights movement has gone as far as it can go. This is the stupidity of some young Negroes who talk about exclusive Negro leadership and all the other black nationalist foolishness. . . . The problem can only be an-swered by thousands of white people pouring into the streets with Negroes. And this is the damnation of this Malcolm X black nationalist foolishness. So if this Negro revolt is not prepared now to join hands and to seek allies and to recognize that a great deal of the problem cannot be solved by Negroes, no matter how great the civil rights movement is, we are in trouble."

Had the Big Six been *willing* to forgive Powell and take him into their planning sessions, they could not have, so viru-lent had been his attacks on them. Privately, they believed that his resort to black nationalism was less a philosophical change-of-heart than an act of petulance growing out of their refusal to defend him following his European junket *à trois*. But he was no longer theirs to save; nor could the Kennedy administration afford to offer him its hand. History was mov-ing too swiftly now, and Powell stood in terrible danger of being left in its backwater.

Rising ahead, like a colossus astride the past and the future, was the proposed March on Washington. The Big Six had already decreed it would be their day, and the professionals—politicians and appointed officialdom—would not be allowed to participate actively. A few editorialists speculated that the decree was aimed specifically at excluding Powell, whose fiery brand of oratory might subvert the demonstration. Still, it would not have been extraordinary for them to make an exception for the man who had kept the civil rights issue alive on the national scene during periods when scarcely any other Negro leaders' words were given a hearing. Powell, facing a nightmarish ostracization, addressed himself to regaining some measure of stature inside the revolt.

On July 28, exactly one month before the scheduled March, Powell led a forum in the basement of Abyssinian Baptist Church on the subject "The Black Revolution." (At the first forum lecture, a month earlier, Powell had presented Malcolm X.) During his remarks, a "new Powell" emerged. Suddenly, all his old hostility toward the Bix Six and their organizations was subtly transmuted into something approaching deference and docility. His audience—which included many Harlem clergymen, as well as Ray Jones and Malcolm X—was variously entertained and bewildered by this new direction. He described civil rights legislation which was then in the Rules Committee and claimed he could expedite its movement to the floor of the House by employing a parliamentary tactic called Calendar Wednesday, a procedure under which a committee chairman may request that a measure be brought immediately to the floor for action, breaking it out of the Rules Committee. Remarkably, and uncharacteristically, Powell said he would first seek the advice of "my leaders"—and proceeded to name the Big Six.

"So on tomorrow at 12:30 p.m." he said, "I have set up a national telephone conference with A. Philip Randolph, Martin Luther King, Roy Wilkins. . . ." He added to the Big Six the names of several prominent Negro civic leaders. ". . . And

I will tell them, as Chairman of the Committee on Education and Labor, what I can do. *And then I will let them tell me what I shall do.* In other words, no white man any more, if they ever have, is going to tell Adam Powell what I should do in the field of civil rights. I'm taking my orders from my black leaders. They're going to tell me what to do. . . ."

Ray Jones, seated just behind the rostrum near Powell, studied the Congressman through narrowed eyes, and grinned. Later, when asked what he thought of Powell's speech, Jones said, "I was tempted to pull Adam's coattails and ask him if he meant what he said. I was always under the impression that no white man ever told Adam what to do. That's what he always said, isn't it?"

A. Philip Randolph, when told that Powell had referred to him as one of "my leaders," laughed in surprise, then recovered quickly and admitted he had never in the past heard Powell call him, or anyone else, his "leader."

Powell's conference telephone call went as planned on the day after the forum. But none of the Negro leaders favored any such precipitous action by Powell on the civil rights legislation as invoking Calendar Wednesday. More significantly, none of them ventured the shadow of an invitation to Powell to lend assistance to the March on Washington planning— much less to address the marchers.

But Powell continued his attempts to associate himself as closely as possible with King, Randolph, and the other leaders. On the Monday before the March, Randolph accepted an invitation to address the National Press Club in Washington —the second American Negro to be so invited, the first having been King—and Powell contrived to be present, seated near Randolph. Such gestures were transparent to the Negro leaders, but they did not bother to refute them. Powell had managed to trap himself, they understood, and was trying desperately to extricate himself. In so doing, he had fallen

into yet another trap: he had assumed the posture of accommodation, become what he had sometimes forced others
around him to be—a sycophant. He was perilously close to becoming an ancient stereotype so odious to Negroes, that of
the black buffoon who appeased without dignity and bartered
self-esteem for imagined advantage.

Pictures of the March were beamed to Europe by television
satellites. Afro-Asian diplomats in London went to the United
States Embassy to present a message supporting the intentions
of the March. In Tel Aviv, 50 Americans paraded past the
American Embassy carrying signs which read: "The Civil
War is Over." The Soviet news agency, *Tass,* said that the
March "rivets attention to the most acute domestic problem
of the biggest capitalist power." A *Ghanaian Times* front
page editorial said, "the voice of the Afro-American cries out
loud for freedom in America." In Cairo, diplomatic representatives of Zanzibar, Northern and Southern Rhodesia,
South Africa, Kenya, Swaziland, Basutoland, and Mozambique
held a two-hour demonstration before the American Embassy,
timed to coincide with the Washington March.

By 9:00 a.m., the marchers in the capital were beginning to
cluster on the meadow at the foot of the Washington Monument. The crowd enlarged until an undulant sea of black
faces—salted with white—hid the grass and overflowed into
Independence and Constitution Avenues. Without signal,
they began the slow parade down those streets, skirting the
reflecting pool between the Monument and the Lincoln Memorial. At first, all that could be heard was the great murmur
of shuffling feet and the shrill cry of locusts in the elm trees
along the avenues. Then a "freedom song" took tentative
hold, and spread up and down the line of march:

> *Deep in my heart, I do believe*
> *We shall overcome someday.*

On the broad steps before the Lincoln Memorial, a succession of speakers and singers celebrated the day with assurances that the spirit of the March would not be lost in the months and years ahead. Adam Clayton Powell sat with some of his fellow Congressmen in a reserved section near the podium. From his position, he could see the upturned faces of that incredible mass of humanity: 200,000 men and women from all corners of the United States. The "marching blacks" were indeed marching, just as he had always said they would. A thin, black line had swelled into this ragtag army, and a hundred years of Emancipation had brought them along the tortuous road to this day.

Powell observed them wordlessly, and, at that moment, appeared infinitely forlorn.

14. At Large in the Great Society

J. Raymond Jones and Adam Clayton Powell severed relations after the March on Washington. The Congressman was in a mood of belligerence. To attack the Bix Six leaders would have been unwise, so Powell—in an exertion of the sort of petulance he frequently displayed in the face of frustration—chose a different target. Jones was running for a seat in the New York City Council and was being contested for the nomination in the Democratic primary, scheduled for September 5—one week after the March. Powell was listed as an honorary chairman of Jones's campaign committee. On his return to Harlem, however, Powell called Jones "a traitor to the black revolution" and accused him of a "personal grab for power," supported by "a flood of white money." But all of Harlem knew the real terms of disagreement: the two men had been bickering for years over whose front organization would win the lucrative sponsorship of certain low income housing projects in Harlem, especially the proposed Esplanade Gardens, a Lenox Avenue development which was still under dispute. In addition, there was the larger divergence growing out of their respective natures: Jones had always labored, in the interests of political unity in Harlem, to prevent his worsening relationship with Powell from erupting in public. But Powell was finding Harlem too small to contain two political titans. Jones had made himself repugnant to the Congressman by facing up to him both in politics and in real estate dealings.

It was no longer possible to perpetuate the myth of unity. The gears which always had aided Powell to a sense of the politic were now running free, stripped by the force of his own rage at being consigned to a backwater of the black revolution.

Jones had no choice but to fight back hard: "Powell is no longer considered a national leader of any importance in the civil rights movement. He can't even get into the conference of the Negro leaders." And again, "He has nothing but contempt for the Negro masses. In relaxed moments, Powell refers to Negroes as 'my slaves.'" Jones buried his sword with the observation that "Powell has had some difficulty deciding whether he is a Negro or a Puerto Rican."

Three days later, Jones won the primary easily over Powell's choice for the nomination. "The white vote" had won it for Jones, Powell insisted. (The councilmanic district comprises both black and white precincts. Jones had, in fact, lost some black election districts two-to-one.) Nonetheless, it was another blow to the Congressman's prestige and another string to Jones's bow.

Even after the general election, which Jones won without extending himself, he continued to worry his old confederate in the duumvirate: The parade has passed [Powell] by. He may not know it, but he'll find it out soon. Adam is contemptuous of Negroes, has always been. He has used them, he has risen to the top on them. Now he's ready to change and become a Puerto Rican."

But even in that direction, Powell's ambitions were being frustrated. The Congress, in 1963, passed a law calling for a joint Puerto Rican-United States Commission composed of two United States senators, two congressmen, and three Presidential appointees; for the island, six members representing variously the partisans of statehood, independence, and commonwealth status. The Commission was ordered to report to the President, the Congress, and the Puerto Rican legislature by January, 1966, at which time it might recommend a plebiscite or simply conclude that one was not desirable. In the meantime, a Senatorship from the island was out of Powell's grasp and, for practical considerations, so was the Governorship. Powell's jousting with Muñoz Marín had established that the Puerto Rican statesman would best the Harlemite in any confrontation on the island. (Muñoz retired in 1964; his protégé, Roberto Sánchez Vilella, succeeded him, polling a substantial plurality.)

At all events, Powell had yet another preoccupation to engage his talents: the so-called HARYOU-ACT youth rehabilitation program, which would funnel more than $110,000,000 into Harlem in a three-year period—the most ambitious social welfare thrust in the ghetto's history. The Kennedy administration, through the President's Committee on Juvenile Delinquency and Crime (headed by Attorney General Robert F. Kennedy), had made the problems of the nation's underprivileged youth a major federal issue. The Attorney General called it "the most ambitious project yet developed to combat delinquency on a broad scale." The Committee authorized programs in 16 communities around the country. Most of them were Negro, but they also included some white, Mexican-American, and American Indian poverty areas. From Harlem—the nation's most impacted slum area, and the archetypal breeding ground of juvenile crime—came requests for Committee aid from two groups: Harlem Youth Opportunities Unlimited, Inc. (HARYOU), headed by the Negro psychologist Dr. Kenneth Clark, who subsequently enlisted the support of Ray Jones; and the Associated Community Teams

(ACT), whose executive director was Livingston Wingate (a one-time aide on Powell's Congressional committee) whose unofficial guiding spirit was Powell himself. The President's Committee had awarded initial grants of $250,000 to ACT (thus incurring Senator Williams's celebrated attack on Powell as an authority on "adult delinquency") and $230,000 to HARYOU—with the proviso that the two groups eventually merge into one organization to supply responsible administration for the great sums of money to be pumped into Harlem. The President's Committee was not unaware of the disaster possibilities in a situation where Adam Powell and Ray Jones were competing for the upper hand and the stakes were $110,000,000. But, in mid-1963, the Committee chose to take the optimistic view that "this community is now working together." Privately, it warned the two camps that if they failed to resolve their differences there might be no program at all; that the President would not tolerate his designs being subverted by petty bickering and political intrusions.

National attention focused on Harlem as the maneuvering proceeded. Dr. Clark produced a 644-page report called *Youth in the Ghetto: a Study of the Consequences of Powerlessness and a Blueprint for Change.* It described Harlem in all its meanness and degradation, the Harlem of the middle 1960's—more than three decades after Adam Clayton Powell first began marching in picket lines on 125th Street. Had the ghetto's condition improved or worsened in those thirty hectic years? A study of the facts in 1963 showed that Harlem's plight was worse by far. For example:

The juvenile delinquency rate in the ghetto the ten years prior to 1963 was consistently twice as high as that in the city as a whole.

The proportion of narcotics users was three to eight times that of the rest of the city. Of New York's 30,000 narcotics addicts, 15,000 to 20,000 live in Harlem. Some of them need up to $75 a day to support their habit and often rob, mug, and sometimes kill to get the money.

Infant mortality, the starkest measure of poor health and nourishment in the ghetto, was twice as high as that of the city.

Both the homicide rate and the rate of venereal disease among youths was six times higher.

Clark's report concluded that three general areas of dilemma underlay the pathology of the ghetto: education, employment, and family life, in that order. Central Harlem had only 20 elementary schools, four junior high schools and no high schools. In the third grade, 30 percent of Harlem's children were performing below expected levels, and by the sixth grade that proportion had increased to an incredible 75 percent. The average Harlem grade-school pupil showed a lack of motivation, a confused and ambiguous self-image, and usually had unrealistic aspirations.

With regard to employment, a far higher proportion of Harlemites were found to be in the "lower occupations": porters, elevator operators, unskilled laborers—the jobs which were available to the uneducated, irrespective of race—the same jobs which were rapidly being eliminated by the advances of automation. In addition, the craft unions, particularly in the building trades, were known to be traditionally unreceptive to absorbing Negroes and Puerto Ricans. Family life in Harlem presented an especially despairing picture: half of all youths under 18 lived with only one parent, usually as the result of abandonment by a father who had no real hope of carrying out his role as husband and provider. A 27-year-old Harlem Negro told one of Kenneth Clark's researchers:

"The man [of the family], not having a sense of pride in self as being a man, is more or less morally destroyed. In other words he will have relationship with a woman and when she becomes pregnant, he will immediately abandon the family because of there being a lack of what you might call a family tie in our community. . . . There are some [such men] who make a racket out of the welfare. [They] walk around and say, man, well I knocked this chick up and now I'm putting her on the welfare, and I knocked this chick up and now I'm putting *her* on the welfare. . . . There's a name for them, they call them the home relief pets, and all he does is go around whenever the check date comes up . . . and he gets so much money from each one of the women. . . ."

Ninety percent of all housing units in Central Harlem were more than a third of a century old in 1963; 40 percent of them were built between 1880 and 1901. One energetic researcher estimated that if the population density of Harlem's worst neighborhoods prevailed throughout New York City, the entire population of the United States would fit into three of the five boroughs. Harlem has few major businesses, although there is a wide variety of small enterprises, most of them owned—if not always operated—by whites. Thirty-five percent of the businesses are involved in consumption of food and drink (bakeries, caterers, grocery stores, liquor stores, luncheonettes, restaurants, bars, and taverns); 27 percent are personal services (barber shops, beauty shops, dry cleaners, and laundries). The largest category of small business is the bar-restaurant—264. Beauty shops are second with 187.

Central Harlem has the highest density of churches of any community in the nation: 418 of them representing 43 denominations. Baptists and Methodists predominate, but a fourth of the churches are unclassifiable—independent congregations who get together in converted movie houses and old stores for their own brand of worship. One Harlemite had this to say about it:

"Churches don't mean us no good. We've been having churches all our lives under the same conditions, and look at the condition we're still in. The church must not have meant anything. See, when you go to church, you don't learn how to read and write and count. . . . You learn that in school. . . . So what good the churches doing us? They are not doing us any good. You could build some factories or something in Harlem and give our people some work near home. That would do us more good than a church."

A 45-year-old woman told HARYOU researchers:

"Whenever you have a lot of preachers of the twentieth century, jumping on their head and rolling on the floor like hogs, I tell you, you can't get no place like that. In the twentieth century, you go there and you see people foaming, your women with dresses up over their heads—My God! You can't get no place like that! The first things we should do, we should all go around and put a padlock on them churches for a hundred years. We got so many churches from the Hudson River to the East River and from 110th Street all the way up to 145th Street right here in Harlem. I don't know how many churches! Holes in the wall, down in the ground, walk-ups and all and we got churches so big they should be factories for the black people."

Investment capital goes into Harlem from white America and profits are taken out of Harlem by white America (not excluding the meaner forms of exploitation, such as narcotics, the numbers racket, and slum real estate, most of which is controlled by whites). The situation is in some ways similar to the historical dilemma of black and yellow colonies of Africa and Asia and their old-line colonial masters: the British, Dutch, Portuguese, Belgians and French. Relatively little long-term capital investment has gone into Harlem so that the community cannot make significant economic advances, nor progress to economic well-being. Northern ghettos traditionally have been vast pools of cheap, unskilled labor. With automation, that pool is less valuable and the human wastage

merely marks time on the ghetto street corners awaiting—
nothing. Unlike colonial natives who lived in the expectation
of territorial independence from their overlords, Harlemites
entertain no such dreams. Their salvation is retarded by pervasive social insensitivity and political power which is not
responsive to their needs. The New York city police force, in
the words of Malcolm X, is "an occupying army" which does
the bidding of the white power structure maintaining the
ghetto as a colony for exploitation by slumlords and *mafiosi*
who pay huge sums of money to law enforcers and city bu-
reaucrats for their "franchise" privileges. Thus, Harlemites
are accustomed, from their earliest years, to seeing the white
enforcers in compromising circumstances. Respect for the law
is eroded, and all promises of a "better deal" for the "natives"
are met with derision and ancient resignation. One white detective in Harlem told a *Time* magazine reporter in July,
1964, "Me and my partner, we pick up junkies, and sometimes we even get a pusher. We want to go further, get to the
wholesaler. Well, mister, we can't move one inch more. If I
move in, I may get busted to patrolman."

That was the ghetto in the middle 1960's, thirty years after
Adam Powell's first promises to lead his people to the promised land. Only the very young were yet vulnerable to salvation. A 15-year-old Negro girl told a HARYOU worker:

". . . One unique product of this system is the young Harlemite, and this Harlem youth is the only one who is in a
position to step back and look at this cycle objectively because
this youth has not yet, because of his age, been so viciously
tainted by the cycle in this system. This youth doesn't have to
risk losing a job because they attempt to fight the powers that
be, so the young person is the only one who can step back and
look at what exists here. And the young person, therefore,
must be the one to channel the frustrations and the anger
away from the bottle and away from the wife and away from

the other children and channel toward the power structure and toward the makers of the cycle."

It was for these reasons that President Kennedy's plans for the rehabilitation of the Northern ghettos were aimed principally at saving the downtrodden youths and contained the implicit conclusion that it was too late to save the adults. At the sound of $110,000,000, however, the predicted infighting broke out in Harlem between the HARYOU (Jones and Clark) partisans and the ACT (Powell and Wingate) axis over who would appoint the executive director of the HARYOU-ACT coalition. Dr. Clark felt that the executive directorship should go to a trained social worker, not a political appointee. He made his position plain: "We can't gamble with our youth any longer. The program must work. It is the city's last hope to save these children from a wasted life." Jones, for his part, said, "To hire someone because he is a politician's fair-haired boy would mean the death of HARYOU. . . . When I became associated with Dr. Clark to put the HARYOU show on the road . . . it was with the understanding that no politics would be involved." (What Jones really meant was that he hoped no *dirty* politics would be involved; the sort of backroom, party-hack patronage hassles which customarily accompany such expensive projects as HARYOU-ACT.) Clark proposed James R. Dumpson, New York City Welfare Commissioner and a professional social worker, for the executive directorship. Powell wanted the job for his one-time aide, Livingston Wingate.

After the death of President Kennedy, the youth program —which drew the fire of conservatives in both chambers of the Congress—became a keystone of President Johnson's anti-poverty campaign. Johnson needed to avoid any public bickering which might jeopardize his entire "Great Society" program, but at the same time, was reluctant to antagonize

Powell before the 1964 Presidential election. Similarly, Mayor Wagner—who was being mentioned as a vice-presidential nominee to run with Johnson—was eager to assert his authority in the HARYOU-ACT maneuvering; to indicate his support of Jones while not making a total enemy of Powell.

Behind the scenes, Powell was calling upon reserves of ingenuity to get control of the youth rehabilitation millions. Partisans of Dr. Clark accused the Congressman of threatening to sabotage the entire HARYOU-ACT venture if he were not allowed to name its administrators. Clark—an academician unaccustomed to big-time political power plays, but determined to preserve his brainchild from traduction—fought back, and asked Wagner to intervene with the White House to restrain Powell. "Anyone who would seek to turn this program into a political pork barrel would be guilty of the most venal type of corruption," he said. "It would be exploiting the misery of the people."

The fury of the feud gathered to full force on June 14. Dr. Clark publicly charged that "emissaries" from Powell had repeatedly threatened to subvert the youth program for Harlem unless Powell were given the upper hand. Clark admitted that Powell had not explicitly said he would use his influence to destroy the program, but in the language of politicians— the "vibrations," once again—the implication was plain. "He's a fascinating man," said Clark. "He has a way of communicating things without being rather direct about it. I mean at the end of a telephone conversation with the Congressman you know pretty well what he was saying, but if you were to say he said this, you would not be technically accurate."

Powell promptly called Clark a "liar" and said the psychologist "would come out of this whole situation making a tremendous sum of money." The controversy reached the floor of the House on June 16, when Iowa Republican H. R. Gross announced regret that the orginal $250,000 had been given to

Powell's ACT in the first place. Republican Peter Freling-huysen of New Jersey said he was concerned on grounds that "there is a political contest" in New York over the funds, and said he had "reservations about expanding the program." Even liberal Republican John V. Lindsay of Manhattan warned that Republicans "will be watching very carefully, and we will raise the roof if there is a continuation, or a be-gining, of political control." On the same day, four of the Big Six—Farmer, Randolph, Wilkins, and Young—entered the feud with a joint statement. "The success or failure of the HARYOU program," they said, "may well set a pattern for what happens in the Harlems throughout America." They viewed its devolution into a political football as "a cruel mockery of the urgent needs of our youth."

Two days later, Mayor Wagner appointed a committee to "report within a few days" the measures needed to end the power struggle. In Washington, Sargent Shriver, director of the President's war on poverty, told the House Labor subcom-mittee that no federal funds would go to Harlem until the ghetto had resolved its internal strife. Finally, ACT and HARYOU bowed to the pressure and agreed on a single charter, naming a temporary seven-member steering com-mittee to run the program until an executive director could be agreed upon. The coalition installed a 59-member board of directors, electing Dr. Arthur C. Logan, who had been on the HARYOU board, as chairman, and Livingston Wingate, of the Powell camp, president. The $25,000-a-year executive directorship remained vacant. The dispute thus ended, mo-mentarily, in a stand-off. Wingate later got the job.

Peace in Harlem appeared imminent, but the truce was short-lived. At the end of July, Dr. Clark angrily resigned from the board of HARYOU-ACT with charges that the pro-gram was being used "to perpetuate political dynasties."

"A couple of months ago, I still had hope that I might be

useful," Clark said. "But when I was shown how completely Mr. Powell has this community all locked up, there was nothing for me to do but go. I now leave all of this to Adam Clayton Powell."

Clark suggested that neither the Mayor nor the White House had been willing to face up to Powell in an election year, and thus support from those two quarters had not materialized. "Superficial is an excellent way to describe that support," Clark said. In his letter of resignation, he called the program "the last chance available for thousands of young people in the [Harlem] community" and described three conditions which were vital to the success of HARYOU-ACT:

"There must be a strong, vigilant, and independent board of directors [willing to resist] all forms of subtle and flagrant pretenses and postures. . . .

"There must be a top staff of qualified people who are identified with the anguish, the frustration, and the affirmative needs of the young people of Harlem.

"[Officials must realize] that the time for lip service, doubletalk, and even well-financed gimmicks has passed [because of] the desperate urgency of the predicament of Harlem's youth."

He added that "the more irritating forms of pretense and the most effective techniques for political control are insidious and tend to come under the guise of 'sweet reasonableness.'" On August 11, Clark delivered his parting shot: "I see Harlem as Adam's plantation, and it will remain so until the people decide differently."

Thus, all the profane squabbling broke out anew, while the ghetto's denizens festered through the hot summer of 1964. Rights leaders had been warning that Harlem was in a dangerously volatile condition, following the overt resistance of many whites in both the North and the South to the new civil rights bill which had been signed into law by President

Johnson on July 2. The new bill had its origin in President Kennedy's new resolve after Birmingham. A further cause of unrest was the nomination for the Presidency by the Republicans of Senator Barry Goldwater, who had voted against the bill.

On Saturday night, July 18, Harlem broke into the most bitter rioting the ghetto had seen since the great eruptions of 1935 and 1943. On five successive nights, Negroes and police battled on streetcorners and rooftops, thousands of rounds of ammunition were fired, and at the end of it, 140 people had been injured, many of them seriously; 520 were arrested, and one man was dead, shot in the head by a policeman. Once again, the city was revolted by the sounds of rioting: wooden clubs raining on black skulls and shoulders; cries of hatred in the streets, "Killers! Murderers! Nazis!"; sirens and alarms as black men raged against white authority.

It had begun, really, on the previous Thursday, as the result of an episode which would have passed almost unnoticed in less pregnant times. A white apartment-house superintendent had turned a hose on a group of Negro summerschool students in Manhattan's East 70's, a predominantly white neighborhood. The children threw rubbish at the man and three of them, including a 15-year-old boy named James Powell, chased him into a doorway. An off-duty policeman heard the disturbance, flashed his badge, and ordered the youths to calm down. According to the police report, the Powell youth then advanced on the patrolman with a knife, and ignored several orders to halt. The officer fired three shots at the boy and two of them found their mark. The youth fell dead.

For two days after that, a pervasive unrest gripped Harlem, as Negroes stood on streetcorners in the hot nights, agreeing that the child's death was another example of police brutality and even deliberate murder. They were unwilling to believe that a 200-pound policeman could not disarm a 15-year-old student without resorting to gunfire. (The officer, a 6-foot, 200-pound veteran of 16 years on the force, was the holder of 19 citations, including several for disarming dangerous suspects.) By Saturday night, their unrest was at a peak. A street rally sponsored by three local chapters of CORE was the scene of harangues by a number of angry speakers, including one Baptist minister who urged the crowd to march on the local precinct station and present their demands—principally the formation of a civilian review board to study the circumstances of the Powell boy's death.

"Let's go! Let's do it now!" the crowd shouted, and started for the station house. Police squads tried to head them off, but the swollen, screaming mob—supported by other Negroes on rooftops throwing bottles and bricks—surged through the streets. Thus it began, and for five nights Harlem was a battleground, utterly unsafe for any white man to enter, ringing with gunfire and the crashing of display windows, as looters carted off armfuls of merchandise. Molotov cocktails, flung by Negroes, arched through the air and sent policemen scrambling. One police officer, asked if he had been frightened during the fighting, replied, "Yes, once when I ran out of ammunition."

Police Commissioner Michael F. Murphy hurriedly issued a statement on the first night of the fighting condemning "vicious, unprovoked attacks against police. In our estimation this is a crime problem and not a social problem." Coming as it did at the beginning of the week of violence, Murphy's statement supplied the Harlemites with a display of the sort of impregnable bureaucratic mentality against which they had been raging for years, and served only to spur on the rioting.

On Sunday night, a rights leader named Jesse Gray, one of Harlem's angriest protesters, addressed an emergency open meeting in a local Presbyterian church, and called for "100 black revolutionaries who are ready to die. There is only one thing that can correct the situation and that's guerilla warfare!" He exhorted these "revolutionaries" to establish platoons and to recruit 100 men each. "This city can be changed by 50,000 well-organized Negroes. They can determine what will happen in New York City!" He was cheered wildly by the 500 Negroes present. A black nationalist issued an appeal that "all you black people that have been in the armed services and know anything about guerilla warfare should come to the aid of our people. If we must die, let us die scientifically!" Such was the mood of the audience that he was hailed with cries of assent.

Incredibly, two of the most militant Negroes of the entire civil rights struggle were booed and jeered when they attempted to address the same meeting. James Farmer of CORE rose and demanded the arrest of the police officer who had shot the Powell boy. The audience rose and cried:

"Let's go! Let's march on the police station now!"

Farmer raised his arms and shouted them down. "If you go out of here—one running one way, one running another—it will be slaughter!" The crowd held, but they jeered Farmer for restraining them.

Bayard Rustin rose and said: "There is nobody in this room who cares more than I do that a young boy was shot down like an animal. . . . There is nobody that has gone to jail more often than I have. I am not ready to die. I want no human being to die or be brutalized!" He was booed off the altar. As he stepped down, a group of Negroes from the audience, supposed to be black nationalists, moved toward him menacingly. Another group formed a protective shield around him.

Farmer went to a local television station on Sunday afternoon and described the riot: "I saw a bloodbath. I saw with

my own eyes violence, a bloody orgy of police . . . a woman
climbing into a taxi and indiscriminately shot in the groin
. . . police shooting into tenement windows and into the
Theresa Hotel. . . . I saw bloodshed as never before . . .
people threw bottles and bricks. I'm not saying they were not
partly to blame. But it is the duty of police to arrest, not indiscriminately shoot and beat."

Harlem had crossed over into irrationality; the terrorism,
looting, and anarchy were a symptom of the underlying de-
mentia. Political radicals unquestionably were fanning the
flames of discontent during the five days of the fighting. No
rationale could gainsay the ancient predisposition of the
ghetto-dwellers to find in violence a language for their dismay.
New York was suffering a vacuum of leadership at the moment: Mayor Wagner was vacationing in Spain; Governor
Rockefeller was relaxing at a family ranch at Jackson Hole,
Wyoming; Malcolm X was in Cairo attending a meeting of
the Organization of African Unity; Adam Powell was in
Switzerland attending a meeting of the International Labor
Organization. Of the four, only Malcolm X could have been
expected to control the mobs in that atmosphere of high
emotionalism.

For the older Harlemites, who remembered the fighting of
1935 and 1943, the rioting of 1964 led to one inescapable conclusion: nothing had really changed. The ghetto was just the
same and probably always would be. Dr. Kenneth Clark articulated that notion in an interview on NBC after the rioting
had spent itself:

"I personally do not have any hope that the events of the
last week will make any difference. Personally, I think what
will happen is that law and order will again prevail, particularly in terms of containing the restless natives, keeping them
within the confines of their ghetto. And once things return
to normal, they will return to normal completely."

Other conclusions, equally troublesome, grew out of the Harlem rioting. Negro leadership was fractionalized and ineffective. In times of stress, Negro masses responded primitively to the visceral appeal of black nationalism and spurned the more moderate, rational leadership, no matter how militant. Even though it could still be stated that, in both the North and the South, the vast majority of Negroes were dedicated to the path of non-violence, certain youthful, intellectual, and disaffiliated elements in the ghetto were fiercely implacable, and their impatience communicated itself to portions of the leadership, goading them to greater expressions of militancy. The Big Six convened in New York after the Harlem riot and issued a plea for a "broad curtailment" of civil rights demonstrations during the summer which might reduce President Johnson's vote in November, and incite further rioting in the northern cities. James Farmer of CORE and John Lewis of SNICK dissented from the appeal, and found themselves in the company of such other dissenters as Malcolm X, Jesse Gray, and Adam Powell. Bayard Rustin spoke for King, Wilkins, Randolph, and Young: "Leadership often has to do what is right, whether or not people like it. Leadership often has to do what is politically sound whether or not people like it." The major civil rights groups realized that they were failing to absorb the *Lumpenproletariat,* the disaffected and dispossessed in the streets, and that the appeal of extremism was mounting instead of lessening. Powell's March 23, 1963, denunciation of the major rights groups as being white-dominated was pointedly addressed to this undercurrent, as was an often-repeated statement of James Baldwin: "There is no role for the white liberal. He is our affliction." The black leadership bloc appeared by mid-1964 to have lost control over segments of black America which—even though they comprised a distinct minority—were crucial to control of the streets. The concessions won for black America by King,

Wilkins, and the others were often not spectacular enough to impress the ghetto-dwellers. The nationalists, with their appeal to race pride, consistently had an impact more immediate and dramatic on this *Lumpenproletariat*.

After the Harlem riots, Bayard Rustin told a national television audience that "nobody knows who had control of the working class of Harlem. It's one of our problems that [none] of us has sufficiently identified with the working classes, and the unemployed there . . . feel they have no leadership. And this is one of the serious lessons . . . we have learned from this tragedy." Perhaps the main lesson was that Negroes were weary of paternalism and tokenism and were determined to wrest from white America those rights which were theirs by nature and by law. Any leader who complemented this determination had their loyalty, and any who attempted to restrain it risked their enmity. As far back as 1961, James Baldwin had written in *Harper's* magazine: ". . . the problem of Negro leadership in this country has always been extremely delicate, dangerous, and complex. The term itself becomes remarkably difficult to define, the moment one realizes that the real role of the Negro leader, in the eyes of the American Republic, was not to make the Negro a first-class citizen but to keep him content as a second-class one. . . . And this problem, which it was the responsibility of the entire country to face, was dumped into the laps of a few men. Some of them were real leaders and some of them were false."

The Big Six—in spite of their intermittent internal disagreements and their cordial association with the white power structure—were still the truest expression of Negro aspirations in the United States: the overpowering urge toward total integration and total equality in the main current of American life. In the great dialogue that accompanied this social revolution, the extremists had their valid role as dissenters, and as articulators of the impatience felt not only by the *Lumpenproletariat* but by the large numbers of Negro intellectuals.

A month after the Harlem rioting, President Johnson signed into law his $947,500,000 anti-poverty bill, promising that "a new day of opportunity is dawning" for the nation's poor. He handed to Adam Clayton Powell, standing behind him, the first of 72 pens he used in signing the historic bill. It was a tacit acknowledgment of Powell's influence as chairman of Education and Labor, and the President's dependence upon the Harlemite's good will.

Other tributes were forthcoming. On September 19, seven weeks before the national elections, some Powell partisans in Harlem arranged an "Adam Clayton Powell Day" to celebrate the Congressman's 20th year in the House of Representatives. An *Amsterdam News* editorial was warmly approving of the project, claiming that if anyone had earned his "Day" in Harlem it was Powell. He was "Mr. Civil Rights," said the editorial, and the "number one crusader for the most burning issue in the hearts and minds of Harlem's teeming thousands." Although he had been born to an affluent manner of life, he had chosen to cast his lot with the downtrodden, said the *Amsterdam News,* and had fought as though the outcome of the struggle depended upon himself alone. "He probably is the most misunderstood public figure in America today. Certainly he is misunderstood and misinterpreted outside of Harlem. And many would have it said that Harlem itself does not really understand Adam Powell."

A parade of sixty cars and four brass bands rolled up Seventh Avenue on Adam Clayton Powell Day. Powell himself led the parade, riding in a black Cadillac convertible. He waved, shouted, and clenched his hands overhead like a victorious boxer. Well-wishers brandished green-and-gold banners bearing the legend: "I Was There—Adam Clayton

Powell Day." The parade ended with a rally opposite St. Nicholas Park, where 23 speakers proffered testimonials to the Congressman. "We here thank God that we were privileged to walk the earth at a time when Adam Clayton Powell walked it too," said one of them. Harry Van Arsdale, President of the Central Trades Council, said: ". . . We in labor are deeply grateful . . . that we have a man of your ability as chairman of the House Education and Labor Committee."

Powell was in good oratorical form that day. He came equipped with a lengthy catalogue of his accomplishments in Congress—the Vocational Education Act, the Manpower Development and Training Act, the National Defense Education Act—plus what he called "the first massive attack on the problems of our teen-agers." Shaking his fist, he warned that he would tolerate "no political shenanigans" with HARYOU-ACT. "I would rather close [it] down than let it become a place to breed 'Uncle Toms.' " Over the crowd's shouts of approval, he said: "I've worked too hard to let some crooks, some downtown politicians and some ivory tower leaders run this thing."

He told the audience that the anti-poverty act was "of much greater importance to the nation and the Negro" than the Civil Rights Act, and described his feelings as he watched the President sign it into law: "I felt a deep sense of pride. For I had steered the bill through my committee. I had fought for it on the floor of the House of Representatives in what, I can tell you, was a bloody battle. That is why President Johnson gave me the first pen when he signed the bill." In a departure from his prepared text, Powell reminded his listeners, to their great delight, that the poverty bill was subject to renewal annually, and that "every year it has to come back to Big Daddy," meaning himself.

He would continue to fight, he told them, "until every single one of *us* is able to live the full life in the Great Society." His closing words, spoken intensely, were: "I am your servant."

A survey published by *The New York Times* a week after the Harlem riots was instructive. Interviews conducted in New York City appeared to indicate that the NAACP was still the most popular Negro organization. Fifty-five percent of those polled said it was the most effective of the rights groups. Twenty-three percent voted for CORE, 14 percent for the National Urban League, and 3 percent for the Black Muslims. Another question was: "Which [Negro leader] do you personally think is doing the best for Negroes?" The respondents gave Martin Luther King 73 percent of the vote, Roy Wilkins 22 percent, Adam Clayton Powell 21 percent, and Malcolm X 6 percent.

Among those leaders, Malcolm X was the one who most consistently called attention to the global nature of the black revolution. He had broken with Elijah Muhammad and the Black Muslims after an internal power struggle, and was setting up two organizations of his own: the Organization of Afro-American Unity, geared to social action, and Muslim Mosque, Inc., a religious group. Malcolm left no avenue unexplored which might lead to a gain in race pride. His father, said Malcolm, had been a devout follower of Marcus Garvey, the aspiring "Black Moses" of the 1920's who had denounced the NAACP and the Urban League for their white associations, just as Adam Powell did almost forty years later. All the serious Negro leadership knew instinctively that what was happening in the United States was a part of a global movement which had been in progress since the end of World War II. Powell had acknowledged that fact when he attended the Bandung Conference of Asian and African nations in 1955. A majority of the world's peoples were non-white: black, yellow, dark Semitic, Indian of East and West. But the whites were in control, either by legal ownership or through the exertion of economic leverages. When the war ended, colonial peoples surged toward independence. First in Asia—India, Pakistan, Burma, Indonesia—and the countries of the Middle East; then Africa in the 1950's, including such North African territories as Algeria and Morocco. It was the black African surge that had a profound impact on Negro-Americans. Until those new nations emerged as independent and sent their diplomatic emissaries abroad, Negro Americans were ashamed of their African ancestry. To them, Africa was—just as it was to the white American—the "dark continent," the great land mass of uncivilized blacks who thrashed about naked and were forever hurling spears and blowing poisoned darts.

The Negro American reacted differently from whites to this stereotyped view of the African continent. He had grown up inside the American culture—in an enclave or subnation having practical colonial status, especially in the ghettos— but was never absorbed into the mainstream of American life. He was viewed, quite simply, as a congenital inferior, a sub-human, and—in the words of A. Philip Randolph—"not wholly a man." The whites found, in the African stereotype, a cor-roboration of their instinctive attitudes toward Negro Amer-icans: they were inferior because their forebears were savages. The Negroes, for their part, were aware of this invidious as-sociation and susceptible to the identical interpretation. They were conditioned by the view of white America that they were indeed inferior because of this ancestry, and thus plainly undeserving of equal footing with whites. So, in self-defense, they entered into the role-playing of inferiority and despaired of ever becoming *someone*.

When the black nations of Africa began stirring for in-dependence, however, their leaders emerged as intelligent, often highly-educated men and, in some instances, given to speaking English with an Oxford accent. They were skillful political operators, urbane and dignified in their demeanor. Most whites had not previously seen the likes of Sir Abubakar Tafawa of Nigeria, Julius K. Nyerere of Tanganyika, Tom Mboya of Kenya, or Kwame Nkrumah of Ghana. Black premiers and ambassadors came to the United States and were welcomed at such hotels as the Waldorf-Astoria in New York and the Shoreham in Washington. They ate in the best restaurants, moved in influential American social circles, and comported themselves with the aplomb of old-world statesmen. They brought tidings from Africa's blacks, and descriptions of backward but aspiring and proud black nations. No longer could such countries be viewed by Negro Americans as uncivilized and inferior.

With the advent of this new source of hope, the ghetto blacks found their own condition increasingly intolerable. Young Negroes in the United States felt an intense sympathy with the dreams of the new nations and a bond of brotherhood with their people. The emerging black Africans, like their counterparts in the United States, were not spared bloodshed and crises of leadership in their thrust for equality.

The late Lorraine Hansberry, whose play, *A Raisin in the Sun,* dramatized some of these notions, told *The New Yorker* in 1959, "One of the reasons I feel so free is that I belong to a world majority—and a very assertive one." George Hauser, executive secretary of the American Committee on Africa, said that same year, "In just two years, American Negroes have developed a new sense of pride in their African origins." At the close of his 1959 American tour, Tom Mboya of Kenya remarked, "The problems of Negroes here are very similar to those we have in Africa. I have found American Negroes more aware of this interrelationship during my trip this time than during my last visit a few years ago."

The attitudes of many Harlemites toward "downtowners" changed subtly in the late 1950's. They were desirous of being recognized as civically responsible. Any white visitor with the merest claim to celebrity might have his presence celebrated in the Negro press. They were eager for recognition from the powers outside the "colony." A reporter on a routine assignment in Harlem might be introduced as "one of the country's foremost correspondents."

Red China began to be an influence in international racism with its estrangement from the Soviet Union. Mao Tse-tung's efforts in Africa were based on anti-white as well as anti-colonial attitudes. Race, as an international propaganda lever, came to the fore in mid-1964 when Red China sought to bar Russian participation in an Asian conference on grounds that Russia was a European country. The euphemisms being translated, the Chinese were saying that the Russians were white and therefore did not belong at a meeting of non-white nations. India, however, took the lead in declaring that Russia was as Asian as it was European and should be invited. Behind it all was the power struggle of two expansionist nations and the unstated thesis that race could be a significant issue in the outcome.

Castro's revolution in Cuba had similar overtones of racism. Cuba has a heavy Indian strain, as well as substantial black and mulatto minorities. During his first year, Castro pointedly brought Negroes and mulattoes into the foreground. When he visited the United States, he stayed at the Hotel Theresa in Harlem, and declared at a press conference that he was "Afro-Cuban." He conferred with Malcolm X. Black nationalists demonstrated in his honor outside the hotel. In Bolivia, where Indian elements have achieved formal political status, many apparent whites—especially if they are politicians—are fond of declaring, "I've got some Indian blood myself."

The latest "immigrant" group to come to the American mainland, the Puerto Ricans, began at the lowest economic level and jostled Negroes for the most menial jobs. But, within a decade, they were achieving substantial integration. Negroes in Manhattan observed that these Puerto Ricans who were below them on the economic scale in the late 1940's were moving ahead of them in the late 1950's. To add insult to that injury, many Puerto Ricans were resentful of politicians—including Adam Powell—who insisted on lumping them together with the Negroes in demands for better opportunity. The association could only retard their absorption into the American middle class, the Puerto Ricans insisted. Some of them accumulated enough substance to move out of the Puerto Rican ghetto of East Harlem.

Thus, what was to be feared was the world-wide polarization of whites and non-whites—including, on the non-white side, the Indians and mestizos of all Latin America. Arnold Toynbee gave it historical perspective in a *New York Times* article of September 29, 1963: "In our present world, race conflict seems to be arousing stronger feelings, and to be producing worse atrocities, than any of the other current conflicts with which mankind is tormenting himself. . . . A glance back at man's history seems to indicate that race consciousness has not loomed so large in the past as it does today. Dare we hope that race conflict will prove to have been an exceptional aberration, confined to a minority of the human race and afflicting even this minority only during a passing phase of its history?" Toynbee discerned three areas from which race conflict might spread: Southeast Asia, where the local peoples were hostile to an immigrant Chinese minority; East, Central, and South Africa, where native blacks were in conflict with an immigrant North European minority; and the United States, where hostilities which had begun in the agricultural Old South were erupting into violence both in the South and in the northern ghettos. He concluded that race hatred was potentially the instrumentation that might "serve a suicidally minded mankind's crazy purpose" for atomic war.

In the United States, extremist and separatist elements were abetting this incipient global racism and toying mischievously with the American Negro's chance for peaceful absorption into American life. The hard-nosed, go-it-alone implacability of many Negro activists who read all whites out of the black revolution, was making the path thornier for the major rights leaders and giving succor to opportunists—political and other- wise—who appealed to the masses with simplist solutions.

Ironically, had Adam Powell not been in Switzerland dur- ing the 1964 Harlem riots, he still probably could not have gone to Harlem to assist in restoring order. Among his many legal difficulties was a libel case against him which he had lost on April 4, 1963. Damages were awarded in the amount of $211,500 (later reduced to $46,500). Not only did Powell refuse to pay, he also refused to appear in court for an ex- amination of his finances. He was cited for contempt on De- cember 27, 1963, and the New York Supreme Court issued an arrest order after repeated efforts to bring the Congressman to account had failed. The charge was criminal contempt. Powell was protected by Congressional immunity while the Congress was in session; and in New York by the illegality of serving a summons on Sunday. For many months, he came to New York only on Sunday to deliver his sermon at Abys- sinian Baptist, leaving the same day.

The lawsuit came about after a television interview on March 6, 1960, during which Powell denounced "organized gambling and police corruption" in Harlem. In so doing, he named one Mrs. Esther James—a 66-year-old Negro domestic —as a "bag woman" (i.e., collector of graft) for the Police Department in Washington Heights. Mrs. James claimed she actually was supplying the police with information on gambling and corruption, and promptly sued Powell for one million dollars. The Congressman took the position that his broadcast remarks were intended to inform his constituents of a speech made earlier on the floor of the House, and claimed Congressional immunity from prosecution under Article I, Section 6 of the Constitution. (". . . For any speech or debate in either House they [Senators and Representatives] shall not be questioned in any other place.") State Supreme Court Justice John L. Flynn determined that, while a congressman has "a qualified privilege of informing his constituents of remarks made by him in Congress so long as the communication to the constituents is made in good faith and without malice," a formal trial would be required to decide whether Powell's broadcast assertion "went beyond the limits of the qualified privilege and was maliciously made."

The trial lasted four days, during which time Powell did not appear. The jury found him guilty after four hours of deliberation and set damages at $211,500 ($200,000 punitive, and $11,500 for damage to Mrs. James's reputation and earning power).

Mrs. James said, "I was afraid of the king in Harlem, but I found out this is America." Later on, displaying a certain dramatic flair, she added, "The king is dead! Adam Clayton Powell is dead! And respectable people will be able to walk in the streets again!" She claimed she really would have settled for a public apology, but Powell was adamant in refusing.

One of the jurors described the secret deliberations: "We had to punish the Congressman so severely not only because of the power his word carries, but also because his job is to uphold the human right and to be responsible for the rights of other human beings." The jury foreman said, "Because of the high office this man holds, he has a public platform for hurting other people . . . without having the true facts. He must know that he is not allowed to do this." But even in the cut-and-dried atmosphere of that court case, in which Powell was pitted against another Negro, a certain segment of the black community was able to find mean motives. A letter writer to the *Amsterdam News* said, ". . . with an all-white jury, a gorilla could have won a libel suit against Powell. It's no secret how most people feel about Powell, including the white press."

By July, it was apparent that Powell did not intend to pay the damages and Mrs. James's collection problem was complicated by the fact that Powell no longer drew a church salary, that he apparently had no New York property in his own name, that his Puerto Rican home was in his wife's name, and that his Congressional salary could not be garnisheed. In addition, the federal government had a prior lien on Powell's property because of old income tax claims, and those were not expected to be settled for three or four years. A subpoena finally was served on Powell ordering him to appear in court on September 20, 1963. He said the subpoena had not been served legally. Mrs. James's attorney said it was, because a copy had been tacked on the door of his legal residence at 120 W. 138th Street and another was mailed to him. The summons ordered him to show cause why he should not be penalized for not paying the judgment.

At year's end, the court held Powell in contempt for ignoring the summons. The court once again ordered him to pay up or to purge himself by appearing in court early in January to have his finances examined. The *New York Herald-Tribune* managed to get Powell on the telephone in Puerto Rico and was rewarded with this exchange:

Q. Will you purge yourself by coming in with $211,500?
A. (laughter)
Q. Well, will you?
A. Merry Christmas.

Q. You were supposed to have been in court September 20, you know.

A. Oh, really? I didn't know that. This has been a wonderful Christmas. I didn't give any Christmas presents and nobody gave me any. Have a happy New Year. It's eighty-two degrees down here right now.

Meanwhile, Mrs. James's lawyers alleged that Powell had transferred a $900 fee for an article in *Esquire* magazine to his wife after the libel judgment had been entered. As a result, Powell was served with a criminal summons outside Abyssinian Baptist one Sunday (a criminal summons can be served at any time). An attorney for Mrs. James claimed that Powell's assets ran "into the millions" in the form of stocks, real estate, cash, and insurance interests, but they were largely in the name of others." Lawyers for the two sides reached an agreement which would permit Powell to return to New York with immunity. Mrs. James agreed to stay all court action until after the Appellate Division ruled on Powell's appeal of the award. Five judges refused to dismiss the judgment, but ruled that the award was "grossly excessive" and reduced it to $46,500. Two contempt charges also were dropped at this time.

Mrs. James was back with another suit on April 8, 1964, charging Powell with "maliciously conspiring" to transfer Puerto Rican property worth $85,000 to his wife's aunt and uncle. She brought yet another one against the Congressman and his ex-wife, Hazel Scott, alleging the transfer of a half-interest in the Westchester house they had lived in. Powell claimed that debate on the civil rights bill in Congress prevented his being in court in New York; but he was in Europe two months later, when the historic bill was passed, and did not vote on it. He also claimed that he was involved with subcommittee hearings on anti-poverty legislation. The State

Supreme Court rejected those arguments and told Powell to be in court on May 1 to permit examination of his assets. Once again, Powell ignored the order. The possibility of his being jailed was increasing now. In the pact under which serving of papers was to be postponed, Powell had agreed to waive his Congressional immunity to arrest. Mrs. James's lawyer asked for the arrest order, saying he knew where to find Powell on that very day. The judge answered, "You're kidding. As soon as I signed it, the word would go out and you'd never find him. . . . Sooner or later this man is going to come to book." But the court did issue an arrest order on May 8, with the recognition that it could not be carried out constitutionally while the House was in session. Justice Thomas C. Chimera described Powell's conduct as being "so flagrantly contemptuous of the authority and dignity of this court as to promote a tragic disrespect for the judicial process as a whole. No man should be allowed to continue in this fashion and it is time for the defendant to answer for it."

But Powell fought on, taking the case to the United States Court of Appeals, and finally to the United States Supreme Court, which declined unanimously on January 18, 1965, to review it. (At that point, 53 different judges sitting in eight courts had considered various aspects of the case.) Theoretically, that was the end of the legal road for Powell in his disputations with Mrs. James, but the Congressman said it was all academic anyway, since he didn't *have* $46,500. He told newsmen, with a smile, that they might refer to him thereafter as "Dead End Powell."

Mrs. James, for her part, merely continued her chorus: "The king is dead! But he won't be buried until I collect that $46,500—and I'm going to get it if I have to stay alive 'til I'm 99." That meant thirty more years of hot pursuit. On February 11, the judgment against Powell was increased by the State Supreme Court to $210,000 because he had transferred the Cerro Gordo villa to his wife's relatives in an attempt to avoid its attachment.

The litigation did have the effect of excluding Powell from the environs of New York during the 1964 Presidential campaigns and election. The Congressman was running for his 11th consecutive term as Harlem's representative, but was unable to campaign at home because of the legalisms. On election day, plainclothes policemen bearing warrants for Powell's arrest were staked out at polling places around Abyssinian Baptist Church. But the Congressman didn't turn up. He claimed subsequently to have cast an absentee ballot.

In spite of the absence, Powell won his own election against three opponents—Liberal, Republican, and Conservative—by the incredible margin of ten to one. "I didn't use anything to win," he declared on election night, "not a postcard, not a pamphlet, not a speech, not a poster." At Powell's headquarters at 145th Street and Seventh Avenue, Odell Clark, chief investigator for the House Education and Labor Committee, said: "This election will teach all of those who want to defeat Adam that the best way to defeat Adam is to leave Adam alone. Adam will win hands up simply because of the enemies he has made." Another co-worker said: "Adam is the greatest. Adam has done more for Negroes than any other single man dead or alive."

In the national campaigns, Powell stumped for Johnson and Humphrey in eight cities. But in New York, he infuriated supporters of Robert F. Kennedy, who was seeking a seat in the United States Senate, by claiming that he and three major county leaders—each of whom was for Kennedy—would name the Democratic nominee. One of Kennedy's closest campaign aides described Powell's intrusion as "gratuitous—it didn't help." Another Kennedy aide said: "With Adam on his side, Bobby doesn't need any enemies." For a time, it appeared that Powell's remarks had jeopardized

Kennedy's chances. Publicly, the former Attorney General stood on a statement made months before: "I have nothing against Congressman Powell."

President Johnson was among the first to acknowledge Powell's importance to his projected Great Society. On December 14—three days before he began receiving labor and business delegations—Johnson met with Powell in an extended private session at the White House. Neither disclosed the weight of their discussion, but Powell was known to have a number of topics on his mind: the expansion of the anti-poverty program to $3 billion in 1965; the appointment of more Negroes to high position in Sargent Shriver's Office of Economic Opportunity, which administers the anti-poverty program; the repeal of section 14B of the Taft-Hartley Act, which permits states to enact so-called "right-to-work" laws prohibiting union shop contracts; the raising of the Federal minimum wage from $1.25 to $2.00 an hour, and the reduction of the standard work week from 40 to 32 hours.

In the week following Powell's meeting with President Johnson, George Meany, head of the AFL-CIO, visited Powell in his Congressional offices to press labor's case, especially for repeal of section 14B. The two men had never been admirers of each other, but now more than ever their purposes were bound together. Powell let it be known that he aimed to be a tough bargainer. He later told an AFL-CIO legislative conference: "I want some assurance from labor that repeal of 14B means that labor will open up its own door, not only to members of my race, but to Mexicans, Jews, and, in some areas of our country, Catholics. . . . It is unseemly for any groups to press their own interests so passionately while they are passive or unduly judicious about the interests of others."

Powell consistently demeaned the Civil Rights Bill—and with it, by implication, the major civil rights leaders such as King, Farmer, and Wilkins—while insisting that the anti-poverty bill (which he frequently called "my bill") was the Negro's best hope. Of what use was access to previously all-white accommodations, he inquired, if the Negro had not ten cents for a cup of coffee. He denounced "ivory tower" Negroes, whom his audiences understood to be the Big Six, and claimed that he was "the only elected leader of all the [Negro] people."

As Powell's position among serious civil rights leaders continued in decline, his position as a legislator of national importance, and a keystone of the Administration's whole domestic legislative program, became impregnable. "Adam is sure one hell of a politician!" a Negro Democrat exclaimed after learning that Powell had bottled up President Johnson's education legislation until the House approved a hefty $440,-000 expense budget for his own Education and Labor Committee. But Administration leaders were not amused. They felt that the longer the hearings were delayed on the $1.3 billion school aid bill, the longer its enemies would have to muster opposition. (President Johnson viewed the measure as one of the two main pieces of legislation in that session, and a cornerstone of his entire anti-poverty war.) Behind-the-scenes efforts were made to ensure that Powell got his money; when he received informal assurances in mid-February, however, he declined to hold the hearings immediately. Instead, he delayed until the money was, in effect, in his hand. But as Johnson's strategists had feared, the bill's opponents were able to use the time to muster their forces against it and bottle it up even longer in the Education and Labor Committee.

Powell's action in holding the bill a hostage jeopardized its passage, and severely nettled Johnson's strategists. But Powell had played his cards coolly and successfully, and prevailed. The bill did pass the House—after the President had kept an unusually close telephone vigil over it.

So confident was Powell of his role in fashioning the Great Society, that he chose the time before the opening of the 89th Congress to enjoy a vacation in Hawaii with his glamorous secretary, Corrine Huff—the same girl who had accompanied him on his celebrated European junket in 1963.

For Adam Powell, it was just the closing of one more cycle, and perhaps the opening of another which would prove as invigorating, and as much fun, as all the others.

15. What Manner of Man?

A few days before the March on Washington, one of the Negro Big Six discussed Adam Powell in private conversation: "He forces us into feeling ambivalent. And he confuses us by the way he does things . . . But he keeps the civil rights issue alive. That's why we don't like to attack him. Sometimes though, he makes it necessary."

A person intimately involved with the HARYOU-ACT said: "The image that stays in my mind is Samson in the temple. . . . He wants to bring destruction not only on himself but on everyone around him."

A prominent woman attorney in Harlem was asked in 1961, "How do you see Adam ending up?" She answered, "Retired in some sunny place, surrounded by a coterie of whites."

The National Broadcasting Company recorded a remarkable exchange between a group of young Negro CORE members while filming a "White Paper" on the Congressman's activities. It is worthy of quotation:

Young man: If Mr. Powell is so different and if . . . he represents us, where is he? Now, we have led every fight in New York for some kind of progress. He's never made a stand with us.

Young man: Whenever Powell is questioned in terms of

his leadership, particularly by the white press . . . he will get to a point and then he will say, "Well, you see, I'm black and you're white and you don't understand." But I'm black and I don't understand. And I would like to know some answers.

Young man: Powell always speaks for this division, "There must be a black leadership. Get away from wilish whites. They will sell you out." Okay, this is fine. He comes in Harlem to divide. To tell you, get away from any of your white friends, regardless of who they might be. Get away from them, then go where? He does not tell you. This is subversive, using his power and prestige . . . as a minister, as a representative of the House to the black people, to subvert them . . . to lead them to a blind alley of emotionalism.

Young woman: He aligns himself with completely negative thinking. Notice, he has never aligned himself with any of the civil rights movements. He has called them down, called them sellouts, et cetera. Because, if he aligns himself with [them], he will have to take some kind of direct action, which he does not want to do. But by aligning himself with Malcolm X and his boys, he does not.

Young man: It gives him the right to say that "I am independent." He can say that "I am the only guy that's independent in Congress." Certainly, he shouldn't owe anything in the Congress. But he owes us something.

Young man: He owes us a lot.

Young man: . . . And I think the tipoff is this: When they attack Powell, they attack him because he goes to Europe and uses government money. But all the Congressmen do that. Now it seems to me that if you represent the largest black community in America, and America is in the middle of a black revolution, as we are, and you are a black Congressman, and all you get criticized for is junketeering, then something's wrong. You see! Something's absolutely out of place. His day has definitely come. He stands and argues. He uses, well, first off, "Look at my record of 19 bills passed. I would have been able to do a lot more but I am one man fighting against. . . ."

You know! At that point he says he's a Negro. . . . He relies on his blackness as an excuse.

Young woman: Look at his record of twenty years and look at King's record of three years. Let us not forget this for a minute.

Young man: Let me say this. You see . . . what is happening here is this: Our revolution is a moral revolution, you see, and those men who are the leaders, the Kings and the Farmers and the Randolphs and all the rest are leaders because they grasp the moral concept . . . because they're men of principles who stand on a philosophy. Now the Powells and the Dawsons and the Eastlands and the Barnetts don't. This, to them, is not a moral revolution. It's just another political fight. And so they apply the run-of-the-mill, everyday American political tactics to our revolution. The difference between Mr. Powell's black revolution . . . and the genuine revolution is that our revolution has goals at the end. Mr. Powell's politics and that whole concept is pragmatic American politics. The black revolution is not based on any pragmatic philosophy. It's based on moral consciousness coupled with political awareness. We are saying this: that in order for us as black people to be free and equal, we are going to have to change some values as they now exist. . . . That's what we mean by revolution. . . . That we finally turn to the white man and say, All right, we understand what you did. And in doing it you destroyed many of us, but those who you didn't destroy you made into beautiful, thinking individuals, to the degree that we can now turn to you and say, not only must you change, but you must not be afraid to change. And to show you . . . we will accept your violence, we will accept your madness and your ignorance because we have a faith in people. And that's what I mean by revolution and I don't think that the Powell concept understands that at all.

It is for such reasons that a catalogue of the peccadillos of which Adam Clayton Powell has been accused through the years is not really important in the long view. More significant is what his life and person tell us about the Negro psyche in these years. He personifies for many blacks the attainment of a bourgeois good life—sports cars, Caribbean retreats, European vacations, fine clothes and good food served with the trappings of refinement. In the 1960's, however, the symbol of such things began to give way to the substance. Tiny fissures appeared in the wall of resistance which had blocked Negro aspirations toward the symbols of middle-class respectability. A day was discernible on the horizon when there would be no more need for symbols. The ghettos would be dismantled and the need even for "Negro politicians" would dissolve. An "irritant" between whites and blacks would only embarrass both races. Negro leaders who symbolized the meaner forms of attainment had already begun to be anachronisms.

Nonetheless, as the black revolution gained momentum, Powell was potentially the most effective single national spokesman for all Negroes. He could speak on more issues with authority than most other leaders and could, if he worked at it, transform many Negro demands into accomplishments. He had often done so with only a telegram when he was still a freshman Congressman. From 1961 onward, he had formal influence in affairs other than racial. He was unique in that he need not dilute his character as a race leader while becoming a national leader for all Americans, black and white. His several power sources challenged him with the opportunity of being a true, multi-dimensioned statesman. If he rose to these opportunities, the name Powell might be burnished on the roster which includes House greats from John Adams to Sam Rayburn, and he would be a historical pride to Americans and a happy complement to the nation's most cherished myth: the man of high influence, risen from a minority people.

By 1961, white leaders such as the Kennedys and Lyndon

Johnson were beginning to understand Negro contempt for white paternalism. They wanted a Negro to achieve success in the national arena on his own merits, and thus be a symbol for that invisible tenth of the nation's population. For 18 months after Adam Powell became the chairman of a key House committee, it appeared that the black revolution had found its focus in the legislative arena. When he walked away from his opportunity, the disappointment was no less severe among sympathetic white leaders than among black.

"What surprises me," said Dr. Kenneth Clark, "is that there have not been more Adam Clayton Powells. . . . We cannot be as pure as Caesar's wife. We are human, too." The double standard of morality which whites instinctively impose upon Negroes has drawn the fire of black men for decades, but it is a concept for which the majority of whites have a peculiar impermeability. White America demands that a Negro, to prove himself, be more able and more moral than a white man in the same circumstances. This fact contains an astonishing paradox. Negroes in America traditionally have been viewed as subhuman, occupying by toleration a subculture inside the affluent and expansive American ambiance. On the other hand, Negroes are expected to be more than human—indeed almost saint-like—to win favor and recognition in business, the arts, the professions, or politics. This condition explains largely why Powell is a uniquely modern hero to Negroes: he has at once shown how capable, how strong, how brilliant, how accomplished, how urbane a Negro can be. He has given a pyrotechnical demonstration of male individuation in the face of the paradox. He has demonstrated—too often, some would say—that a prominent Negro suffers public flagellation for his breaches of good order and discipline far more quickly than does an offending white leader. (The *Congressional Quarterly* in 1962 indicated that six Congressmen had spent more money in European junketeering than had Powell.)

White men of high achievement are traditionally allowed their foibles, and even vices, on grounds that "they're only human." But the white community denies, in most subtle fashion, that a Negro can be fully human—and Powell is a symbol of the Negro American.

Yet Powell attempts to carry this rationale one step further, and it is in that attenuation that his logic suffers. Adam Powell is not just another influential Congressional figure: He sought to be a national party leader, with his committee chairmanship as the font of his authority. Similarly, he is not just another Negro leader: He sought to be a national spokesman for all Negro Americans—their articulator, as they lived suppressed, depressed, frustrated and with their anger turning to despair and hopelessness. His stated purpose was to bring them to a realization that they were potentially powerful behind the proper leader; that, individually, they could become "someone" and, collectively, they could meld with American society and thus win its material and spiritual benefits.

No other contemporary American has held such an opportunity to succeed. Powell had it in his grasp to be a national figure who happened to be a Negro and a Negro race leader who happened to be a powerful legislator—all at a time when the black revolution, of which he was a prophet, was cresting in the nation, both North and South.

Confronted with this opportunity, Powell demanded his right as an individual to indulge himself the same as any other man. His demand for full equality included the right to be as bad as the worst white man—not merely in the hours of the week that he could claim as his own, but at times when there were clear obligations to his high state. This became his doctrine of freeism—this view of what he, as a whole man, must try to be. Powell effectively denied that a great leader, whatever his race, should conform to a more rigid ethic; that the way of high leadership is often tortuous and lonely and in need of the severest self-discipline. In that denial, Negro Americans lost the man who was potentially the greatest race leader of the century.

At the same time, Powell's abrasiveness, egocentricity, and desire for power cannot be held against him, in the long view. The most exalted of contemporary leaders—Winston Churchill and Konrad Adenauer, for example—have been prickly and difficult in personal relationships. Theodore Roosevelt was more unpredictable and a greater maverick than Powell; Franklin Roosevelt was in possession of more truly demagogic characteristics; John Kennedy was a more politically canny animal. But those men always contrived to enlist their total selves—the bad and the good—in the cause of the public weal. Their "humanity" abetted them to high leadership rather than inhibited them. The archetypal leader is a man who unself-consciously lusts for power and authority. That is what makes him a leader. If no restrictions are placed upon his lust—either self-imposed or inherent in the political system— he may cross into irrationality and become an adventurer, leading masses of adulating people to a perilous end. It has been the genius of American self-government that practical checks and balances have kept the greatest leaders—some of whom have revelled in the exercise of power—on the track of wholesome public-mindedness. And their great gifts as leaders thus were expended for the common good.

Powell's most telling weakness revealed itself in his incapacity to work in harness with other Negroes as co-equals. When Ray Jones emerged as a political force in his own right in New York City and insisted on a full share of the leverage of Harlem, Powell tried to destroy him as a leader. As it developed, Jones survived and Powell was weakened. When the Congressman moved to Puerto Rico, instead of using his influence as a complement to the remarkably vigorous and popular Muñoz Marín, he turned it against Muñoz and maneuvered to weaken him; neither Harlem nor Puerto Rico was large enough for two leaders, if one of them happened to be Powell. When the Negro Big Six organized the epic March on Washington and carried it off without miscue, Powell was enraged that it could be done without him. And when Dr. Kenneth Clark—a respected scholar and social scientist—conceived and engineered an unprecedented scheme to save Harlem's wasted youth, Powell fought him to the earth and succeeded in driving him from the terrain. Earlier, when A. Philip Randolph, the oldest and longest continuously active Negro leader in the country, sought to organize black workers into the Negro American Labor Council, Powell called him a "captive" of persons outside black America, and impugned his motives with the charge that Randolph's own labor union (the Brotherhood of Sleeping Car Porters) was growing weak, and he thus needed a new organization to perpetuate himself as a leader.

All of these sorties are illuminating. Powell charged Jones with relying on white money and white votes to win his councilmanic election. Did Powell desire to attract greater support and campaign contributions from the white Democratic elements of Manhattan?

Powell charged all civil rights organizations with domination from outside the Negro community. Did he want to dominate those organizations himself?

Powell demanded statehood for Puerto Rico so that the islanders could be free. Did he mean free of Muñoz, so that he could become chief spokesman for the island himself, either as Governor or as United States Senator?

Powell accused Dr. Clark of being personally interested in the money that would come to Harlem through the HAR-YOU-ACT program. Did Powell covet that money for himself?

Powell said Randolph was trying to strengthen himself as a national leader by forming the NALC. Did Powell have a vision of an all-new, nation-wide black workers' organization with himself at the head of it?

A peculiar pattern of self-destructiveness came into focus with Powell's embracing of Malcolm X and the concomitant espousal of the cause of separatism over that of black-white cooperation. Highly-placed appointees in the Kennedy administration were eager to salvage Powell after his disastrous European junket in 1962. He was worth saving, they insisted, both as a keystone of the New Frontier legislative program and as an invaluable bridge to black America. But for Powell, the acceptance of such largesse would have meant a degree of accommodation, and to that he could not adapt. It ran counter to his notions of freeism. He would no longer have been as free as, let us say, Huckleberry Finn on a raft in the Mississippi—out of reach of the onerous and confining proscriptions of a society he never made.

But then came Birmingham, the bench mark of the black revolution. All the ancient forces of Negro discontent gathered to a hard determination and then moved forward in unison. Powell was shouldered aside by forces he could no longer either control or impress.

Powell fell as a leader but remained as a symbol. Negro Americans will adore him forever for what he gave them: a sense of self and of self-esteem, of full malehood, of having wombs to give birth to fully male humans. Powell, for his part, was the creature of the black ghetto and of a manner of life designed, enforced, and perpetuated by white men. The fatal dualism in him is, in fact, a symptom of the double moral standard and, ultimately, of the hypocrisy of white America.

When Negroes first landed on these shores and began absorbing the Bible stories which their slavemasters told them, they were quick to discover parallelisms between their own predicament and that of the Jews in Egypt. Deliverance became the theme of a thousand songs and folk tales, and a part of the "blues" which were sung in cotton fields and on dirt farms in the Southland:

> *Go down, Moses,*
> *Way down in Egypt land.*
> *Tell old Pharaoh,*
> *Let my people go.*

And:

> *Jordan's river is chilly and wide,*
> *Greener pastures on the other side.*

And:

> *See them chillun dressed in white,*
> *It must be the chillun of the Israelite,*
> *See them chillun dressed in red,*
> *It must be the chillun that Moses led.*

Unknown to their white overlords, the blacks prayed for a Moses to lead them to the promised land. No such man ever assumed that role; only a handful tried. In the present century, one "Black Moses," Marcus Garvey, came closer than any leader before him to mustering the nation's black men for a march up freedom's road; but he was a flawed Moses, and failed. Adam Powell issued a clear, siren call to the nation's marching blacks to follow him on the path to selfhood and glory. But the call faltered, and finally faded.

It may yet be that the Black Moses of the American Negro dream is some such leader as Martin Luther King, or another successor to the passing generation of fighters led by Randolph and Wilkins and Farmer; or perhaps he is a young Negro whose name is not yet known, and who, even now, is playing child's games on the streets of the ghetto.

Selected Bibliography

Bennett, Lerone, Jr. *Before the Mayflower.* Chicago: Johnson Publishing Company, 1962.

Cronon, Edmund David. *Black Moses.* Madison, Wisconsin: University of Wisconsin Press, 1955.

Ginzberg, Eli. *The Negro Potential.* New York: Columbia University Press, 1962.

Greenberg, Jack. *Race Relations and American Law.* New York: Columbia University Press, 1962.

Kardiner, Abram, and Ovesey, Lionel. *Mark of Oppression: A Psychological Study of the American Negro.* New York: Norton, 1951.

Lewis, Claude. *Adam Clayton Powell.* (Gold Medal) New York: Fawcett Publications, Inc., 1964.

Lincoln, C. Eric. *The Black Muslims of America.* Boston: Beacon Press, 1961.

Lomax, Louis. *The Negro Revolt.* New York: Harper & Row, Publishers, 1962.

Myrdal, Gunnar. *An American Dilemma: The Negro Problem and Modern Democracy.* New York: Harper & Row, Publishers, 1944.

Powell, Adam Clayton, Jr. *Marching Blacks.* New York: Dial Press, 1945.

Powell, Adam Clayton, Sr. *Against the Tide.* New York: R. R. Smith, 1938.

———. *Riots and Ruins.* New York: R. R. Smith, 1945.

Senior, Clarence. *Strangers Then Neighbors.* New York: Freedom Books (Anti-Defamation League of B'nai B'rith), 1961.

Silver, James W. *Mississippi: The Closed Society.* New York: Harcourt, Brace & World, Inc., 1964.

Thompson, Daniel C. *The Negro Leadership Class.* Englewood Cliffs, N.J.: Prentice-Hall, Inc., 1963.

Weaver, Robert C. *Negro Labor: A National Problem.* New York: Harcourt, Brace & World, Inc., 1946.

White, Theodore H. *The Making of a President.* New York: Atheneum, 1961.

Wilson, James Q. *Negro Politics: The Search for Leadership.* Chicago: The Free Press of Glencoe, 1960.

Clark, Kenneth B. *Youth in the Ghetto: A Study of the Consequences of Powerlessness and a Blueprint for Change*. New York: Harlem Youth Opportunities Unlimited, Inc., 1964.
Hapwood, David. "The Purge that Failed: Tammany v. Powell." *Case Studies in Practical Politics*. Eagleton Institute. New York: Holt, Rinehart and Winston, 1959.

Magazines
Bennett, Lerone, Jr. "Adam Clayton Powell: Enigma on Capitol Hill." *Ebony* (June, 1963).
Dunbar, Ernest. "The Audacious World of Adam Powell." *Look* (May 7, 1963).
Powell, Adam Clayton, Jr. "The Duties and Responsibilities of a Congressman." *Esquire* (September, 1963).
Wakefield, Dan. "Adam Clayton Powell, Jr.: the Angry Voice of Harlem." *Esquire* (November, 1959).

Television
CBS News Special Report. "117th Street, New York, New York." July, 29, 1964.
NBC White Paper. "Adam Clayton Powell." March 12, 1964.
NBC Television. The Open Mind. "Congressman Adam Clayton Powell Talks with Eric F. Goldman." April 21, 1963.
WCBS-TV News. New York Forum. (Congressman Adam Clayton Powell as guest.)
WOR-TV. John Wingate's 6:15 News Extra. June 6, 1958.

Other
"Puerto Rico: A Report on Business and Trade." New York: The First National City Bank of New York. February, 1958.
"An America to Serve the World." Speech by Luis Muñoz Marín, Governor of the Commonwealth of Puerto Rico, to the Annual Convention of the Associated Harvard Clubs. Coral Gables, Florida. April 7, 1956.
Untitled address by Governor Muñoz at the Hotel Commodore. New York City, N.Y. January 18, 1963.
Untitled address by Governor Muñoz at the University of Kansas City on the occasion of receiving the Honorary Degree of Doctor of Law. Kansas City, Kansas. April 23, 1955.
Hearing on a bill to provide for amendments to the compact between the people of Puerto Rico and the United States. The Committee on Interior and Insular Affairs, United States Senate. June 9, 1959.

Index

DATE DUE

F			
MAR 3 '68			
In library			
MAY 8 '68			
OCT 1 '68			
OCT 15 '68			
FEB 23 '70			
GAYLORD			PRINTED IN U.S.A.